The Road to Samarkand

Delius in 1907, age forty-five

The Road to Samarkand

Frederick Delius and His Music

by Gloria Jahoda

Charles Scribner's Sons   New York

For Margaret Vessey

"Do not be jealous, lover of truth, because of these inflexible and oppressive men. Truth has never yet clung to the arm of an inflexible man."

Thus Spoke Zarathustra

Contents

List of Illustrations

Acknowledgments

Many people have made this book possible. My greatest debt is to Frederick Delius's niece, Margaret Vessey, of Salisbury, Wiltshire, England, a dedicated co-worker who has written me more than a hundred and fifty manuscript pages about her life with her uncle during his later years. She has also furnished me with four recorded tapes, made by her, on him and his family and his music. Her enthusiasm has been unflagging, and her sacrifice of time great.

To her, and to the estate of her mother Clare Delius Allan-Black, I owe permission to reproduce all photographs with the following exceptions: The one of Delius at the age of twelve has been taken by permission from *Frederick Delius*, a booklet published by the Bradford, Yorkshire, City Art Gallery and Museums in 1962. The photographs of Virginia Ann Watkins, of Delius during the First World War, of Jutta Bell-Ranske, and of Jelka Delius (alone) were supplied by the Delius Collection, Haydon Burns Library, Jacksonville, Florida. "A Card Party at Leipzig" appears by permission of the Grieg Museum, Troldhaugen, Norway, and its director Mr. Sigmund Torsteinson. "Høifagerli" has been graciously provided by H. M. King Olav of Norway. The Daniel de Monfreid portrait of Delius is reproduced by permission of Mr. and Mrs. Derek Hudson of London, its owners, and the photograph of Julius Delius (now in possession of Mrs. Margaret Vessey) is used also by permission of Nicholson and Watson, Ltd., London. That of Ilkley from the moors, also in possession of Mrs. Vessey, has been authorized by the Lilywhite Co. of Brighouse, Yorkshire. The photograph of the Delius cottage at Jacksonville University was taken by the author.

Any Delius biographer must be indebted, as I am, to several sources in particular, though all except the first stress his English rather than his American ties: *Frederick Delius—Memories of My Brother* by Clare Delius (London, Nicholson and Watson, 1935);

A Mingled Chime by Sir Thomas Beecham (New York, Putnam, 1943); *Frederick Delius*, by Sir Thomas Beecham (London, Hutchinson, 1959; New York, Knopf, 1960); *Delius As I Knew Him* by Eric Fenby (London, Bell, 1936; London, Icon Books, 1966; Philadelphia, Editions Dufour, 1966); *Delius* by Peter Warlock (London, The Bodley Head, 1923); *Norman O'Neill* by Derek Hudson (London, Quality Press, 1936); *Peter Warlock* by Cecil Gray (London, Cape, 1934); *Musical Chairs* by Cecil Gray (London, Home and Van Thal, 1948); *Delius* by A. J. B. Hutchings (London, Macmillan, 1949); *Thomas Beecham* by Charles Reid (London, Gollancz, 1962; New York, Dutton, 1962); *Portraits With Backgrounds* by Catherine Barjansky (New York, Macmillan, 1947); and *Overture and Beginners* by Sir Eugene Goossens (London, Methuen, 1951).

I am indebted to Boosey and Hawkes, Inc., New York, for permission to quote sections of *Appalachia*, words and music by Frederick Delius, copyright 1907, 1927 by Universal Edition, renewed 1935, 1954, copyright renewal assigned to Boosey and Hawkes Music Publishers Ltd.; *A Village Romeo and Juliet*, words by Jelka Rosen Delius and music by Frederick Delius, copyright 1910 by Universal Edition, renewed 1938, copyright and renewal assigned to Boosey and Hawkes Music Publishers Ltd.; *Requiem*, words and music by Frederick Delius, copyright 1921 by Universal Edition, renewed 1948, copyright and renewal assigned to Boosey and Hawkes Music Publishers Ltd.; and "La Calinda" from *Koanga*, piano reduction by Harold Perry, copyright 1935 by Hawkes and Son, London, copyright arrangement 1949 for all countries by Hawkes and Son, London, assigned to Boosey and Hawkes Music Publishers Ltd.

I am grateful to Miss Margaret Harrison of Smallfield, Horley, Surrey, England, for providing me with her written memories of Frederick Delius, and, through the kindness of Mr. Francis Bickley, to Mr. Lionel Ovenden of London for the same reason. To H. M. King Olav of Norway and his private secretary, Mr. V. Bommen, I owe thanks for invaluable help in gathering information on Delius's years at Lesjaskog. Mr. Ola Molmen of Lesjaskog also generously provided me with written reminiscences of Delius; Miss Kristin Feyling of Tallahassee was good enough to translate them for me. Mr. Otto Molmen of Englewood, Florida, kindly supplemented his nephew's account with his own.

In New Orleans I was assisted by Mr. Richard B. Allen of the American Jazz Archive, Tulane University, and by Mr. Alcide Pavageau; I owe thanks also to Mr. Jeff Driggers of the Haydon Burns Library, Mr. William Chalker of the Jacksonville University Library, and the Delius Association of Florida, Jacksonville; the Rev. Fred Dickey, Tallahassee; the late Mrs. Julia Alvarez Sanks, West St. Augustine; Mr. David Everhart of the Cincinnati Symphony, Cincinnati; Mrs. Sam Patterson of New York; Mrs. J. Pratt of Brooklyn; Mrs. Vernon G. Ramey of the Danville Public Library, Danville, Virginia; Mr. C. H. Hainton and Mr. K. A. Priestly of the Borough Road Training College, Isleworth, Middlesex; Mr. B. N. Aldridge of the London Borough of Hounslow Library Services; Mr. G. Thomason, editor of the *Middlesex Chronicle*; Mr. Jon Embretson of the Royal Norwegian Information Service; Boosey and Hawkes, Inc., New York, for making available to me the score of *Koanga,* words by Charles Keary and music by Frederick Delius; the Oxford University Press, New York, for the loan of the score of *A Dance of Life* by Frederick Delius; Mr. Carroll Wade and the Library of Congress for *Anatomy and Physiology of the Orchestra* by Frederick Delius and "Papus"; Monsieur J. C. Boixière and the staff of the Mairie at Grez-sur-Loing for copies of documents and for newspaper files and other information.

Permission to quote directly from the sources listed below has been granted by the publishers indicated: Alfred Knopf, Inc. for extracts from *Hassan, or the Golden Journey to Samarkand* by James Elroy Flecker; Heinemann Educational Books Ltd. for an extract from James Forsyth's translation of *Brand,* by Henrik Ibsen; Cambridge University Press for lines from "All the Hills and Vales Along" in *Marlborough and Other Poems* by Charles Sorley; the Bodley Head for extracts from *Delius* by Peter Warlock; Penguin Books Ltd. for extracts from R. J. Hollingdale's translation of *Thus Spoke Zarathustra,* by Friedrich Nietzsche; Doubleday and Co. and Mr. Robert Lewis Taylor for an extract from *The Running Pianist* by Robert Lewis Taylor; the *Musical Times,* London, for extracts from "Delius's First Performance" by Rachel Lowe; and Victor Gollancz, Ltd. for extracts from *Thomas Beecham* by Charles Reid.

Gloria Jahoda

1 ✐ Music of Tomorrow

Outside, on the mild evening of May 30, 1899, you could smell the lilacs. Street lamps in London squares were starting to shine down into the green branches where fresh blossoms were clustered. A few last birds still sang. But St. James Hall was packed with concert-goers. Inside, the smells were of fresh varnish and perfume and lingering tobacco smoke. The sounds were violins and oboes tuning up. Scattered throughout sat the critics, their note-pads ready to receive the jottings they would be making for reviews in the next morning's newspapers. Women fingered the laces and chiffons of their collars beside men in dark evening dress. On the gray heads of stately dowagers, tiaras glittered. Most of the professional musicians and students and managers had gathered in the back rows. Now they were murmuring to each other as they studied their programs.

It was no ordinary concert, everyone knew. Seldom had a night at St. James Hall been filled with the works of one composer, and for that matter a composer few people had ever heard of except as a scandal. There were rumors of that among the gossips once again. Fritz Delius—wasn't he the man who had been shot at in a Norwegian theater two years before? His *Norwegian Suite* had included a burlesque of Norway's national anthem. He had been hissed and catcalled as he conducted it, and when the gunfire had started, he had had to flee the orchestra pit for refuge in a hotel next door. There had been headlines about the riot which followed. It hadn't stopped him, apparently. The same parody was on tonight's program, though he wouldn't be conducting it himself.

Exactly who was he? Marchers sandwiched in board posters had been promoting his English debut, yet the posters had given no personal information. In musical circles talk recalled an orchestra leader who had dared to play a Delius piece in Germany and had nearly been fired by the town council for it. That time the audience had called Delius outrageous. Those gathered now in St. James Hall had come less to enjoy a pleasant evening than to listen to the output of a mystery man. Fritz Delius lived in France. His name was German. But the tale went that he had been born in England.

The performers had gathered on the stage: bald men in frock coats who played arpeggios on their harps and scales on their clarinets, a youth half-staggering under the bulk of a tuba, violinists and cellists adjusting their chairs and the scores on their racks. The composer was present, it was said, but he wasn't on the stage and nobody knew what he looked like. When the lights went down there was a rustle of programs, then a hush. Stout, black-bearded Maestro Alfred Hertz, of Germany's Breslau Opera House, mounted the podium to prolonged applause. There was no mystery about Maestro Hertz. He had enough prestige to make his London hearers receptive, and the unknown music was probably worth something if he liked it enough to give a whole concert of it. He straightened his glasses over the bridge of his nose and then tapped his baton. Softly the strings began the first faint melody of *Over the Hills and Far Away*, billed as "a Fantasia."

To hear it it was necessary to be utterly still. A haunting tune began wandering through the orchestra until the pitch mounted into harsh chords in the brasses gleaming behind hot footlights. Up and up the music went, a beckoning dance that evoked wind-swept moors and austere fir trees and cold rivers and always a range to be climbed beyond. Obviously it

was difficult to play. The musicians were wiping their fore-
heads when the piece ended and into the fresh silence broke
loud applause. What weird harmonies! Had the audience
heard as many wrong notes as it thought? Yet the fantasia
had held them and made them want to hear more. It had begun luring them into a world of sound they understood was
like no other they had ever known: at once wistful, violent,
bittersweet, and mocking.

In the movements of the *Norwegian Suite* which followed
there was satire; in a violin solo, homesickness; in a set of
Scandinavian songs, shadowy discords; in a solemn chorus,
meditations on human life. Most of it was less than catchy;
you couldn't hum it easily. By intermission the critics were
scribbling furiously, students were arguing, and visiting concert managers were frowning. Would the public go on wanting this stuff as they seemed to, or were they just momentarily hypnotized? Yet nothing in the first part of the program
prepared anybody for the second.

Delius had writen an opera—a Negro opera, set in America where no operas were ever set. Surely Negroes were for
minstrel shows, jolly men in blackface who sang ditties and
tap-danced. But these Negroes were real. Though there was
no scenery, and the opera was being sung piecemeal in concert, and the singers were white, a drama of slavery on a
southern plantation began to unfold in melodies that were
passionate with understanding of an African prince in chains,
a slave woman betrayed by white overseers, and the bitterness of separation when human lives were bought and sold
because the victims' skins were black. *Koanga* was tragic on a
grand scale and so were its characters: Koanga the prince,
Palmyra the mixed-blood woman he loved and who joined
him in death, white men corrupted by the system of bondage
they had created. Once the orchestra burst into the abandon-
ment of a Negro dance, the Calinda, that called up images of

torchlit clearings in dark swamps as tambourines and a banjo beat out the hard rhythms. (One of the students listening knew a singer up front; during rehearsal the soloists had all had to hold their fingers in their ears, so outlandish were the Negro music and its instruments.)

Yet when the last notes of *Koanga* had died away the applause was louder than ever. The crowd began to clamor for the composer. If they were puzzled, they were now also consumed with curiosity. As a man sitting near the aisle rose and began to make his way to the platform they strained forward. On stage, he turned to them: dark-haired and tall and slender, probably in his late thirties, immaculate in carefully tailored evening clothes, his smile slight and startled, his blue eyes shrewd and intense in a pallid face. But how positively elegant he looked for a musician! Several times he bowed, gravely but hesitantly. Then he quickly vanished into the throng, and they saw no more of him. The evening was over.

Next morning the newspapers were full of the event. Some of the reviewers were savage: "There is nothing beautiful in ugliness, though Mr. Delius is evidently not of my way of thinking. The ugliness of his music is really masterly. It is his duty to cheer up. Life itself gives one one's share of 'the blues.' " "Discordant, harsh, uninviting." "The music is bizarre and cacophonous to a degree almost unapproached." Some were frankly baffled: "What the devil to make of this music?" Some were moved: "It sends the blood tingling through one's veins. It is music of today, or, rather, of tomorrow." Some wrote extravagantly of "signs of greatness," "heaven-sent," a new era in opera. One added soberly:

> England ought to know something about one of the few composers of genius she has the good fortune to possess . . . I have used the word genius, a rash action,

but no one present at the Delius concert could have
had it far from his lips.

Fritz Delius was indeed English—a Yorkshireman of German ancestry who had traveled in Scandinavia and now
lived in a tiny French village—but English nevertheless. Why
then had he chosen to give such a bitter picture of southern
American slavery in *Koanga?* When the truth was learned it
was more unexpected than the music had been, for all its
blue notes and banjo twangs. Fritz Delius had once also
been a southern planter—a grower of oranges in Florida.
He had learned his harmonies from the Negroes themselves.
He had lived among them, known them as individuals, and
thought they were artists with a music to give the world.
What he had taken from them was not only their spirituals
but echoes of Africa in the work songs they had gone on
singing as a conquered people. Their blues and rags and
chants, he believed, were for concert halls. The musical history of their sufferings and of their triumph over them could
no longer be ignored.

The newspaper accounts gradually filtered into English
counties—especially Yorkshire. One morning in the textile
city of Bradford a rich wool merchant sat at his breakfast
table reading the *Yorkshire Post.* Ranged in a row were his
large family of daughters and his wife, and in their dark gowns
on which he permitted no embroidery they all waited in silence
as he rustled page after page. They had lived in fear of his
tyranny long enough to know they must be spoken to before
speaking. There had been sons, but all of them had left. Julius
Delius, the ruler of Claremont, a forbidding brick mansion in Horton Lane, was now carefully scanning the textile
and stock market reports. Then there was the foreign news:
the threat of war between the English and the South African
Dutch, a speech by the quarrelsome German Kaiser. From

time to time Julius Delius cleared his throat in disapproval.
When he had finished sipping his tea he folded up his paper,
laid it neatly beside his plate, and rose to leave for the office.
He was never late. Briefly he paused to inspect his row of
womenfolk with a stare. Then he spoke a single icy sentence:
"I see Fritz has given a concert."

The subject, they knew, was closed.

2 &* Yorkshire

Fritz, the second son of Julius Friedrich Wilhelm Delius and
his wife Elise, had been born in Bradford thirty-seven years
before. January 29, 1862, had been a grim afternoon when
Yorkshire fog and factory dust were mingled outside Claremont's narrow windows in a thick pall. From the mansion's
high chimneys wound spirals of coal smoke; fires had to
crackle brightly in Claremont grates during the long season of
cold. The wide lawn behind an iron fence lay brown from
frost and sunless days. At its summer best, industrial Bradford
was never inspiring. At its winter worst, it was depressing. By
day the smog was gray, faintly sour. At night, where the city's
lights flickered through, it hung down an eerie greenish-white.

Fritz Théodor Albert Delius was baptized into the Church
of England in solemn ceremony. With his brother Ernest, six
years older, he would go into the family business. That much
had been decided by their parents long before either of the
boys had lain in their cradles. All their lives they would live
where the tall smokestacks and telegraph poles stretched in a
grimy forest for miles on the banks of a small tributary of the
Aire river. Beyond and above the factories of Bradford
brooded the stony Pennine hills on whose slopes noisy steam
trains chugged past heaps of smoldering slag, the discarded
refuse of mill furnaces. The tops of the Pennines were moors,
treeless and somber and thick with clumps of bilberry bushes
and the heather native Yorkshiremen called ling. Sheep for-
aged for sedge grass beside small Pennine streams. The out-
lying landscape was as rough and downright as its people,

with their broad speech and their faces reddened by the rigors
of the weather they had endured.

But Julius and Elise Delius themselves had not been born in
Yorkshire's West Riding—or thirding, in an older English
dialect. They had both come from Germany. Elise's family, the
Krönigs, were romantic. Her father prided himself on his
patronage of artists. Her mother, a famous beauty, came of
royal blood. A prince of the Swedish dynasty of Vasa had
renounced his title to marry a commoner he loved, and Elise's
mother was descended from that union. On his deathbed the
prince had charged his children: "You need bow the knee to
none but God." Afterwards, from the turrets of his castle,
Schwarzenraben, the Swedish royal standard had flown at
half mast. Elise's mother had inherited the silver and claret
coach the long-ago pair had eloped in. It stood resplendent in
the Krönig stables. Elise also had a relative who was safely
married to a French count but who had once been a singer on
the concert stage. Julius Delius strongly disapproved. He loved
music, but musicians were people you hired to brighten your
leisure hours in the drawing room. Never were they social
equals. How could a family related to royalty permit such a
degradation?

The Deliuses were as ancient as the Krönigs, if not as well
documented. Julius had grown up on what his kinsmen all
called "the scarlet and gold tapestry of the Delius legend."
Had not the Greek god Apollo, of the island of Delos, been
called the Delian Apollo? Had not Julius Caesar's sister married a Roman general named Caius Delius, one of the first of
the family to bear arms for king and country? Caius Delius's
was an example to live up to. The Delius name was one of the
few unchanged throughout history, Julius told his children.
The Caesars claimed the Delian Apollo as the god of their
imperial line. Julius Delius himself was Julius Caesar's name-
sake. "There is more genealogy in the shape of a nose than in

papers," he would say wisely. He looked like the Caesars: his features were strong and clear-cut, his nose aquiline, his mouth thin and hard.

In the middle ages a Delius had served as chaplain to the King of England. Later Deliuses had married into several artistic European families: the Esterhazys, patrons of Franz Josef Haydn, and the von Arnims, patrons of Ludwig van Beethoven. A branch of the Delius family also migrated to Spain. One of its leaders became a subject for society scandalizing as The Red Delius of Malaga. The Red Delius was dashing, had auburn hair, deep blue eyes, and a long nose— family traits—and loved a Spanish countess married to another man. Most of Julius's closer relatives and forbears were less memorable, but all knew their name dated back to the mists of antiquity and also that the Deliuses were capable on occasion of producing men and women of strong temperament, fierce independence, and even recklessness.

Julius's immediate ancestors had been university professors and clergymen. None had had any experience as manufacturers. His father, an officer in the Prussian army, had helped fight off the hordes of Napoleon. During one battle he had been carrying a large repeater watch in his pocket and the watch had stopped a French bullet from killing him. Julius Delius treasured the keepsake, its glass broken and dial scorched, its hands pointing forever at seven minutes to seven. Deliuses were brave, he said, ready under God's providence for heavy responsibility. If they glittered in "the scarlet and gold tapestry" of their legend, they were also prepared for the world's daily duties.

In the German military town of Bielefeld, where Julius Delius and Elise Krönig had spent their childhoods, soldiers had paraded stiffly in front of gray barracks. Nearby Bielefeld factories turned out linens and glassware, and Julius noted that their rich owners had even more power than the highest-ranking officers. As a young man he longed to build an industrial empire of his own, to share that power. Unlike the aristocrats of England, those of Germany saw no shame in commerce. When his oldest brother emigrated to Manchester, in the heart of England's industrial belt, to establish a wool business Julius followed him, borrowing money to found a branch of the business at Bradford. Bradford was north of Manchester, not far from Leeds. Already Bradford had a large colony of German merchants who traded profitably with Manchester, Leeds, and the Fatherland. After Julius revisited Bielefeld to marry Elise Krönig, he took her back to Yorkshire and they both became subjects of the English Queen, Victoria. Elise brought with her an autographed portrait of Prussia's Chancellor, Bismarck, a family friend, and hung it over her bed. "Dear Uncle Otto," she would sigh when she was homesick. Julius insisted that the pillows below be sprinkled nightly with German cologne.

But whether Julius and Elise Delius lived their lives as German or English hardly mattered. Queen Victoria herself had more German blood than English, and the two countries had been staunch allies for most of their history. Together, a half century before, Germany and England had stopped the ravages of Napoleon. Now they shared their commerce and a moral code that prized hard work and its reward, wealth. In Bradford, lines of mill-hands bent each day over clacking looms and at night they tended the furnace fires that flamed up orange in the valley. It was all very congenial to Julius Delius. He took seriously his obligation as a citizen, helping to found the town's first orphanage and its first children's hospital. In Bradford a man could see the results of his labor. Elise, who loved her husband but also feared him, agreed. She was stern and proud. He was sterner and prouder.

The small brown river that swished and swirled through The Flat, Bradford's center, was polluted with chemical refuse.

In it was rinsed the fleece that came from West Riding shepherds but also from ranches as far away as the colonies of Australia and New Zealand. After the fleece was rinsed it was carded into wool. The short fibers separated out during the carding were called noils. Delius and Company, Wool and Noil Merchants, sold the raw material from which sturdy Yorkshire yarns were spun and then woven into worsted, serge, and alpaca. Julius Delius was canny and dedicated. His cardings were always "up to sample"—as good as the first batch. Not long after he had settled in Bradford he had paid back his loan and was doing an international business which continued to swell his bank accounts. By the time his son Fritz was born he was able to hire whole orchestras for the elaborate evening parties he and Elise gave at Claremont for the rest of Bradford's tycoons and their wives.

Pleasure, Julius believed, ought to be as disciplined and regulated as work. He sent for music masters to teach his children correct fingering and the classics as they grew up. Ernest, the oldest, showed ability on the cello. Clare, a daughter, sang. Such talents were all very well in their way. Julius took his children to Manchester to hear Sir Charles Hallé conduct the symphony he had founded, the Hallé orchestra, of which Julius was a patron, and to the Theatre Royal in Leeds to see the ballet. Sometimes at night he permitted the children to leave the nursery door open and listen to the chamber music concerts below. One evening when Fritz was five he was spellbound by a violinist.

"I want a violin," he announced the next morning.

Julius was startled. The child wasn't even old enough for regular school lessons. "What can you do with a violin, Fritz?"

"I can play it," Fritz told him firmly.

At his son's determination Julius permitted himself to smile. It was a trait he wanted to encourage. Fritz would need it in Delius and Company. If the boy turned out to be a good player, Julius would see that he had a violin of the best quality —a Cremona, perhaps, costing hundreds of pounds, but worthy of a Delius. Fritz was made to learn all the family traditions. He adored them from the start.

Julius also smiled when Fritz climbed onto the stool in front of the battered Erard upright piano in the nursery classroom. Fritz was able to remember tunes, it seemed. Very well; he should have lessons immediately. It was a pity he preferred trying snatches of his own to practicing finger exercises. "You must learn to play correctly," his father warned him. "Haydn, Mozart, Beethoven, and drill." His mother bought him a black velvet suit and when she had company she would order Fritz's governess to dress him and bring him downstairs.

"Now make up something," she would coax, pleased at his lack of shyness in front of her friends. Of all her sons and daughters—there would eventually be twelve—Fritz had the sunniest disposition. Ernest could be sullen and withdrawn. Clare was a dreamer. Fritz's eyes, a clear, dark Delius blue, sparkled when he laughed. His hair was auburn and he had inherited the wiry build of his ancestors.

Fritz was also a favorite with his godparents. One of them, his uncle Théodor Delius, had never married. In the beginning Théodor had been a partner in Delius and Company, but recently he had preferred to leave the business to Julius and had settled in Paris, from which he brought toys and candy to Fritz on Bradford visits. Julius now resented Théodor; it was not right that any man should live in idleness. Everybody knew the French were light-minded and extravagant. Théodor was rumored to be having love affairs. Fritz's godmother was a better example. Aunt Albertine Delius had married a Krönig relative and lived in Bielefeld. She too visited Bradford from time to time. She had made careful investments with her inheritance and was almost rich herself. She was pleased when she learned that Fritz enjoyed going to Bradford's All Saints

Church and paying close attention to the hymns. She herself was religious and musical. She played the piano.

As he continued his church attendance Fritz became devout. He began to mark religious feast days on his calendar, and when they came he observed them in his prayers. Each year at Christmas he and Ernest and Clare sang hymns and carols for their parents. The Church of England, its rhythms and pageants, its dignified forms, appealed strongly to the children. Fritz himself began a habit of meditation about God and the world of nature He had made. This meditation was intense and emotional, and he could lose himself in it easily when he practiced it.

Not for a moment did Julius Delius permit his family to forget that the center of their world was Delius and Company. From it came all their luxuries, music included. To it they owed their respect, the boys their careers. He was thankful when his third son Max was born. Who knew what heights Delius and Company might reach with three strong sons to run it? When he sent them successively to Mr. Frankland's Day School in Horton Lane near Claremont, he gave directions that they were to concentrate on mathematics, the basis of office routine. Ernest, slow at figures, was to have extra help if necessary. After school Julius enjoyed leading his sons gravely through ornately bordered doors to the carding rooms where rows of machines banged away beside small-paned windows. The factory foremen bowed and stood aside. Poor lads, they thought as they watched Ernest and Fritz and Max marching ahead of their father like little soldiers. They would have to look sharp to stay out of trouble with Julius Delius's temper.

Most of Bradford felt sorry for the Delius children. Sometimes when their governess was herding her charges down the city's main street she would hear the sudden tinkling of a shop doorbell and a hurried friendly whisper: "Oh, miss, miss!

You'd better bring the children inside. I see Mr. Delius coming!"

This was because whenever Julius met his children in public, he inspected them. He checked the bonnets of the girls and the caps of the boys for frayed edges. He squinted to see if there were any shiny places on the elbows and collars of their coats. Particularly he examined their feet. If he found a run-down heel or a scuffed toe, he exploded into an angry torrent and then led his brood off to the bootmaker's for new shoes. Back at Claremont, Elise protested at "this glut of footwear." After all, old shoes could be repaired.

"Madam," her husband warned her, "the children must be dressed correctly." He himself patronized the tailor of the royal family in London. A Delius was expected to be perfect. Governesses came and went under the strain. The townspeople of Bradford murmured to each other in deep-throated West Riding accents that the pale little girls might turn out well enough, but the boys might rebel: "Happen the lads will go wrong." Surely there were some lurking high spirits behind those bright blue eyes.

The mill hands weren't surprised when they began to find Fritz and Max playing tag in the warehouses where high bales of fleece were wrapped against moth damage. Fritz was the leader. The Delius employees didn't want to betray him, and he decided they were "fine fellows" for it. He was bored with the endless arithmetic of his classroom. He and Max liked to spend their time thinking of what it would be like to run away and join the circus. They had seen a traveling carnival in Bradford. Signor Luigi, in tights and spangles, had performed daredevil bareback feats. Fritz got up a circus in the Delius nursery, teaching Max and Clare to swing from brass curtain rods to the top poles of their canopied beds. When Elise found out about the circus, she was too late to prevent the irreparable damage it had done to the bedframes.

Fritz enjoyed inventing things. He and Max loved *The Arabian Nights* and its legends of the East, but especially they loved penny-dreadfuls, cheap paperbound adventure stories like *Buffalo Bill* and *Sweeny Todd, The Demon Barber*. In this tale the barber's customers disappeared one by one through a trap door and were taken away to be converted into pork pies. The only time to read *Sweeny Todd* in peace was at night. Fritz fixed up a string and pulley machine which could turn down the gas whenever his parents passed the nursery door. Elise discovered the machine during a housecleaning session, and Fritz was lectured by his father for wilful disobedience.

There was also the affair of a neighbor's ducks. They quacked noisily while Fritz was practicing the piano. One day he decided he had had enough quacking and stole out to mix some of his father's best rum with the ducks' feeding mash. Soon afterward they were sprawled quackless in what the neighbor at first thought was a strange and possibly fatal disease—until he came close enough to smell the trough. The culprit was all too easy to guess: the second Delius boy, the brightest one. Rebellion was natural in the house of iron-willed Julius Delius, as arrogant as any fallen angel in mythology. "Here comes Lucifer!" the members of his Bradford club would whisper when he entered the club's lounge. No one dared to sit beside him.

One summer day in 1870, when Fritz was eight and Max was six, they decided the time had come to leave Bradford. Fritz filched a supply of candy from the Claremont kitchen. "We have to have the necessary provisions," he explained to Max. At four o'clock in the morning the boys sneaked downstairs and set out on foot for the neighboring village of Ilkley. When they arrived bedraggled and thirsty after a climb of several miles over the moors, they were discovered by a friend of their father's and handed over to the guard of the Bradford train. Julius, a telegram in hand, met the train himself. "How do you dare?" he thundered at his sons. "Why do you leave home?"

"To have an adventure," Fritz answered truthfully. There were few enough chances for adventuring at Claremont.

His favorite excursions were to the hamlet of Haworth, a few miles west of Bradford, where a family named Brontë had lived in the rectory. At Haworth, Emily Brontë had written a novel, *Wuthering Heights,* and after Clare had read it, she told Fritz and Max about it. She loved tramping over the moor to Withens Farm, the novel's real-life setting. Sometimes too the Deliuses took their children to Skipton, which boasted one of the few real castles in the West Riding. At Skipton there were the echoes of a nearby waterfall to hear, silent guardrooms to explore, ancient lead-framed glass windows to stare up at, and dead knights and ladies to imagine. Noble and strange names were carved into the worn tombstones in the church: bygone barons and earls, the forgotten henchmen of kings. It was all like one of the verses Fritz had read, Tennyson's *The Princess*:

> The splendour falls on castle walls
> And snowy summits old in story . . .

It was easy to think of splendors at Skipton over the moors.

Rombald's Moor, near Ilkley, was one of the wildest of them. It stretched black in the harsh light of day, but its shrubs turned golden-brown and lavender in the softness of dawns and twilights. Fritz's parents never noticed an odd habit he was developing, but Max and Clare did. Sometimes on Rombald's Moor he would stop and stand perfectly still for a few minutes while the wind sang in the sedges or a plover cried. Then he would hike on, talking and laughing, as if the incident hadn't happened. Smiling, he would shake his head and refuse to explain what had held him.

He savored autumn, when he could trudge with Max and

Clare after school over damp turf paths. In the pale blue sky overhead the distant clouds were massed like fortresses. The smell of the heather was sharp and spicy. He was unafraid of cold evenings when the few stunted moor oaks shivered in winds full of snow flurries. In April the oaks' bare branches moaned in the rain but he was heedless of its falling, wishing he could stay on the moors forever and forget the factories below. What was their ugliness compared to the march of spring across the Pennines?

Such thoughts were foolish, he realized. Besides, his father would be angry if he knew them. Uncle Théodor had also disliked factories. Now he was frittering his life away in Paris. What was the use, Julius wanted to know? What would be the results? Fritz must apply himself—at the piano, for instance. What was the purpose of hiring the expensive Mr. Haddock of Leeds to teach Fritz proper technique if Fritz mooned about with his own improvising instead? The reports of Mr. Bauerkeller, the violin master from the Hallé orchestra, were more encouraging. They proved Fritz could concentrate if he tried.

Each year, late in the summer, Julius and Elise Delius took their children to the East Riding for their health. The air of the coast, they believed, was beneficial. Julius hired a private railroad car and when it arrived at the port of Filey crammed with children, governesses, nannies and under-nannies, the station master would nod: "The season has begun. The Deliuses are here." Steep red bluffs towered over the rough North Sea at Filey and foamy spray scattered crashing on the rocks in fitful sunlight. In The Crescent, Julius rented a fashionable cream-colored stone house which had a piano. Fritz and Max and Clare spent their days scrambling over windswept cliffs. Once Fritz found a sailor on the docks who talked of what he had seen on his merchant ship in the farthest corners of the world: street bazaars and palm trees and coral reefs and brown-skinned natives. Breathlessly Fritz hurried home and played new melodies to Max and Clare: "Listen! That's a wood, hanging on the shore of a coral island . . . That's where the river meets the sea. And listen! That's a bird . . . This is sunset in the tropics . . . This is the dawn."

Filey Bay was a large curve protected by a ledge of rock, the Brig, which was exposed only at low tide. One afternoon some local boys begged Fritz to go out to the Brig with them. When he ran eagerly to get permission from Julius, Julius refused. Resentfully Fritz watched the boys swimming away from the beach. At home he was sullen. The next morning the boys' bodies were washed ashore. They had been trapped out of their depth among scraping reefs and turbulent waves while bell buoys clanged and the spray roared. Fritz was stunned. What was death? Could it happen to you by chance that way? How were its victims chosen? For a long time he brooded about the tragedy. His father could not resist an "I told you so," but he encouraged him to begin playing cricket with farm hands in the nearby villages of Gristhorpe and Hunmanby. Finally the experience receded.

Fritz, in high spirits one afternoon, persuaded Clare and another sister to try wearing their satin sashes around their hips instead of their waists. It was smarter, he said. When the girls went downstairs Julius roared at them: "Put your sashes where God meant them to be!" and guessed the culprit. Once more Fritz was in trouble, though his father was soon mollified by watching Fritz's developing skill at cricket. Deliuses must excel; Julius was pleased, and when the family returned to Bradford, he bought Fritz a horse, Black Bess.

She was a tall and shining beauty, and forgetting the consequences of daring Fritz rode her hard. She was also skittish; she would shy at a piece of paper on the ground. Over Rombald's Moor the red grouse scurried away from Black Bess's hooves, and lapwings soared and plunged ahead above the heather against the haze of the hills beyond. Faster and faster he urged the mare to gallop at breakneck speed. When he stood up in the saddle to try a riding trick, she stumbled. He was thrown and knocked unconscious, dragged for yards over scrub and rocks, and was found lying in a pool of blood. His head was a mass of matted hair and scraped flesh. Afterwards at Claremont he had to spend long days in bed recovering from what the doctor said was a serious injury, possibly to his brain.

Julius worried and paced his study. What was the matter with the boy? Why couldn't he be moderate? Julius lectured and punished. Time after time, when Fritz had recovered, miraculously unscarred, he had to be sent to his room. To live at Claremont was "like living on a volcano," whispered Clare. What made Julius's temper worse was the growing disinterest of Ernest in his studies at the Bradford Grammar School. Ernest seemed hardly to care whether he was fit for Delius and Company or not. Several nights, to discipline him, Julius locked him out of Claremont. It was Clare who stole down to let him in when the house was dark. Fritz would be made to care about Delius and Company more than anything on earth.

In 1874, when he was twelve, he entered the Bradford Grammar School himself. He was tall for his age, with a shock of dark hair, quick eyes, a long nose, and a mouth that more often than not was smiling. His teachers liked him, but he wasn't a very good student, they reported. Like Ernest, he hated arithmetic. In geography he was bright enough, but even here he had a tendency to recoil from learning details. He preferred planning imaginary voyages. Julius was furious because he knew Fritz could remember astonishing details when he cared. One holiday afternoon Fritz and Clare and Max had been permitted to attend a Bradford performance of the Christy Minstrels, an American troup of singers. The minstrels were white men who had blacked their faces to look like Negroes, and they danced out what the program said were Negro songs or "Ethiopian melodies":

> I wheel about, I turn about,
> I do jist so!
> And ebery time I turn about
> I jump Jim Crow!

Afterwards Fritz had been able to play every number.

There had been the time, too, when one of Julius's friends had introduced Fritz to the modern Romantic composers. The friend had played a lilting Chopin waltz. Fritz was able to play it back after hearing it only twice, his father noted. "Not, of course, very correctly," Fritz had at least admitted. Chopin was pleasant but light stuff, his father thought. The trouble with Fritz was that he didn't settle down to what mattered.

Only once was Julius really proud of him. That was the evening when the great German violinist Joseph Joachim came to play at Claremont for a gala entertainment. When he arrived, bearded and ponderous, his bushy eyebrows upslanted at the corners, it turned out that he needed a second violin to accompany him in one of his pieces. Fritz himself volunteered. Concentrating fixedly on the music rack and the score it held, he got through without a mistake. "Splendid!" Joachim congratulated him. "You have great musical feeling." It was time, decided Julius, to buy Fritz the Cremona violin. The boy's mastery of his hobby should be rewarded. Now he would have to be driven harder to master his schoolwork.

For a while Fritz stayed "out of hot water," as Clare put it. But the newly pleasant atmosphere at Claremont was soon shattered. Ernest had gone into the offices of Delius and Company and was doing badly. One night there was a sudden and terrible conflict between father and son. He hated Delius and Company, Ernest shouted at his father. He didn't care if he ever saw it again. What did a book-keeping mistake matter? He wanted to leave Bradford and Yorkshire forever. He would go anywhere to avoid the factory whose routine was driving him out of his mind. He couldn't stand the torment of Bradford and his father's rigid control any longer.

Perhaps, suggested Julius after a frightening silence, Ernest was fit to raise sheep? Perhaps that was all he was fit for? Perhaps he would accept some money to sail out to New Zealand, since a Delius could hardly be permitted to beg? Let Ernest try his luck as a rancher. He would be given a single chance. That was all.

Ernest went up to the nursery to say good-by. "Dear little Clare." He bent over his sister. "You are the only one I really care a damn about." Fritz heard him and never forgot. Ernest cared nothing for him, he understood.

After Ernest had left, his name was seldom mentioned. Julius's disappointment was deep and bitter. Elise was heart-broken. Then Julius made an announcement. Fritz was the oldest son now, the heir. He was fourteen. It was time he left his grammar school for greater educational opportunities. He was young to go, but so were most English boys. He must be prepared for leadership in international finance. For this a special sort of institution was required, and Julius, after a careful search, believed he had found just the one. Its students were drilled in modern languages, natural history, and chemistry according to the advanced theories of Britain's most eminent scientist, Thomas Henry Huxley, who was chairman of the International Education Society. The society had its own college at Isleworth, a London suburb. Perhaps now and then Fritz might even have time to hear a concert.

3 ⚭ "The Shades of the Prison-House"

On his way down to enroll at the International College Fritz stopped in London. His father had given him permission to stay at the Langham Hotel, one of the city's newest and most elaborate. He would be allowed to attend an evening of modern music in the Covent Garden Opera House. *Lohengrin,* by the German Richard Wagner, was currently being performed to shocked audiences who were protesting that Wagner broke all the rules of harmony with his strident brasses. The opera was more than twenty-five years old, but to the English its composer remained a heretic. Wagner, they said, was not graceful like the Italians, Bellini and Rossini. There were no beguiling melodies to whistle as you left the theater. Instead of sparkling arias like those which adorned Rossini's *Barber of Seville,* Wagner gave his public gods and heroes torn by the real-life emotions of ambition, passion, and revenge. He was impure, complained moralists horrified by his frank depictions of love. Nevertheless *Lohengrin* was playing to packed houses. Everybody wanted to be offended in person.

Fritz surprised himself by a suddenly poignant homesickness in his carpeted room at the Langham. London was vast and impersonal. Beggars and flower-girls jostled each other in its narrow streets, and hansom cabs rattled by in an endless procession. The tangy odor of chrysanthemums in the window boxes of town houses larger than Claremont was mixed with the fishiness of the river Thames and the closeness of coal smoke. In Bradford he had known every building; he had been able to call most of his father's workers by name. When he had walked in the streets, men had doffed their hats to the future head of Delius and Company, and their wives had smiled. In London he was only a fourteen-year-old of no importance. The city's people were oblivious of him.

The night of the *Lohengrin* performance he was dazzled by the glow of gas lamps and the jewels and furs of the women who sat in their boxes at Covent Garden. Awed and shy, he slipped into his seat, feeling lonelier than ever in the midst of a crowd which had surely heard music he hardly knew by name. When the house lights lowered, he had no idea of what he was going to be listening to. In Bradford the Deliuses had been the town's musical authorities. Here, he was afraid, they would be dismissed as provincial, behind the times.

Then the miracle happened. He forgot his homesickness and his family and even himself. The soaring voices began to sweep him away from all reality into glittering dreams. What daring, in the rich orchestration with its complex divisions of the strings. It was impossible simply to watch the opera; you became a part of its characters and all the things that happened to them and what they felt. Was not the mysterious knight Lohengrin, with his secret past, like any musician or artist who demanded to be valued for himself alone? The tumultuous cadences went on pouring out and by intermission time Fritz knew he would be under their spell for years to come. Beethoven was dry stuff, Mozart now seemed stilted. Mozart had made operas; Wagner made worlds.

Fritz knew, too, that he could never give up spending hours a day at his own music. He would continue violin lessons at the International College, and he would save his allowance for as many trips to London as he could manage. He had to go on hearing Wagner and Chopin as well as discovering the other romantics who were little more than names to him; Edvard Grieg the Norwegian, Berlioz the Frenchman. Abruptly the chamber concerts Julius Delius had given at Bradford seemed insignificant. Even the Hallé orchestra, with its heavily traditional programs, could never matter half as much as the enchanted nights Fritz meant to spend whenever he got the chance in Covent Garden and St. James Hall. The music for him was the music of emotion, not form. And it was life, not recreation.

His housemaster at the International College soon decided he was a curious combination, this boy from Yorkshire. He was alternately shy and enthusiastic, full of laughter, but thoughtful too. He was an experienced cricketer, and surely he would lead the school to future victories. Yet he also said he was a music student and immediately signed up for violin practice with Mr. Deichmann, the music master, whose white whiskers had earned him the nickname of The Walrus. When The Walrus told Fritz that an amateur orchestra had been formed at the nearby town of Chiswick he begged to join. The orchestra played once a week under the direction of a Mr. Sommers, who found the boy from Yorkshire as startling as the college authorities had. Fritz Delius was obsessively dedicated for anybody destined for the buying and selling of wool—too dedicated, perhaps, too intense. Startling also was his rough Yorkshire accent, peppered occasionally and un-expectedly with German. He called boys and girls lads and lasses, yet he said *orchester* instead of orchestra, and it took some figuring to understand that when he spoke of an "ayderadoon" he meant an eiderdown quilt. Sometimes he talked longingly of home and the moors (yet the father in the case was a Tartar, one heard). Quickly Fritz made friends with his classmates and began punishing balls with unmerciful regularity on the cricket grounds. He played the fielding posi-tion of slip, close to the batter, and had never, he boasted proudly, dropped a catch.

He had surprised the masters and students of the college; the college surprised him even more. Its main building was a hideously towered sham-gothic pile of yellow brick. Imitation medieval stonework bordered the doors and windows of the central block and both wings. It had been erected at a cost of £15,000 ten years earlier and had been opened by the Prince of Wales himself. Originally the International Education Society had set up three separate colleges, one in France and one in Germany as well as the one in England at Isleworth. All would have the same curriculum; the students would spend part of their time at each college and would thereby become proficient in three languages. Such cosmopolitan intimacy would, hoped Thomas Henry Huxley and his fellow-educators, "put an end to war and the rumors of war." The original dream had lasted just until 1870 and the Franco-Prussian war when German soldiers had besieged and conquered Paris. The French and German colleges had been closed down for lack of students interested in peace.

But the one at Isleworth survived to advertise bravely in the *London Times*: "Unfettered by traditional usage, this College, while preserving what is good in the older institutions, assigns a prominent place to subjects of the utmost importance in our time." The Headmaster, Dr. Leonhard Schmitz, was the Prince of Wales's former tutor. He ruled with a rod of iron like the militarist that he was, and he directed the teaching of subjects never heard of at staid schools like Eton or Harrow, both of which stressed Latin and Greek. The International College boasted natural history, "advanced experimental physics," and something called social science, which included "the Theory of Commerce, Law, and Government." The college's fees were impressively high. The single characteristic it shared with every other boys' school in Britain was the worship of athletes who could win trophies.

As revolutionary as the courses were the students. The International Education Society had insisted no restrictions on race or nationality were to be tolerated. French, German,

Spanish, and Portuguese boys mixed with breezy Americans and temperamental Brazilians and Nicaraguans, many of them in the habit of settling their youthful rivalries with knives. Dr. Schmitz castigated them, and sometimes they rebelled at his edicts about stern diets and ice-cold baths. On one occasion they barricaded their doors against him in a self-imposed siege. At night they let down ropes from their windows. Supplies were loaded into the hanging baskets from the nearest pub by scouts stationed outside. When Dr. Schmitz found his orders to open up unheeded, he called the police, who broke down the doors with billy clubs and then withstood a barrage of paper balls soaked in brandy. Ten of the ringleaders were expelled that particular time, but the "mixed bag" of boys who remained continued to tax Dr. Schmitz's temper. The English taught cricket and soccer to the Latin Americans, one of whom "raged over the ground like a goaded bull" during the games. "His tackle's like an octopus swallowing you whole," complained one of his victims.

The Latin Americans in turn taught the English how to smoke. One, a Chilean named Perez, was feared by his teachers as "a wizened, preternaturally wise old youth." In this gathering of cigar-chewing teenagers from all over the world, something had happened to Thomas Henry Huxley's ideal of the tranquil Brotherhood of Man. Instead, a high-spirited confederacy of mischief-makers continually challenged disciplinarians who shouted rules in ferocious succession. The weaker masters admitted to real terror. Settling the boys down to *Paradise Lost* and the Law of International Commerce took ingenuity. Delius from Yorkshire was at least civilized. If he was eccentric enough to want to play his violin and take the train to Chiswick once a week to be in concerts instead of laboring over his schoolbooks, what could be done? Also, he was the best cricketer the International College had ever had.

Julius Delius, of course, had no idea of the wild goings-on

at Isleworth: the brandy in the dormitories, the summoning of police, the knives in students' trouser pockets, and the classroom heckling. Like other parents he had been sent glowing reports of the great skill of the staff and the healthfulness of the site, nearly a mile away from the Thames. Isleworth itself was full of the greenhouses of market gardeners and of apple orchards where laden branches were propped up every autumn by long sticks. Isleworth skies were blue and clear. There were two industries, a soap factory and a brewery, but the town was still rural. It had seen one vivid event of history centuries before when Lady Jane Grey had accepted the crown of England at the Duke of Northumberland's mansion, Syon House. Now Syon House drowsed behind a tall iron fence, and away from it stretched a park full of venerable beech trees.

Fritz and his friends took long walks in chestnut-shaded country lanes and fished for trout in a tiny branch of the Thames. He joined them in their less spectacular pranks: giggling down a pompous bishop in chapel, for instance. Soon he missed the moors of the West Riding less and enjoyed the gentler local landscape and also the admiration of his classmates. All of his courses he found dull; he worked only enough to get by. The least boring, as usual, were languages and geography. In mathematics he was still hopeless. His masters might have grown angrier at him had they not repeatedly been thrilled during cricket matches when they heard him cheered at the bat and watched him score his runs with effortless ease. For his part he found it delightful to be a hero instead of the target of his father's wrath. The only things he wanted to work at besides cricket were the Cremona and the college piano.

The fellow-students who fascinated him most were the Negroes, who came from the West Indian islands of Bermuda, Jamaica, and St. Kitts. He had seen the Christy Minstrels and heard their Ethiopian melodies, but at the International College the Negroes talked of a music he had never known about before: drumming and island dances like the Bamboula and the Calinda, one of the wildest, which men danced stripped to the waist while they brandished heavy sticks in mock battle. Sometimes the battles became real, and in America the Calinda had been outlawed as too dangerous for southern plantations, where Negro workers were already intoxicated at their recent emancipation from slavery. In the West Indies emancipation had taken place over forty years before, and many Negroes had prospered enough to send their sons abroad for schooling. Moaning chants of "Aie, ya, yaie!" would sometimes echo in the college's corridors and Fritz wondered what it would be like to hear them on tropic islands to the insistent beating of log drums. Wagner had been strange, but the Negro music was stranger. Across the western ocean lay a new world of which the old was ignorant. Clearly there was more to its music than the tunes and jigs of Christy. Some day he would go there, to the wide white beaches where French, Spanish, and African music were combined in a heady mixture.

The Negroes at the college were strapping fellows, magnificently strong. There was an ancient dignity about them Fritz had never expected, in spite of their straining at boarding school discipline. They longed only to return to havens that sounded like the Garden of Eden: sugar mills, fruit groves, seaports full of onetime pirates. The Negro boys talked and Fritz listened; then he would go to the piano, trying new improvisations that echoed their alien world, just as he had tried years before to paint in music the far-off landscapes evoked by sailors beached on the Yorkshire coast.

In 1877, he was confirmed in the Church of England by the Bishop of London. It was customary. As a boy he had been religious, keeping the Church's feast days. Lately however he had begun to have strong doubts about the Book of Genesis. The recent experience of hearing a Bradford atheist challenging God to strike him dead in two minutes if He existed hadn't helped. The crowd had waited breathlessly, but God had done nothing. The emotion Fritz had once put into religion he was now putting into music. The confirmation was a gesture to please his parents, who were becoming sharp about his schoolwork.

They were sharper the summer he came home and began his duties as a wool sorter in the Craven and Company Mill at Thornton, just outside the Bradford city limits. He despised the work: poring over piles of rough fleece that reeked of rancid sheep oil, fingering sticky strands in a stifling warehouse. Daily he dreaded his streetcar trip to the torture where his only consolation was the companionship of the factory laborers. He found himself actually longing for the beginning of school, and when he left Bradford for Isleworth again he felt only relief. He hoped he had done his stint in the sorting operation forever.

But as a scholar he showed no improvement. His father wrote a stream of angry letters. Soon the letters became anxious. During a cricket game on the school field one of the boys tossed aside a heavy wooden wicket. It struck Fritz hard in the temple in a blinding flash of pain, knocking him senseless. In the school infirmary the doctors' verdict was concussion of the brain. When he rallied from his coma, he was told he must spend weeks in bed. It was the second bad head injury he had suffered in the space of a few years. Unless he rested completely, the doctors warned, they would not be responsible for the consequences. Day after day he lay propped up on his pillows in a drab room where he watched golden sunlight playing on the brown leaves still clinging to oak branches beyond the window. Agonizing headaches made him long for sleep. When the worst of them passed, he marked time by trying to remember the scores he had studied in the Chiswick orchestra. One afternoon he begged the nursing sister for music paper. He wanted to write something of his own. Feverishly he scribbled nearly illegible notes to the words of a trite, if popular, poem:

> When other lips and other hearts
> Their tales of love shall tell,
> In language whose excess imparts
> The power they feel so well,
> There may perhaps in such a scene
> A recollection be,
> Of days that have as happy been,
> And you'll remember me.

That the poem, by one Alfred Bunn, had already been set to music by another composer didn't bother him. His own music, he decided with a creator's arrogance, would be better. When he had finished, he experienced a mixture of tension and relief, as if a burden had been lifted from his shoulders. The music had been in him and had had to break out. He had known how to let it. Elated, he mailed the song to Clare. She would sing it like an angel; at Claremont she was spending more and more time at the piano.

At last the consulting physicians declared that the injury was probably not permanent. Fritz was permitted to get up. During the summer which followed he had a respite from wool-sorting. His father became unusually gentle and reasonable; Fritz had had a brush with death. Now he passed his days on Rombald's Moor with Clare and Max, climbing his favorite path to a rocky hill near Ilkley. In the autumn Max returned with him to Isleworth. Once more Fritz began to play cricket. Soon he became the official school champion and Dr. Schmitz presented him with a prize certificate and a new bat. Max was beginning his school years in Fritz's reflected glory. That Fritz was a poor student was freshly accepted because of his recent illness. He seemed strong and well, but he had had a shock. The sports-minded masters were grateful his play hadn't suffered. Surely, they reasoned, he could succeed in the wool business without fully understanding the Theory of International Commerce, for he was developing the dash and verve of a salesman. When graduation day came, he heard real regret in their voices when they said good-by to him.

He had always hated schoolwork. Now, at eighteen, he realized his boyhood was over. The music there was in Bradford wouldn't be as splendid as the music in Covent Garden and St. James Hall had been. He would hear cheers in the cricket grounds in Easby Road near Claremont, but they would be only occasional. His time as a hero was over too. The June day he left for home was warm and green and gentle. Farm women in coarse cotton skirts were bundling early asparagus in the fields. The crops were bound for market in a Covent Garden district he might not see for years. But he made up his mind that unlike Ernest and Uncle Théodor he would do his best to succeed in Delius and Company. What else was he fitted for? Oxford and Cambridge universities were out of the question; his grades were too low. Many men earned their livings at things they hated. He was sure he could manage. The first real panic came only when his father told him he had decided to start him in a back office as an accountant. "The shades of the prison-house begin to close," he murmured out of Julius's hearing.

He tried hard at first. The employees watched with dawning compassion as he battled debits and credits in the huge ledgers at which he had to squint, perched on a high stool. They corrected his mistakes for him. When his factory day was over, he fled to the drawing room piano at Claremont, a polished Broadwood grand. Max still remained at Isleworth and Clare had gone to her first boarding school. He was alone, hemmed in. Not a soul in Bradford cared for the things he did—opera, theater, the French painting he was discovering in a few stray magazines that came to the town. Delius and Company officials noted his increasing depression and restlessness. By the autumn of 1881, his work had deteriorated to the point where one of them suggested gently to Julius that his heir really wasn't making any progress. Perhaps he would do better as a salesman. A tight-lipped Julius reluctantly agreed. Fritz was assigned to the Gloucestershire town of Stroud as a traveling agent or "bagman." He was instructed to be as charming as possible to potential customers and to push Delius wool on a full-time basis.

Stroud was a relief. Set in the midst of hills whose beech woods smoldered reddish-gold, it had been a cloth center since the middle ages, but there were few factories processing the raw wool in the town itself. That was done in the north, and Stroud's ravines and lanes were still bordered by high firs and thick hedgerows. There were a hundred walks to take into the Cotswold hills, past gabled cottages, past the canal where you could hear the boatmen singing as donkeys towed their fleece-laden barges past. Robins and cuckoos called overhead. In the pubs Fritz heard tales of bygone highwaymen and of the days when, before Yorkshire and its factories, Stroud had produced so much wool that its valley was called the Golden Valley for the fortunes it had garnered.

The local merchants welcomed him. "What a boy he is!" one of them exclaimed. "The handsomest I ever saw in my life." He adorned dinner tables, was courtly to wives and daughters, and told witty stories about Isleworth escapades. Mothers regarded him with narrowing eyes and soft smiles. The inheritor of a rich industry, possessor of a noble pedigree, full of humor, apparently even-tempered, fond of music, and able to sing after-dinner songs in his light baritone: what better prospective husband could there be? Orders poured in to Delius and Company, and an increased allowance made it possible for Fritz to begin taking the London train for important concerts of Chopin, Wagner, and Grieg. His father, who knew nothing of the trips to London, decided the time for actually promoting him in the firm was near. Instructions came to Stroud for Fritz to report to Wilhelm Vogel and Company in Chemnitz, Germany, as an unpaid apprentice. He would need to see as many phases of the cloth business as he could. In Chemnitz he would have plenty of pocket money, and perhaps he would like the Saxony city which had a variety of after-hours amusements to offer. Also he would be able to visit his godmother, Aunt Albertine Krönig.

Wilhelm Vogel and Company was as taken with him as Stroud had been. His duties, however, were undefined. In Chemnitz he made discoveries. Every such German provincial town had its own theater and opera, and Chemnitz and nearby Dresden had several of the best. In Dresden he heard Wagner's *Die Meistersinger* for the first time. Its robust troubadours' choruses were more stirring than the choruses of *Lohengrin* had been. There were also theater cafés where he met music students and could talk for the first time about Wagner's experiments. And did he know that one of Germany's most famous violinists, Hans Sitt, taught in Chemnitz? In a flush of excitement he began lessons with the master. He preferred the piano for his improvising, but it was well to be able to perform. His fingers were too long for clean piano runs, Sitt said, yet on the violin he had real talent. Had he ever thought of making his living in music?

The idea was preposterous. Musicians earned no decent salaries; Fritz could imagine what his father would say at the very thought. He didn't confide it to Aunt Albertine when he stayed with her on a holiday. But because there was really so little to do at Wilhelm Vogel and Company, he began to ignore it altogether, go to several Chemnitz concerts a week, practice for Sitt until his fingers ached, and wander among Saxon rococo palaces and formal gardens that redeemed the ugliness of nearby mills and linen-bleaching grounds. He heard Karl Goldmark's opera *The Queen of Sheba* and studied the score, marveling at the intricate fitting-together of the orchestra's parts. Would he ever be able to learn the technique of it, the better to understand the effects of large masses of sound? While he lost himself in the Goldmark opera, his superiors sent a sad report to Bradford. Young Herr Delius was most amiable and accomplished, but he could hardly be said to care for wool. He had in fact ceased his connection with it.

A stormy telegram recalled him to Bradford. Before leaving he found a dachshund for Clare, Rip, and the frivolous gift further proved his lack of responsibility to Julius Delius. His father began to find fault with everything about him—his friends, for instance. When a young Bradford merchant came to dinner and after Elise Delius had retired to the drawing room pulled out a pipe, Julius glared at Fritz. Later he shouted: "That man never comes into this house again!" Julius disapproved of pipes.

When neither father nor son could stand the strain of controlling their tempers any longer, Fritz was sent to the Swedish wool town of Norköpping, once more as a bagman. There was no music in Norköpping, so he repeated his successes of Stroud. But when the concert season began in Stockholm, he took to commuting. His orders quickly stopped. He rambled down the old city's cobbled streets, through royal galleries and museums, over the islands around which the silver-blue water of Lake Mälar flowed. Statues of victorious kings—his own kinsmen—and Vikings adorned the squares. He reveled in it all; the crisp air, the hospitable people. Perhaps his father would let him extend this vacation. Actually he had gotten several large orders at first. Impulsively he set out for the mountains of Norway on a hiking tour.

Sweden had been delightful; Norway, with its steep fjords and jagged spruce-covered peaks, was breathtaking. He climbed with a pack on his back to lonely heights where clouds swathed trackless forests. He was free; it was all that mattered. He thrived on country cheeses he bought from mountain farmers in gaily decorated chalets, each with its tidy courtyard. He began to learn Norwegian. In one of the towns he passed through he found a book by a contemporary playwright, Henrik Ibsen. The book was a verse drama, *Brand*, the hero of which was a clergyman who preached emancipation from outworn conventions and from slavery to tyrants. Brand spoke in thunder:

> One thing a man cannot give: his soul.
> He cannot deny his calling.
> He dare not block that river's course;
> It forces its way to the ocean . . .
> A place on the earth where one can be wholly oneself:
> That is Man's right, and I ask no more.

They were disturbing words to a twenty-year-old reared in luxuries it had never occurred to him to do without.

In Bradford that autumn his father's rage was at white heat. Play the truant, would he? Now Julius cut his allowance and sent him to a place where there were no concert halls or tempting landscapes to which he could flee. In addition he would be watched and reported on. St. Etienne, near Lyons, was known as "the Leeds of France." It was an endless chain of cloth factories and coal mines. When Fritz came to it, a salesman with little money and a temper once more edgy, he found its only legacy of romance was the shell of a ruined castle presiding forlornly over the grime. St. Etienne was so thickly settled that at night it was a blur of lamps. Every move he made, every place he went—and where was there to go but from factory to factory?—he knew was put in thick memoranda sent to Delius and Company.

He survived it all for a few weeks; then he had a brainstorm. At Monte Carlo on the Riviera there was a gambling casino. He left his lodgings, boarded a train, and soon arrived in the cliff-hung Mediterranean principality of Monaco. That evening he laid the small store of coins he still had on the roulette table and while the wheel rolled under high chandeliers he waited with clenched hands. Women in low-cut velvet gowns and men in dinner jackets were watching him, amused. When his number won, they were astonished. It was a run of luck, they assured him. He ought to try again. When the night was over, he had amassed enough to live on for weeks, basking in the sunshine, strolling palm-lined boulevards by day, and after dark attending the concerts sponsored by Monaco's Prince and Princess. The idyll lasted until a Delius and Company agent arrived to haul him back to St. Etienne; his railway ticket had been traced. Telegram after angry telegram arrived once more from Bradford. Again he bolted, this time to Uncle Théodor in Paris.

Théodor Delius was alarmed. His nephew was obviously overstrained, and bitterly unhappy. In sympathy he listened while Fritz told him of his hatred for business, his longing for a life filled with the arts. He had even tried composing written music, he confided. Now, of course, he knew his song wasn't very good. But what was he to do?

Théodor, a stiffly elegant bachelor, tall and spare, smiled reminiscently. So much of this had happened before, to himself. He had been able to settle in the French capital to find the society of a world free from counting houses. Yet Fritz was without means. "You must go away from Bradford, certainly," Théodor counseled. "Go where you can be at peace for a while. I will write to your father. Perhaps eventually you

can try the business once more. At all costs avoid a break
with him. How could you live?"

Back in Bradford, Julius peered in fresh perplexity at his
son. Definitely there was something seriously wrong with
the boy. Théodor's letter about Fritz's nerves had made that
clear. Perhaps the head injuries were the cause. Trying to
subdue his anger, Julius dispatched him once more to Norway.
There would be one or two cities to visit for orders; then Fritz
might stay in the countryside and rest until he reported for
work at the Manchester branch of Delius and Company, now
under Julius's control since his oldest brother had died. There
Fritz would be tried as an assistant office manager. He might
at least know how to deal with troublesome underlings.

He did, to the point of trading jobs with one of them. In a
matter of weeks the Manchester office was in chaos. Fritz had
no executive capacity. The firm begged its head in Bradford
to recall him. He was a menace to discipline. Julius realized
he had on his hands a misfit, incapable even of dealing with
his own inheritance. Now Fritz was saying openly that he was
more than willing to renounce Delius and Company forever.
"I might be a musician," he added. "A violinist."

Julius gaped. Fiddlers weren't gentlemen! You enjoyed hearing clever people like Joseph Joachim, but you didn't follow
their careers. Did Fritz realize some of the greatest performers
of the century, not only Joachim but Ignaz Moscheles the
pianist, had had to enter the London houses they entertained
in by the service stairs, and when they reached the drawing
room they were separated from the guests by a cord stretched
across it? Even Ignaz Moscheles, head of the Leipzig music
conservatory, the greatest in the world.

Claremont continued to seethe with the undeclared war
under its roof, and during the day while his father was in his
office Fritz thumbed aimlessly through books in the family
library. He tried to amuse his younger sisters, he practiced,

and he walked dejectedly in the streets of a city he had grown to despise for its money-grubbing and its distance from everything he cared for except the Pennines and their open stretches of heather. When Clare came home on vacation they rode together on Rombald's Moor. Clare too was troubled. Her teachers had told her she might become not only a good but a great singer. It was hopeless, of course. As for Max, he was still in school. Max alone wanted to do what had been planned for him. Or did he?

On a walk through The Flat, Bradford's Center, one afternoon Fritz's eye was caught by a poster. The Florida Land and Mortgage Company, Limited, had recently set up a branch in Bradford. The company's chairman, the Earl of Huntingdon, announced "two millions of acres of farming, orange, timber and grazing lands situated in 29 counties. The lands have not been picked over. No part has been reserved in any manner and the whole is open for sale."

Several times Fritz had stared at the distant American peninsula on the library globe. It was a wilderness still, a vast jungle far from most of the human race. It was fragrant with magnolias, the sun shone perpetually, and the Indians and Negroes were unspoiled children of nature with mysterious music of their own, music he had heard hints of at Isleworth. Oranges grew even in the forests. Surely it couldn't be hard to run an orange plantation. He had already been cut off from concert halls; a wilderness couldn't be worse than Bradford. If he had to be a failure, he might at least fail far away from the cruelly probing eyes of his mother and father. At dinner that night he broke his news. "I would like to grow oranges in America." For Florida would be what, like Brand, he had to have: a place on the earth where a man could be wholly himself.

"Oranges?" Julius Delius echoed. But that was farming, a lowly occupation about which no Delius knew anything at all.

And at the other end of the world? Ridiculous, a further proof of Fritz's lunacy. The project was not to be spoken of again. And yet, as the evening wore on, Julius began to wonder. He too had heard of Florida; the land that knew no winter, its evergreen acres ready for the taking. The American Civil War had ended nearly two decades ago. Now investors from all over the world were thronging to what had been a sleepy Southern Confederacy. The Earl of Huntingdon, for instance, was no fool. Certainly Florida was hardly civilized. Yet this meant there would be no theaters, no concert halls, no tinseled temptations for a wayward son. St. Etienne had been isolated, but not isolated enough. In Florida there would be the barrier of an ocean. An orange grower would have to stay in his grove because there would be nowhere else to go. God alone knew what Ernest was doing in New Zealand; he never wrote. Fritz had some remnants of conscience; he would at least keep in touch. Was his plan really as wild as it sounded?

Years before, Julius himself had left Bielefeld to found a textile house in Bradford. Perhaps Fritz would be striking out on his own to become a Florida orange baron, an American millionaire. He would need less arithmetic and office routine than he would salesmanship, his only business ability when he cared to use it. And he would have to use it on a frontier: no Stockholms, no Rivieras, no Norwegian mountains could tempt him away from toil and duty. If only there were some way to keep him under observation, to make sure he wouldn't daydream in the soothing mildness of the subtropics. Then Julius thought of a Bradford firm which had been having the same problem as Delius and Company. Douglas and Company, Dye Merchants, had been trying to cope with the indifference of young Charles Douglas, who wanted no part of textiles either.

What would Douglas Senior say to the experiment of helping to finance both boys in the orange business? Would

Florida lure Charles Douglas, too, to its mysterious shores? Julius made up his mind to do some investigating. Fritz and Charles knew each other only casually, but both had a taste for outdoor life and sports. That would help keep them fit in their exile.

By the time Julius got around to visiting the offices of the Florida Land and Mortgage Company his mind was almost made up. Charles Douglas was bored with Bradford and enthusiastic about Florida. His father would put up an equal share of money. Always Charles had longed to try his independent luck in America. Even Fritz was reading everything he could about citrus fruit, as he assured his father. While Julius listened to the blandishments of the Florida Land and Mortgage Company's boosters he grew positively optimistic.

It was easy to grow oranges, they told him. Florida enjoyed a perpetual boom. Some of the choicest grove land lay between the small city of Jacksonville, on the St. Johns river in the northern part of the state, and St. Augustine, the onetime Spanish capital of the old East Florida territory. For years winters on the St. Johns had been balmy, yet at night there was enough snap in the air to keep the fruit trees vigorous and hardy, unwilted by a too-steady heat. On the St. Johns, millionaire Frederick DeBary had made his fortune, not only in fruit but in steamships. DeBary oranges were being shipped west from Jacksonville by rail and north by DeBary's own vessels. What a DeBary had done, a Delius could do. Labor was plentiful and cheap; ex-slaves would work for a pittance and they stayed happy on diets of pork, black-eyed peas and sugar cane. Really there was no possible way Fritz and Charles could make a mistake in choosing the St. Johns. Any way you looked at the area, it was a gold mine.

Fritz was at first elated at his father's consent. He had always liked Charles Douglas, who was reserved and sensible. With him he would be exploring the lands of his imaginings, the enchanted lands the sailors and West Indians had told him about. By the time he visited Clare in her boarding school, however, he was having second thoughts. There would be no Clare in Florida and no concerts either. The only classical music would be what he made on his Cremona. He wanted solitude, but did he want that much of it? He and Clare promised to write; he would tell her all about America and his life there. "The thing to do is chuck up everything and go," he assured her. When he sailed with Charles Douglas on the Cunard liner *Gallia*, the English March afternoon was blustery, the dampness as sharp as a knife. Ahead lay endless summer. The knowledge was comforting.

4 ✑ Florida

The two young men had no time to see New York. From the steamship docks it looked like Bradford: dreary, modern, full of hurrying workers clutching overcoats and shawls. Fritz and Charles transferred their suitcases to a steamer bound for Fernandina, on the Georgia-Florida border, and soon the ship was moving into calmer waters and softer weather. It came into its Florida port on a morning full of golden sunlight and sparkling blue-green sea. In wonder Fritz and Charles stared about them. Everywhere waved the long fronds of cabbage palms. Yellow-green banana trees rustled their huge floppy leaves. Yucca needles were clattering against each other in the hesitant rises of the south Atlantic trade wind. On the waterfront Negro stevedores rolled turpentine barrels and hauled bales of cotton. Fernandina was full of the smell of blooming jasmine and tart pines from the forests at its edge. The ocean itself was incredibly clear and lukewarm. Through side streets floated the voices of the Negroes, and sometimes one or another would rise above the rest: "Heyo, heyo, halleo . . ."

In a surge of enthusiasm Fritz knew he had done the right thing. Florida was going to be a paradise after all. On the way to the Fernandina railroad station he and Charles passed white frame houses with tall pillars half hidden behind darkly glossy dooryard trees where green-gold oranges hung like Christmas balls. From November to July the fruit would ripen in a succession of varieties. Friendly passers-by struck up conversations about orange-growing with Fritz and Charles as they paused. This year as usual, they assured them, there had been a bumper crop.

In Jacksonville the railroad depot and freight yards edged the wide St. Johns itself, and Fritz and Charles saw crate after crate being loaded into boxcars and onto the decks of north-bound steamers: bushels of Parson Browns, Valencias, Mandarins, Satsumas. Soft-spoken gentlemen in white suits repeated the strange names and bowed courteously as the two young men asked directions to the offices where they were to sign the rental agreement for their grove. Mockingbirds were singing in the liveoaks which shaded dusty streets. Fresh cries echoed: "Ba-na-na, ba-na-na!" Always the black men seemed to be singing. Instead of being empty of music Florida was full of it. But the music was bewildering in its sliding tones, and at times it turned as melancholy as the moaning whistles of Seaboard Line trains bound for the pinewoods of the interior.

Julius Delius had made long-distance arrangements with a man named Guy Pride, the owner of an orange plantation called Solano Grove. Pride was cheerfully casual as Fritz and Charles signed their lease and an option to buy. The place had once belonged to a Spanish settler, Mateo Solano of St. Augustine. It was about forty miles south of Jacksonville. Oh, yes, Pride said, there was a road, but usually you couldn't use it because it was poorly drained. Lately there had been rain. In the coming summer there would be more. The only way to get to Solano Grove was by riverboat. The house was small. On an adjoining property lived another Englishman, Captain Bell. In the shed at Solano Grove there was a buckboard wagon. Every Sunday a mule pulled you through the forest on a narrow track the five miles to Picolata Landing to get your mail—when the track was passable, that is.

What Fritz and Charles still expected as they listened to Guy Pride's nonchalant admissions of isolation were tidy rows of orange trees like those they had seen in Fernandina. Solano Grove surely would be well-cleared, the house perhaps newly painted for its tenants. But as their DeBary ship churned its way south up the river they could make out only vast and dim forests where broad-leaved vines looped through the tallest trees either had ever seen. Rarely they noted tiny houses half-choked by overgrowth. When the steamer drew up to a stretching dock they were told was Solano Grove's there was nothing but the eternal jungle they had been skirting. And as they carried their bags along the dock's rickety length toward shore, the departing steamer whistled. But they could find no house. There was only a small peeling shack behind a cluster of palms and magnolias. It was sheltered by an immense liveoak tree with a spread of at least ninety feet. A pungent smell lingered nearby. At once Fritz realized what it was; rancid oranges and large, yellow shaddocks, which the Americans called grapefruit. "Some are the size of footballs!" he called out. In shock he and Charles began to wander around the shack itself. The fruit trees were behind it, but all their fruit had dropped, untended, to rot. Between the trees the weeds were gigantic. Thin branches sagged half-suffocated by long strands of Spanish moss, the air-plant swaying eerily in a wind which grew steadily hotter during the afternoon. Beyond the tiny grove—what there was of it—was a virgin timberland where black and red and white woodpeckers the size of crows were rapping at the pines. No other house existed, Fritz and Charles understood. Home was the shack in front of them, full of cobwebs and buzzing insects when they opened its creaking unlocked door.

Some of the moldings in the four tiny rooms were curiously ornate, legacies perhaps of better days. But Fritz and Charles found no bathroom and no wardrobe chests. The kitchen was separated from the house by a half-covered passage, and it boasted a wood stove. Now the heat had become stifling.

Fortunately on the two porches, front and back, it was at least possible to escape to breathe. The beds were narrowly spartan. They and a few tables and chairs were the only furniture the shack had. Beyond the house and kitchen stood a shed full of half-rusted farm tools, a pair of guns someone had recently oiled, and a splitting wagon. This, then, was where the citrus enterprise of Delius and Douglas was to be founded. Fritz and Charles laughed at their disillusionment because they could do nothing else. In the middle of the shambles lay the case which held Fritz's Cremona violin, token of another life forever renounced.

After a few hours a young Negro appeared. He introduced himself as Elbert Anderson. He and his wife, Eliza, lived deeper in the pines in a shack of their own. Eliza's young sister, Julia, stayed with them and could do her share of chores. The three were the only help on the place unless you counted old Mary Ferguson who had done Mr. Pride's washing when he'd lived at Solano Grove. Elbert, Eliza, and Julia could cook and clean and garden and hoe if need be among the trees, and Mary could scrub shirts on her washboard at the river's edge. Surely, the trees had been let go, but now that the grove had a master again Elbert Anderson would work hard. He and his family had been living off their garden patch: collards, turnips, corn, tomatoes. They had the Solano mule, and a few chickens, and some razorback hogs which had been roaming the woods. Elbert Anderson was the single ray of hope in a ludicrous mess and Fritz and Charles seized on the hope eagerly. They promised him all the jobs he could handle. They could pay him a dollar and a half a day, which was above the standard wage, if only he would help them get the house and the grove back in order.

After a dinner of pork and yellow field peas, which tall turbaned Eliza Anderson served moving as silently as a shadow, Charles disconsolately went to his cot. Fritz was tired too, but his mixed despair and fascination made him sit late on the front porch smoking cigar after cigar. He stared at the scarlet glow of twilight over the St. Johns in the west. He heard the tiny stinging buzzes of strange warblers nesting in palm tops that gradually grew blacker in silhouette until they were lost in a night sky as deep as lapis lazuli. The stars came out, distant and coolly white. He sank into a half-trance, stunned by the insignificance of men in the rankness he had come to. A chorus of frogs and crickets began. Then came another chorus drifting from the woods, the strangest he had ever heard. The Anderson family were singing. Their melodies wandered from note to note, rising and falling in shifting discords that were hypnotic. Sometimes the discords were backed by an echo of plucked strings. The words were full of the sorrow of slavery—the separation of families, the fear of being sold:

> Oh, honey, I am going down the river in the morning.
> Heyo, heyo, down the mighty river,
> And don't you be too lonesome, love . . .

Soon the music changed. The voices joined in the hallelujahs of spirituals. They cried out from the pines and mounted to a climax of faith until the darkness itself was transfigured for Fritz in a light made of the pure washes of jubilant sound. He was swept into a wondering worship of all creation. The music he was hearing became the music of the universe and he longed to answer it. When it stopped, he was exhausted by the intensity of what he had felt. In those blinding seconds his future had been shown him. He would be a composer, of course, because nothing else was possible. He would absorb the music of the Negroes of Florida because it rang more clearly than any other with the truth of human endurance. As nature continually renewed itself, so did men's spirits. That was what the force of life really was; that was what the word eternity meant.

"A state of illumination," he later called the experience on the porch. It had been the ecstasy of a mystic, a contemplation he realized he could never teach anyone else and hardly understood himself. What the Andersons and Florida had already shown him was his own destiny. The soul of every man made a pilgrimage and he knew what his own was to be. The distance of Solano Grove had begun to turn him inward, throwing him on the resources in himself. The revelation of the porch couldn't be betrayed. His worship of life would become his religion. What arrogance in those Bradford and Isleworth churches that had preached their doctrines of salvation by a rigid creed. Salvation, whatever it was, could come only from understanding the whole world and everyone in it, not just a single race or a single nation. More than the physical labor of the Andersons he needed their friendship as well as instruction in the beauty of their musical inheritance. And he knew he must earn these things by his sympathy with them as artists and as people capable of suffering and love.

5 *"Language of Another World"*

Charles Douglas, who began to sense a change in Fritz by his new quietness, was puzzled. What about the orange business? Why didn't they all begin clearing the ground under the trees? But Fritz took to spending his days in the cabin of the Andersons, listening to Elbert and Eliza and small Julia Alvarez, her sister, singing hymns. Eliza and Julia had Spanish blood and Indian too; their eyes were darkly remote, their noses hawklike. Shyly the Andersons taught Fritz the work calls of the fields, and in the evening they listened with him to the farewells of other Negroes in the pines: "See, them boys is friends, they say goodnight." They showed him the instruments they had been using: banjos, seed pods, cowbells, a log drum. In the cities rich Negroes with pocket change had cornets and snare drums they could buy in back-street pawnshops. In the country you used what was at hand. You could, for instance, stretch a cord across a washtub and anchor the string with a braced stick. By varying the stick's tightness you could make the cord vibrate in different tones, because the tub's bottom served as a sounding board. It was a homemade and serviceable bass fiddle.

At night Elbert Anderson took Fritz quail shooting. Once, in a thicket of tough saw palmettoes, Anderson grabbed his arm with such force that his gun went off. He had saved Fritz from stepping on a rattlesnake five feet long. A sullen Charles joined them for the alligator hunts which at least were a distracting adventure in his frustration over the grove. Anderson would silently paddle a rowboat along the shore of the St. Johns while Charles held a strong rope and Fritz a gun. For their searchlight they used a lantern tied onto the top of Fritz's head. Whenever it surprised a lurking alligator in the eel-grass the hounded animal's eyes glowed like rubies. You had to keep the boat directed toward his head, for a whisk of his tail could swamp you. Fritz shot several alligators at close range. He loved the challenge of their size and iron jaws. On the way back to the house Elbert Anderson rowed to a new rhythm. It came from the Fanti people of West Africa, for many Florida slaves had had Fanti parents and grandparents:

The immediate result of the alligator hunting for both Fritz and Charles was malaria. Fritz escaped with a relatively light seige of fever and chills, but Charles grew sicker daily, his teeth chattering and his limbs aching. His depression over Fritz's refusal to work and the slow progress the Andersons were making at clearing the grove didn't help. Also, the oranges were showing signs of blight. One afternoon he was gripped by a freshly violent fit of the shakes. Anderson gave him a foul-tasting concoction to drink, but it didn't do any good. Alarmed, Anderson went in the wagon for the mistress of a more prosperous plantation at Picolata Landing, Mrs. Montgomery Corse. When Mrs. Corse arrived at Solano Grove she decided that Fritz must go to Jacksonville to get a doctor. She was southern and maternal; her husband had been a Confederate brigadier general. She had been familiar with malaria all her life. What Charles needed was quinine.

The doctor's address was on Bay Street, on the Jacksonville riverfront. When Fritz knocked, a maid told him the doctor was out. Annoyed, he scribbled a message that he would return and started to stroll down the street to kill time. A sign caught his eye: "Merryday and Payne, Music." Behind a large glass window he saw a row of pianos. He had been playing his violin, but he hadn't touched a keyboard since Bradford. If he were going to teach himself to compose, surely he had to have a piano. Here was the very place to rent one. Excited, he hurried in to introduce himself to the clerk at the counter, who told him to try all the instruments to see which one he liked. It was the first chance he had had to play Anderson's spirituals and chants. To his disappointment, they didn't sound right. Most of the time Anderson sang a five-note scale instead of an eight-note, as if a piano player were to use only the black keys and not the white ones. But the combinations were trickier than Fritz had believed possible. Still, the music he was playing now was different from any other. He knew it, and the knowledge intoxicated him. The clerk was regarding him fixedly and before long he heard another man coughing. When he looked up it was to see a gaunt stranger who was actually staring.

"Where have you heard that?" the stranger demanded sharply.

"Oh—it's just a tune I was making."

"*You* were making?" The man introduced himself. He was Thomas F. Ward, organist in the Catholic cathedral at St. Augustine, and sometimes he played and taught in Jacksonville. Hadn't Fritz seen his advertisement in the *St. Augustine Chronicle*?

> *Learn to sing at sight.* Thomas F. Ward, organist in the Cathedral, has organized a singing class which will meet once a week. Those desirous of thorough instruction should join at once. A few pupils will also be received for private instruction in sight reading or on the piano or organ.

When Fritz explained he saw no newspapers and no people except plantation Negroes and Charles Douglas, Ward was astonished. Why on earth had he been living like a hermit? There were scores of people near Jacksonville who loved music. William Jahn, who clerked at the Campbell music shop down the street, had studied composition at Stuttgart in Germany. The German Susskind family often had chamber concerts, and perhaps one of the most talented local musicians of all was Mrs. Charles Edward Bell, who lived upriver. Surely she must be a very near neighbor at Solano Grove. Her English husband, Captain Bell, was trying to grow oranges. He had been lured by one of those land companies that advertised abroad. Doubtless Fritz knew the sort. Ruefully, he admitted he himself had been sung a siren song of gold in paradise. Instead he had found a forest; but in that forest he had discovered a music he was now desperate to understand. He was trying to, and he couldn't.

Ward, lanky and pale, was a New Yorker. He announced frankly that he was the illegitimate son of a Spanish priest and an Irish kitchenmaid. The Catholic church had cared for him and trained him in music. He had been a Brooklyn organist when a racking cough had begun to trouble him. The parish had sent him to Florida for his health and one of its priests had found him the St. Augustine job. He rented lodgings near the cathedral plaza. But he was willing to come to stay with Fritz at Solano Grove and, for nothing, teach him the fundamentals of harmony and counterpoint.

"I'll make you work," he warned. Out poured his questions, and Charles Douglas's malaria was forgotten completely. Had Fritz read Hector Berlioz's book on orchestration? He hadn't? Hadn't he done anything at all in music besides performing? Did he keep a notebook? No musician could grope in the dark. Fritz was caught up in the sweep of his new friend's plans. He protested he didn't want to impose. Dryly and briefly Ward answered his objections: "I think you will prove to be a pupil of an uncommon kind."

When Fritz finally did remember Charles's need for a doctor, he was chagrined. He and Ward hurried down Bay Street where they found the doctor baffled by a message which had left no address. But the doctor was willing to go with them to Solano Grove, and the three boarded a river steamer at its Bay Street dock. In Fritz's pocket rustled the rental contract for a Merryday and Payne piano. All the way upriver he and Tom Ward talked excitedly, Ward of the music he was going to teach him and Fritz of the performances he had heard in England and Europe. Ward was hungry for details of Joachim and Sir Charles Hallé and Hans Sitt. He listened sympathetically when Fritz told him about Julius Delius's opposition to music. From time to time Ward coughed. He had tuberculosis, Fritz realized. Florida was supposed to cure it. But Ward confessed he wasn't getting any better. If he could have one outstanding pupil before he died, he would feel he had accomplished something. Fritz would surely be that pupil. Ward's conversation was racing with names and projects: Bach's counterpoint and chorales, Mendelssohn's oratorios, a plan for trying to take down Elbert Anderson's music in conventional notation, violin concertos and piano exercises and musical evenings with Captain Bell and his pretty Norwegian wife, Jutta. The doctor listened bewildered; his prospective patient's friend seemed curiously indifferent to an errand of mercy.

At Solano Grove four hours later the trio were met by a furious Mrs. Corse. Where had Fritz been? When an earlier riverboat had passed, she had become seriously worried about Charles, now delirious. When the doctor had treated him and he had rallied, he learned what had happened. Fritz had forgotten him. Fritz and his music again! Charles could have been dying, and yet Fritz had been renting a damned piano! Charles would be hanged if he'd have that tunesmith Tom Ward in the already cramped shack. And where, he would like to know, was anybody going to put an instrument they would all three be tripping over? His mind was made up. He was going to move out. He would apply his father's money to another grove. Fritz could explain to Julius Delius what had happened. Yet Fritz wasn't dismayed. Bradford was across the sea. It would be some time before his father heard the news, and then perhaps he would think it was just as well for Fritz to have a place of his own. "Everything will come right," Fritz grinned cheerfully. He was counting on Elbert Anderson for the orange harvest. For his own part, life would be a continuous round of music and he would revel in it.

When the piano arrived, he and Ward and Elbert Anderson pushed its square bulk gingerly along the dock through the weeds of the yard into one of the front rooms. The shack's tiny tables were all soon littered with score paper. Ward established a schedule: so much time for technique, so much for composition. In the notebook Fritz began he tried repeatedly to analyze the melodies of Anderson: the skipped beats, the minor refrains. For relaxation he and Ward and Anderson went boating. Anderson also had a friend who came by with a banjo and tried to teach Fritz its tunes for his violin. At night Fritz slept exhausted through the torrid humidity of the rainy season, when the steady beat of downpours on the roof was soothing. Often he did the cooking. He had never known happiness like this. What he had dabbled in he was now beginning to master. He composed an orthodox accompaniment for a Norwegian poem, "Over the Mountains High," and he knew the song was better than "When Other Lips." He had been able to get all the parts of the piece to move because his counterpoint lessons had shown him how to back his melody. What baffled him was that when Tom Ward began to take him to visit other musical friends, they were all openly con-

temptuous of the Negroes' folksongs and laughed at his
interest.

Jutta Bell, for instance, was astonished at his familiarity
with the Andersons. She was tall and fair, with round eyes,
a full mouth, and a lilting voice. Fritz was twenty-two and
she was twenty-seven, a fastidious woman of sophistication,
buried deep in the country. She wore laces and fine sheer dress
fabrics, loved theatricals, and had founded a troup of players
in Jacksonville. She also planned to begin teaching voice there,
taking the name of Madame Bell-Ranske because Americans
expected their culture to come from very foreign shores. Jutta
Bell could laugh at the necessity of her proposed name, yet
she saw nothing of any value in American music. Two respect-
able but obscure American composers had tried writing American operas, both based on the legend of Rip Van Winkle's
sleep in the Catskills. Both had been dismal failures. All good
music came from northern Europe, especially Germany. Surely
as the son of German parents Fritz ought to know that, and
certainly he was wasting his time listening to his blacks and
also to the banjo-picking poor whites, called Crackers because
they ate cracked corn. The Crackers had taken to stopping by
Solano Grove to join in the singing good times.

But Fritz—and Tom Ward—couldn't agree. Had no serious
composer ever tapped the richness of Negro and Cracker traditions? There had been one, Tom Ward said, a New Orleans
concert pianist named Louis Moreau Gottschalk. Gottschalk
had died in the 1860's, but he had written pieces based on
New Orleans street cries and dances: *The Bamboula, The
Banana Tree*. Gottschalk had toured Europe and had been a
rousing success. He had been dark-eyed, heavy-lidded and
moustached, and women had swooned over him. His melodies
were gay, showy reproductions, many of them using the
rhythm of a dance called the cakewalk. Now the Negroes were
calling the cakewalk the rag. Gottschalk, though, hadn't ever

tried what Fritz wanted to try; capturing the psychology of
the Negro and rural white people themselves in music, all the
tragedy they had known which found expression in their
blues and chants, all the joy they felt in worship. And
Gottschalk hadn't used the flatted notes the Negroes called
blue notes. He had turned out novelties, never poems. All
were presently as dead as the dodo. The surviving Gottschalk music was a tear-jerking parlor ballad called *The Last
Hope*.

Not only were Americans disdainful of the Negroes' music.
When they were confronted with a genius like that of the
sightless Negro pianist Blind Tom, they couldn't believe the
performance they saw and heard. The *Florida Times-Union*
described Blind Tom in a Jacksonville concert: "Without
emotion of his own, this idiot Negro with painful fidelity
reproduces the expressions of emotion of others. He is unconscious of art. He counterfeits with humiliating exactness
its most splendid achievements." The attitude wasn't confined
to the South. It was national, Tom Ward assured Fritz.
Stephen Foster was looked on as frivolous because he wrote
mostly for minstrel shows. Foster had composed banjo music
and piano ballads, but even he, American though he was, had
never dared blue tonality. He had hardly dared the delayed
beats of Negro syncopation.

The center of Negro music in America was New Orleans,
a city which had been first French, then Spanish, belatedly
American. But Fritz hadn't a hope of going there. As usual,
his allowance was meager, just enough to live on. Solano
Grove brought in nothing because it was producing almost no
oranges. When the Florida Fruit Growers' Association held its
meetings in Jacksonville they were not being supported by
Delius of Solano Grove. Instead, besides absorbing himself in
music with Tom Ward, Delius of Solano Grove was reading
everything about New Orleans he could lay his hands on:

its *vodun* or voodoo dances, its rituals, its beautiful white Creole and mixed-blood quadroon women, its flamboyant jewels and large sugar plantations. Many of the ex-slaves near Solano Grove had originally been sold from New Orleans, and they told Fritz legends of Marie Laveau, the voodoo priestess, and Bras-Coupé, the African prince captured by slave traders. Bras-Coupé had called himself, in French, Arm-Cut-Off because his freedom had gone. But he later escaped his bondage to haunt Louisiana swamps, and he chanted curses on his former masters. His tribesmen still danced their snake dances in a New Orleans square, the *Place Congo*. "Morally hideous!" pronounced white American witnesses. "As dark and horrid as bestialized savagery could make the adoration of serpents!"

Sometimes Seminoles stopped by at Solano Grove for food and rest, and Fritz found them possessed of a solemn grace. They were gentlemen, he wrote to Clare. He also wrote her about the various varieties of oranges he meant to grow when he got time: Did she know the blood orange wasn't really rotten at all, as the English thought? It was sweet and rich, its reddish pulp full of juice. But perhaps Clare wouldn't be fooled by his good intentions.

All the time he never forgot the moment of revelation on the porch. Nothing like it had happened since, yet at his piano he tried often to recapture its exaltation. Always the chords faded away; they never ended loudly and suddenly, because nothing in nature ended that way, and he wanted his music to be faithful to nature. In St. Augustine, with its high gates and sand-beige Spanish buildings and red-tiled roofs, he often went to listen to Tom Ward play in the cathedral on Sundays. For hours afterward the cathedral bells rang in his ears. Back at Solano Grove late at night he and Ward would visit small clapboarded Negro Churches, "praise-houses."

Sometimes the meetings were outdoors. Around a red-gold

pine stump fire in a forest clearing would gather half-clad field hands and turbaned women, dandy house servants and barefooted girls. They would all shuffle around the flames in a ring-shout, some of the singers keeping time in the bass and others calling the melody out as they clapped hands. Rarely did they sing the same words to the same spiritual twice in succession. "Hanh! Anh hanh!" responses would echo. Several of the singers kept their fingers in their ears not to lose their own variations of the melody. Tambourines rattled, guitars strummed out. All of it blended into the lushness and moisture and heat of the woodland. The white settlers of the cities fought nature. The Crackers and Indians and Negroes accepted it, worshiped it, as Fritz himself did.

As for the Negroes, they were baffled. Old Mary Ferguson the laundress, for instance, couldn't make him out at all. When she kept back eleven of his fourteen handkerchiefs in the wash one week, he didn't shrug and say all Negroes, being savages, stole things and what could you do? He asked instead to have them back. They both owed each other honesty, he told her. "Otherwise I must fire you, and I don't want to do that." Her bluff called, she returned the handkerchiefs and then burst out laughing: "Oh, sar! You is a funny gentleman."

The musical enchantment at Solano Grove could not endure forever. Julius Delius, in Bradford, tried at first to believe the infrequency of his son's letters was due to the briskness of the orange trade. Then he heard of the departure of Charles Douglas. There was only one thing to be done. He ordered one of his managers, a Mr. Sucksmith, to go to Florida and read an ultimatum. No oranges, no allowance. At the last minute Mr. Sucksmith was unable to go and in his place went a Mr. Tattersfield. What Mr. Tattersfield found when he stepped off the riverboat at Solano Grove was as grotesquely Dickens-like as his name. The grove was littered with decaying fruit. Solano's master played the piano and violin all day long, and when he wasn't doing these things he was listening to Elbert Anderson sing slave songs in a rowboat. Mr. Tattersfield was horrified. "He is bubbling over with a furious energy," he scribbled to Bradford. But not, alas, for oranges. One whiff of the rotten fruit was enough to turn the stomach. And Fritz spent whole afternoons lolling while a darky sang! He now wanted, he said, to be a composer of music. He hadn't Gone Native, as his father had feared. Instead he had gone mad.

Fritz and Tom Ward conferred. Julius would soon know the worst from his emissary, who had been ordered to exercise the option to buy the grove and thus chain Fritz to it forever. Perhaps it was time to brave Julius Delius before it was too late. "I've taught you all I can," Ward mused. "Now you need to go to the only conservatory that can do justice to training you—Leipzig."

Leipzig . . . Where Felix Mendelssohn and Robert Schumann had founded the most famous concerts in the world, where Ignaz Moscheles had played, where even now Brahms and Grieg conducted . . . In a last desperate gesture Fritz begged his father to send him there. He wrote about the Merryday and Payne piano, about Tom Ward, about his composing. To go to Leipzig—and he had to go—he needed money. His father was a rich man. As passionately as he knew how, he pleaded his case. The result, weeks later, was a cablegram of refusal. The grove had been purchased outright and Fritz was to raise oranges forever. That was that.

He was "completely demoralized." It would be years before he could ever finish his studies. He knew he would finish them, for he was now burning with ambition. The only thing to do was to walk out the door of the shack and never return. He could give up his allowance forever and live by his wits. Jutta Bell, for instance, knew Jacksonville matrons who would hire him to teach their daughters the violin. It was time to be

Delius the musician, not Fritz the scapegrace son. He should have begun on his own years before. He had been spoiled by the Delius fortune. Now he must learn always to live the austere life he had been leading in the shack at Solano Grove—but even without money for trips, books, sheet music, and piano tuners. It bothered him, though, to be leaving his father's property untended. That wasn't right. And Elbert Anderson had to have wages.

He debated his dilemma with Tom Ward until an autumn afternoon when he heard a Yorkshire voice singing on the St. Johns River, its glassy surface dotted with fallen pecan leaves. Unbelieving, he rushed to the dock. The rowboat made for it, and the figure inside waved, holding up a jug of moonshine. It was his brother Ernest. Ernest had failed in sheep in New Zealand and had written to Clare, who had told him where his younger brother had, himself, fled from Bradford. To Ernest in New Zealand Julius had sent a splendid suit of clothes to help him out; Ernest had auctioned the ensemble off at the dock, which is how he had gotten passage money. Now he wanted to try easy oranges in Florida. Could he stay at Solano Grove? He knew his father would never take him back. His failure had broken him, and he needed another chance. He had lately been drinking too much; he admitted it.

It was a stroke of luck as odd as any descent of the gods in a Greek comedy. Ernest's once-scorned younger brother was now expected to be his benefactor. Well, Ernest could indeed have a chance at the grove—all of it. His arrival had solved a problem. "Only, Ernest—" the benefactor pleaded with an eye on the moonshine jug, "don't paint the place red!" Fritz Delius, teacher of music, needed the armor of respectability, not a carousing relative.

Solano Grove, where his life had changed . . . As he strolled its evergreen paths once more he looked at it with new eyes. He was twenty-three. Its hardships had made a man of him.

Its Negroes and Indians and Crackers had given him the gift of their music and their toughness. The moss hanging from the immense liveoaks swayed, as always, in a warm wind. Pine needles were quivering with light, and a thousand wildflowers bloomed under the saplings in the forest. The stiff cones of magnolias stood erect in dark branches. Would he ever live at Solano Grove again? He thought not. But he would always be trying to recapture the "moment of illumination" he had had in the darkness of a summer night on the shack's porch. His last evening he sat alone there once more, listening to the frogs and crickets, to the thin wail of Elbert Anderson's harmonica, and to the distant echo of a field-horn calling workers home. The river lapped against the pilings of the dock and the driftwood and sand of the narrow shore. He had loved Solano Grove's people. But even more he had loved its solitudes.

When Tom Ward gave him a book of Byron's poems as a going-away present, he soon marked a passage in *Manfred:*

> I linger yet with nature, for the night
> Hath been to me a more familiar face
> Than that of man; and in her starry shade
> Of dim and solitary loveliness
> I learned the language of another world.

Philipp von Wolf,
great-great grandfather of Delius

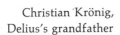

Christian Krönig,
Delius's grandfather

Ilkley from the moors

Ilkley in the seventies

Julius Delius

Elise Delius at seventy

Delius at twelve

Delius house restored at Jacksonville University

6 ❧ "The Celebrated Professor Delius"

In Jacksonville, Delius had two immediate problems he had never had before—food and shelter. Between hunger and his vision of composing lay only what he had saved from his last allowance check. Now he would never get another. With a young bachelor Jutta Bell had recommended he rented a suite of rooms at the Bingham House, a downtown hotel on Forsyth Street. From there the two men placed an advertisement in the *Florida Times-Union*:

F. Delius,
Teacher of the Violin.
Stephen G. Sesser,
Teacher of Foreign Languages.

It was to be hoped that a path would promptly be beaten to their door.

At first Delius was not disappointed. A bevy of young women, unmarried, came with their mothers to look him over and then enthusiastically signed up for a course of instruction. The fees they were willing to pay were less flattering than their smiles. The money he would earn, he understood, would at most enable him to break even. Through Jutta he was introduced to other contacts among what Jacksonville considered its musical elite: the Susskinds, the Jahns, a retired Italian opera singer named Severo Strini. Delius's obvious talents on the violin, the daring of his flight from Solano Grove, and his breeziness charmed everybody. He teased people with tall stories of how he had shot a twenty-one-foot alligator, and when they challenged him he laughed with as much mockery of himself as of his listeners.

But Rabbi Marx Moses detected the worry beneath the jokes. Did he need a second job? When he admitted that he did, he became the first and only Gentile cantor of Temple Ahavath Chesed. The temple's name, in translation from the Hebrew, meant Lovers of Justice. Rabbi Moses had saved the day.

Jacksonville was a strange mixture: half-elegant resort town, with galleried hotels where crystal sconces glittered in the halls, and half-raw, roaring outpost. The trunks of the city's liveoaks and palms still bore the scars of bullet holes from the Seminole wars. The streets, mostly unpaved, were full of rivermen, backwoods farmers come to market, and toughs who had wandered in from surrounding lumber camps on a spree. Gambling dens and saloons flourished seven days of the week. Whiskey was sold from open barrels in all the grocery stores, and scrawny cows ran wild in alleys where pigs rooted through reeking piles of garbage.

On holidays young bucks mounted their horses and chased each other through town, whooping as they shot pistols off into the air. There were forty hotels and an annual tourist trade of 75,000 in this "winter city of the summer land," whose regular population numbered 20,000. The rich guests tried to ignore the roistering around them as they promenaded down Bay Street to shop in bazaars that sold shell ornaments, alligator teeth made into jewelry, rattlesnake skins and palmetto canes. For Clare, Delius bought what he was assured were genuine snake rattles in a box which a Seminole chief had once made from a pioneer's scalp. Clare, he knew, would shiver with delight as she showed her trophies to her schoolmates. He didn't want to stop to think how long it might be before he saw Clare again.

He had taken a plunge into a new universe. Swindlers and

confidence men methodically worked the hotels and fleeced the visitors. Jacksonville was a haven for adventurers. Its arts were dismissed as *"culc*haw" by local buffoons, and when the tourists gave themselves over to culture at all, it was mostly to hear pianists who could perform such feats as playing "Yankee Doodle" with one hand and "The Sailor's Hornpipe" with the other. "The music furnished by our local artist was good," pronounced the *Florida Times-Union* after a hotel concert. "So was the boy with the ice cream. The baby that cried during the love song was not." One Jacksonville music teacher signed his name "M.D." (Musical Doctor) and after his hurried escape from town was found to have gotten himself engaged to several of his pupils at once and stolen the rings they had taken off their fingers before they practiced.

For Delius, who had played with Joachim and spent his winters listening to Sir Charles Hallé conduct Bach, Jacksonville was a comedown. "America's interest in the arts may be fatal to 'em," he began to joke. But Jacksonville was also a challenge. He translated its violence into freshly dissonant chords as he improvised at whatever piano he could find to play. He hadn't the courage to put the strange new chords to paper, however. His first composition intended for sale was a polka, "At the Carnival." He persuaded Alexander Campbell's music printing shop on Bay Street to buy it; Campbell set the price at sixty cents a copy. Among Jacksonville's parlor pianists it sounded strange enough. Did some of the passages have mistakes, or had Mr. Delius really meant to use the halftones their cooks and gardeners sang?

The real music in Jacksonville, he knew, was the music on the wrong side of town. Jutta Bell kept calling it vulgar, "preposterous." But more and more he found himself going into La Villa, the Negro neighborhood where the Union Cornet Band marched in the streets during sun-drenched days and piano rags full of syncopation poured out of tiny open parlors on steaming nights heavy with the fragrance of ginger lilies. Again he was irresistibly drawn to the Negroes, and again they welcomed him, the "funny gentleman" so English and so serious about their music, and so young.

"I am a musician," he would tell them simply. "I would like to learn your songs. Can you teach me?"

In La Villa, too, he could watch Negro funerals where uniformed drummers marched slowly ahead of the bands toward the graves and afterwards stepped high on the way back while every musician became a soloist and improvised his "licks" to the drums' muffled beat. Spanish customs, also, were left in La Villa; serenades under balconies, and the lilting tangos of a Spanish-Negro-Italian fiddler:

> And when he touched familiar notes, the sober and
>   the staid
> Just felt the music in their heels, when Marcellini
>   played.

It was a Jacksonville ballad. Under the palms and chinaberry trees rang the cries of the fruit-sellers: "Sweet oranges! Sweeter than the honey in the comb! Sweet oranges!" Down by the railroad yards, to the clanking of steel couplings and the rolling of package trucks and the moans of long whistles, there were blues drifting over the smell of turpentine barrels:

> I woke up this morning
> With the same thing on my mind,
> Thinking 'bout my high brown
> Down on the Seaboard Line.

Back in his bed at Bingham House, Delius still heard the trains wailing away in the stifling dark. Again he was full of wanderlust, longing to hear more of the melodies of a country which ignored them. On his violin, between his struggles to teach fingering to southern belles, he tried new blues and some of the accented off-beats he had heard in La Villa rags. He haunted Merryday and Payne's and Campbell's where he spent free hours at unsold pianos making chromatic slidings. Mule-drawn streetcars clanged beyond the windows and gawking tourists stared through the pane at him. At such times he felt unutterably lonely, as lonely as his music was becoming. Often, fighting to keep his hands out of his jacket pockets because he wanted to look older and dignified, he could be seen walking the streets as apricot-streaked skies set sparrows to their last chatterings in city squares.

In November, 1884, he joined a few other performers in a concert sponsored by the Hebrew Musical Union. He played a solo, Schumann's violin *Romance*, and then joined fellow-artists to sing "The Soldiers' Farewell." Signor Strini pronounced his voice pleasant. A scant audience of thirty was impressed. Rabbi Moses had come to give moral support, and the next morning the *Times-Union* praised the proceedings for being "of a high order."

The concert did have the desired result of bringing in more students. Delius got, in fact, all he could handle. Most of them were flirting girls with crushes on him. He smiled and stayed aloof, but their parents were beginning to ferret out the truth about him, mostly from Jutta Bell. Their daughters' music master was not only well-born and had titled relatives in Europe, but he would perhaps be heir to one of England's textile fortunes if he ever patched up his quarrel with his father.

How enchanting! Suddenly F. Delius, Teacher of the Violin and Sabbath Cantor in Temple Ahavath Chesed, found himself being pursued as at Stroud by ambitious mothers with gleams in their eyes and pious things to say about his need for asking his father's forgiveness. "There's no real living in music, Mr. Delius," they warned. "It's only foolishness."

He tried to change the subject without being rude, but when

an advertisement appeared one day in the *Times-Union*, he was ripe for it. It was from a Professor Ruckert of Danville, Virginia, who desired a permanent music teacher not only for his daughters but for all of the Roanoke Female College, "a Finishing School for Young Ladies of the Baptist Denomination."

Perhaps the Baptists in Virginia would be different, and their daughters serious. Besides, Ernest Delius was cutting up with benders at Solano Grove and then came to visit Jacksonville drinking dens; he was being generally embarrassing. "You're doing everything you can to annoy and tease me!" Delius protested. The Danville job would be regular and distant, with a guaranteed salary uncomplicated by tourist and off seasons. Virginia would be full of Negro music too. In Jacksonville, Delius knew, his father would probably soon find him, but if he disappeared into the vastness of the continental United States he would really be free of Bradford forever, free of Ernest too. He hadn't been able to save much. Rapidly he calculated the fare to Danville. He had it with a dollar to spare. When he applied for the job, Tom Ward and Rabbi Moses wrote him glowing testimonials.

Professor Ruckert wired him to come immediately. After a quick trip to Solano Grove and St. Augustine to say good-by to Ernest and Jutta Bell and Tom Ward, he boarded a steamer with his suitcase and violin and tickets and the dollar. As the steamer moved away from Bay Street, he believed he was seeing Jacksonville for the last time in his life. He was still carrying Clare's unmailed snake rattles.

The ship took him as far up the coast as Charleston, South Carolina, where he found boulevards full of high mansions and grill-framed galleries leaning over hidden gardens. Lacy entrance gates stood locked and forbidding. It was an older South than Jacksonville had been. An outsider, he walked to the station and climbed onto his connecting train. Traveling salesmen dozed in plush seats, and as darkness fell the coaches jerked along a trestle over a Southern marsh dotted by palm clumps—the last, he knew. He woke with a start hours later as the conductor called out: "Dan—ville!" A blast of cold air hit his face, and his breath steamed white. It was the middle of the night. In pitch blackness he tried to make out the shapes of baggage racks and benches at the depot while the train disappeared.

Presently he saw advancing toward him a towering man whose carrot-red goatee was pointed and grotesque in the light of the lantern he carried. It was Professor Ruckert, who pumped his hand genially and said he had already gotten him a number of private students. The Roanoke Female College was anxious for him to begin teaching counterpoint and violin and piano and harmony and composition—at once, all at the same time; French and German too. Arrangements had been made for him to board with another teacher on Danville's north side in a private home. Meals would be sent up each evening, and Delius would be able to practice and compose in his spare time—if he had any.

When his landlady delivered the Danville newspaper to him next morning, he had a fresh shock. His eyes fell on a flamboyant advertisement: Professor Ruckert was pleased to announce the arrival in Danville of "the Celebrated Professor Delius," who was prepared to teach anything whatever about music and languages Danville wanted to know. Danville was reminded, in tall print, how lucky it was that Professor Delius, the eminent European virtuoso, should choose southside Virginia in which to live and work.

Danville, Delius learned, was no haven of the old Virginian aristocracy. As in Jacksonville, anybody who wanted to be a professor could be and was. George Washington and Thomas Jefferson, those genteel Virginia presidents, had lived far away. The city to which he had come was poised on low hills over a wide bend in the River Dan just on the edge of North Carolina—a valley of humiliation, wags said, between the two mountains of conceit that were Virginia and South Carolina. Danville was grimy from the thick smoke of the Riverside and Morotock cotton mills lying on weedy stream banks. Red brick tobacco warehouses sprawled into the countryside where there was no tropical exuberance but inland winter, a stark landscape of tawny broom sedge and slash pines. Danville was less than thirty years old, but its slogan was "Danville Does Things." It was briskly scornful of history. In the last few days of the Civil War it had been the capital of the dying Confederacy. Now it was anxious to shake off the very memory. When it wanted culture, it was prepared to hire it handsomely. This was where The Celebrated Professor Delius came in.

He was taken to visit the part-time head of the music department at the Roanoke Female College, Robert S. Phifer. A sharp wind cut at him from the street corners, and the windows of the red brick college rattled in fitful gusts. He met his first pupils: girls of fifteen and sixteen who wanted to learn graceful accomplishments like *The Last Hope* and *Hearts and Flowers.* The weather was frigid, but Professor Ruckert and Robert Phifer and their young charges broke the chill. What the girls clamored to play was appalling, Delius thought privately, but all of them at least appeared modest and teachable, the Ruckert girls included. Robert Phifer invited him to his house where they spent the first of many evenings together over Chopin and Schumann and Mendelssohn with Phifer at the piano and Delius at the violin.

Phifer was consumed with curiosity. How came it that a traveling music teacher owned a Cremona violin? Delius only smiled noncommittally, but Phifer decided that in time it would be interesting to learn more of this pleasant young man who had appeared out of nowhere with only a dollar in his pocket. Phifer's daughter Willa, still in long braids, was delighted by Delius's laughter and his slow Yorkshire speech. He said "leetle" for little, and after he had heard her father play he would exclaim: "That was grr—and!" She giggled, too, at his habit of scratching out music on handy scraps of paper, and she collected the tiny piles he had forgotten. Her mother began to feel solicitous. Belle Phifer as well as her husband was puzzled by the Cremona, especially when Delius played it brilliantly one evening at a college concert.

He had chosen Mendelssohn's sparkling E minor violin concerto, and when he had finished to Phifer's accompaniment the audience rose spontaneously to its feet to cheer him. The auditorium's gas lamps flickered in the winter draught, but Delius was perspiring after the technical display of the last movement. Who had taught him, everyone wondered? Surely not some plodding country music master in the north of England. "My parents are German but I'm a Yorkshire lad," he had explained; he had said no more.

With the Ruckerts and especially with the Phifers he began to experience in Danville the first comfortable family life he had ever known. He was more often with the Phifers than in his boarding house. They were gay and easy with each other; no fear shadowed their lives together. On the evenings he managed to save for them, the crystal wineglasses ranged on their sideboard glinted with sherry, and Mrs. Phifer and her Negro cook baked cakes and rolled cookies. Cheerfully the cook sang all the hymns Delius wanted to hear. In the parlor Robert Phifer and his friends, tobacco planters and mill officials, smoked pungent Virginia tobacco in their pipes and nobody minded. The men nodded with approval the frosty morning they learned Delius could sit a horse as well as any of them and that he could ride as recklessly and shoot as far as they could. Where had he learned? The music master was clearly a gentleman.

What he preferred was to tramp in the woods by himself over the beech and hickory leaves crackling underfoot. Sometimes the afternoons were smoky from farm field clearing fires nearby. Beyond Danville, the gullied clay roads cut north to a distant range of hills, the Appalachians. High cedars drooped beside magnolias in the dooryards of green-shuttered and whitewashed houses where he gave lessons after school. The plantations' romantic histories of splendor and war stirred his imagination. As in Jacksonville, the girls began to fall in love with him. This time he wasn't immune. Danville's welcome had touched him too deeply and had weakened his reserve.

One of the families which had hired him was named Watkins. Their daughter Virginia Ann was only fifteen, but she wore her brown hair piled high on her head in grown-up style. Dark brown eyes shone in her rosy face. A wide mouth and a pointed chin lent piquancy to her expression. She was fond of fichus and white gloves, and when she spoke, it was with Virginian softness. Like every other southern debutante she had learned early to flirt with subtlety and grace. Now, full force, she turned her charms on her music master. Her parents approved. He was prospering in Danville. Girls married young in the South. As he began to dream of Virginia Ann, he wrote her a song, "Two Brown Eyes." Several times master and pupil were alone together in front of a flickering fire in the Watkins parlor. As he watched her move and heard her sing and listened to her crystalline laughter he fell deeper and deeper in love. What couldn't he do with this child-woman at his side, believing in him as she said she did? He had new friends, warm and loyal and willing to judge him as he was. The Dan valley reminded him of West Riding dales. With Virginia Ann he lost himself in a round of plantation dances and dinners, and he discarded like an outworn garment the loneliness which had haunted him in Jacksonville. Two other men were in love with her too. In a mixture of shyness and coquetry which enchanted him she danced across polished ballrooms, her tiny waist swaying, her hands slender and beckoning. He could not lose her. Impulsively he hurried downtown and bought her a ring, and late one evening he asked her to wear it. Yes, she promised astonishingly. She too was in love. And he would settle in Danville, and he would write great music, and she would adore him. America would be at his feet some day. She was sure of it.

Leipzig? Perhaps Paris, crowded European opera houses and theatres, as much music as he wanted, played by the greatest orchestras of the world? The vision faded and rose up again. But he would take her with him. There would be some way to support her; he would keep saving his salary, and he would make her see that she had to leave her home because of his music. He would not tell her just yet; it would frighten her. But gradually he would earn her trust and she would follow him where he had to go. Meanwhile his ring gleamed on her small finger, though their engagement wasn't announced and she didn't use the word. They "went together," she said American-style.

He was happier than he had been in months. He told Robert Phifer about her and confided his history to them both. He had played the Mendelssohn concerto as well as he had because his teacher had been Bauerkeller of the Hallé Orchestra. He himself had accompanied Joachim. Hans Sitt had worked with him. He had escaped his father and the wool business and orange-growing. At Solano Grove he had found his vocation.

Robert Phifer was sympathetic, if not surprised. He had suspected a rich and tyrannical father and a rebellious son. Of course Delius must go to Leipzig. His friend Ward had believed it, Phifer believed it. Delius was a social and financial success now and his father might be impressed. One night Phifer sat down at his study desk and wrote a strong letter to Julius Delius. You have a son to be proud of, he told him; you must help him instead of standing in his way. Quietly then Phifer waited for an answer without telling Delius what he had done. It was only to his daughter Willa that he confided some of his misgivings: "Delius has a strange sort of music in his mind. Some of the harmony is so involved that when it's set down it's impossible to play." But Leipzig would remedy that by stressing orthodox German rules.

Gossiping Danville girls didn't fail to notice Delius's romance with Virginia Ann. Some were jealous, some flippant. "Just wait. What he really cares about is composing. She doesn't know her own mind." Didn't he already spend free time listening to Negroes sing in the tobacco stemmeries when he could have been with his betrothed? In the stemmeries bare-shouldered men stood in rows to strip veins from the tobacco leaves that were the mainstay of the American cigarette market. Because so many work songs were chanted at the stemmeries' stripping counters, the rooms where the workers stood were called "singing rooms." Again Delius tried to transcribe the harmonies in his notebook. But he was beginning to realize that perhaps he could never get them exact. European notation wasn't capable of showing African tone systems. It didn't matter. What he was after more than accuracy was the emotion behind them, and that he could learn to convey.

Again too he sought out small ramshackle churches in the country to hear prayers intoned: "Pile up them great black clouds of yours, Lord! Let you lightnin' skip about, blow 'em over this way an' then let 'em dreen theirselves down on our fields till the springs is full and the streams got back their strength and the corn untwist itself and the tobacco raise up its head once more and the earth be drenched." The words were like those of a lyric drama. He tried to make Virginia Ann understand why he wanted to learn them all.

The rains came, and a season of white dogwood merged into a hot sandy June. He took her on picnics with the Phifers in wooded meadows and always the talk was of concerts and folksongs and composition. Phifer remained silent about his letter to Julius Delius. It had never been answered. The man was blind, Phifer decided. Music didn't "interest" his son; it hounded him ruthlessly. For the moment he was in Danville gathering strength, but this was only an interlude. And how could the little Watkins girl understand that?

Delius himself tried at last to tell her. Wide-eyed and bewildered she listened, shaking her head. She belonged in Danville; her friends were here. Leipzig was foreign. He couldn't ask her to go. How could she leave her parents? Slowly she twisted his ring from her hand and gave it back to him. They weren't really engaged at all. She'd only said she'd wear his ring. Now she couldn't. Besides, there were still the other boys, and *they* didn't leave her to listen to darkies. She wanted balls and bouquets and house parties, fun and friends and home.

Even in Delius's infatuation he knew the truth when he heard it. He couldn't give up the dream of Leipzig for any woman. Perhaps it was crazy for a musician to think of marrying at all. As an artist he should be "free as the winds," ready to follow where his art called him. Love was "a madness that played itself out, a fireworks" that flared hotly and then fizzled away. The happiness of creating and learning lasted . . . Yes, he and Virginia Ann could remain friends. He would come to see her and she would continue her lessons with him. But he knew the episode of Danville was drawing to a close. Danville was a way station on the road he had to travel.

All summer and fall he worked furiously, banking dollars by the pile. Christmas 1885 was gay, full of holly wreaths and punch and fir trees and supper parties inside Main Street's brick houses. Sleighbells jangled in a fresh fall of snow. The mill whistles blew out recess and briefly the stemmeries were empty. He saw several girls beside Virginia Ann, and they laughed at his jokes and listened to him play. He had never known a Christmas like it; he wouldn't forget. But he knew he must go farther, this time to New York, where musicians' salaries were higher than anywhere in America. He could finish his saving for Leipzig in a few years. The knowledge of his need for training haunted him.

Once again he began scanning newspapers. This time he found a call for a church organist in Brooklyn. He could play the organ after a fashion; Tom Ward had taught him how to use the pedals in the cathedral at St. Augustine. In New York he would hear the music of a great city: ocean liners, the songs of nations. His friends in Danville protested, but he promised to write. Once more he took his suitcase and his violin and, this time, a bank draft, and he boarded a train north.

Weeks passed. The Phifers heard nothing and neither did anyone else, even Virginia Ann. Finally Robert Phifer got a brief card. Delius had a job and planned to live on Long Island for a while. The card was followed by a thick letter postmarked Bradford, Yorkshire. Julius Delius announced to Phifer that he had hired detectives who had advised him his son had now disappeared from Danville and was untraceable. This had distressed Madam his mother and his Aunt Albertine as well. Therefore Julius was reconsidering. It was staggering enough, after all, to learn that his son had succeeded at something—anything. So the fellow was coining money out of teaching Americans! It had taken time to get used to the idea. If Mr. Phifer would be so kind as to inform Julius punctually where the boy could be reached, Julius would summon him home in preparation for the proper course of instruction in Germany. Once again, Robert Phifer sat down to his desk to give a father the latest news of his son.

For Delius it was out of the blue that his father's detectives presented themselves on Long Island. They handed over passage money to England and explained that Julius's plans now included Leipzig, eighteen months' study, and a diploma in musical theory. Further orders would be delivered personally in Bradford.

Dazed and triumphant, Delius packed. He had won! He would take Leipzig any way he could get it, but now his father knew he was capable of standing alone. Never again would there be slavery to Bradford. He had no idea why his father had surrendered, but he had. Of the two, the younger Delius had actually been the stronger. Now his ears were ringing with the rhythms of America and he was going to finish learning how to let those rhythms speak to the older world he meant to conquer with their help.

7 ⟡ *Leipzig and Edvard Grieg*

On a clear morning in August, 1886, an express train crossed the Dutch frontier. Aboard it was Fritz Delius, fresh from Bradford and a reunion with Max and Clare. His eyes scanned eagerly the range of high mountains in the distance. Soon he made out a pass and beside the river which had carved it, his train steamed into a spectacular gateway to Germany. Back in Yorkshire, Max was laboring in Delius and Company and Clare was "at home," a debutante waiting to marry, singing only for herself. Far away in Florida, Ernest was halfheartedly trying to grow vegetables. Fritz alone had gotten what he wanted. The coaches rumbled on, across broad fields and down into steep-sided valleys. When they slowed to a crawl in a series of industrial suburbs, his excitement mounted. At last came the magic moment: the screeching of brakes, the grating of hitches, and the platform sign: LEIPZIG. He had reached what he was sure was the city of his dreams.

He was supposed to earn his diploma as quickly as he could, and then return to America to teach. Julius had made that clear in Bradford. But Delius had resolved from the start he would never live away from Europe again. In a year and a half there would be another battle. He would fight it when the time came, no sooner. And again he would win. He had to be near really professional orchestras, mingle with accomplished musicians, try his wings as a composer where he could be seen and heard. Leipzig would give him everything he needed.

The boardinghouse he had arranged to live in was shabby and dark. The only running water trickled from a kitchen tap, but he wasn't discouraged. When he had deposited his suit-case and his violin, he set out to explore winding, narrow streets. The warm sun of late afternoon was falling on the mellow bricks fronting rows of high houses with tiled roofs. It fell too on the copper-clad pinnacles of the old city hall, the Rathaus, and the sturdy tower of the Pleissenburg fortress beside the Pleisse river in the city's medieval center. Nearby, in the Thomas-kirche, Johann Sebastian Bach had been cantor. In the Thomasschule he had taught his choirs. The Conserva-tory itself loomed gray and solemn, close to the Gewandhaus, the cloth-merchants' hall. Every Thursday evening in winter there would be the Gewandhaus concerts to which musicians like Johannes Brahms and the Russian, Peter Tchaikovsky, came to conduct their works. Delius knew the stiff Gewand-haus tradition: the string section was not allowed to sit during any of the performances. Years ago Mendelssohn had decreed they must stand. Mendelssohn had been dead for nearly forty years, his teacher and friend Moscheles for sixteen. But their legends lingered on. They had made the Gewandhaus and the Conservatory the musical center of the world.

As Delius roamed he stared up at the street signs: Beetho-venstrasse, Mozartstrasse, Haydnstrasse, Schumannstrasse. He passed the ornately fronted Booksellers' Exchange. Leipzig was also the capital of Europe's literary world. Every spring and fall there were gigantic fairs to which booksellers came with their wares. Garish booths lined the sidewalks then and scholars jostled Saxon peasant couples in laced native cos-tumes. Wily old merchants in fur-trimmed cloaks hawked trinkets, and lager beer flowed like water in the cafés. In the formally symmetrical Rosenthal park stood the Restaurant Rosenthal, where the elite of the Conservatory and Leipzig University lingered most afternoons over ham rolls and cheese and talked of Schiller, who had written his *Ode to Joy* in Leipzig. Beethoven had made this the choral finale of his

Ninth Symphony. In Leipzig, too, Goethe had set several
scenes of *Faust*. Gee'de, the Leipzigers pronounced his name
with Saxon slurring. Reminders of greatness towered wherever Fritz went. It was impossible not to be awed.

In the Conservatory he knew he wouldn't feel completely strange. His onetime teacher Hans Sitt was now holding violin classes there, and he would continue lessons with
him. His two other professors would be Carl Reinecke, a
prolific composer of concertos in Mozart's style, and Salomon
Jadassohn. Reinecke taught composition. Jadassohn was an
authority on harmony and counterpoint; he would carry on
where Tom Ward had left off. Delius was in a fever for
classes to begin. The only distraction from music was his
discovery the first night in his room that the wooden furniture
was crawling with bedbugs. He beat a hasty retreat to a
garret in the Harkortstrasse closer to the Conservatory and
the Gewandhaus. Here he began to meet students who had
bedbug stories of their own. Leipzig was medieval in more
ways than one.

It was also expensive. When the fall session began, the
Conservatory doorkeeper exacted tips for opening and shut-
ting the gate. Café food was rich and heavy and high-priced.
Julius's allowance wouldn't pay for many kraut-stuffed par-
tridges. Most of the students lived on sausage and ambition.
Few were English. The most talked-about English musician
was a Conservatory graduate, a woman. Ethel Smyth smoked
cigars and stalked down the aisles of the Gewandhaus with a
huge black mongrel dog who had once jumped on one of the
violinists. She was bluff and strenuous, but Delius liked her
when they met. He respected her demand to be treated as an
equal on the ground of music. She had every right; several of
her compositions had been performed, and the widow of
Schumann said she was brilliantly gifted. What disturbed him
was her airy dismissal of the Conservatory. "It's trading on

its reputation now. The great days are over." The opinion infuriated Conservatory wives like Frau Reinecke, who boiled with rage when critics said Brahms was greater than her husband.

Reinecke disliked coming to the Conservatory. Instead he made his students climb to his flat, where frizzle-haired Frau Reinecke greeted them with a stiff bow and then gestured helplessly toward the debris her brood had strewn over the floor. Reinecke had been married three times, and each wife had presented him with a family. The first two had died in the process. Reinecke was used to composing in the midst of drying wash and legions of toy soldiers. Politely he accepted his students' exercises and usually handed them back without comment. Delius was puzzled. He kept cramming his notebooks in the hope that Reinecke would guide him toward his first long composition, a suite he planned to call *Florida*. But Reinecke peered, nodded, and with thinly concealed impatience went back to his own music at a littered desk. Delius was advised vaguely to persevere.

Salomon Jadassohn came to class, but he was always fifteen minutes late. When he arrived he began telling jokes with a lisp, his back to an antique iron stove. Everything his students needed to know was in his harmony textbook, he said. Every few years he revised it. Like Reinecke he disliked marking papers and seldom did. When he got around to the job, he would simply scrawl "False!" across what he said were mistakes. He gave no explanations. Instead he reminisced about a colleague who had proclaimed: "Play diligently the old masters: Haydn, Mozart, Beethoven, and me!"

It was all very entertaining; but Delius reluctantly began to understand that Ethel Smyth was right. He was actually learning little Tom Ward hadn't taught him in Florida. Hans Sitt was helping him improve his violin playing, but he hadn't come to Leipzig to perform. Reinecke gave him piles of piano

exercises and told him he must unlearn the technique he had
taught himself. He was making small progress; his fingers
were simply too long and thin for crisp playing, and he began
to believe Reinecke was destroying what skill he had. He
hadn't thought the Conservatory would be like this. Where
was the help he needed for *Florida*? He knew the effects he
wanted but as usual couldn't get them on paper. When the
belated reaction of Salomon Jadassohn came, it was curt:
"These chromatics!" What was Delius trying to do? "False!"
scribbled Jadassohn, and then went back to telling jokes.

If the classes didn't matter at Leipzig, the music itself did:
the chance to hear it and talk it all day long and half the
night. Delius began to study the scores of Wagner in detail.
He would have to find for himself a method of orchestral
shading and coloring. The fiery conducting of Wagner's Leipzig champion, Artur Nikisch, was a revelation. Offstage,
Nikisch flirted with professors' daughters and was known as
Jack the Maiden Killer, but when he mounted the podium,
even outraged fathers forgave him. Whenever he conducted
Tristan and Isolde, the result next morning was a nearly empty
Conservatory. "*Tristan* again," and teachers would smile dryly
as they faced a handful of pupils. Sometimes a hollow-chested
young Austrian, Gustav Mahler, came to lead the Gewandhaus orchestra; he drove them like a gang of slaves, they
complained. Delius met Tchaikovsky, who didn't like the
Gewandhaus programs. "Too classical!" he sneered. But the
violin playing of a quartet in Leipzig's Chamber Music Hall
had the unexpected effect of making Delius admire Beethoven
once more. The later Beethoven quartets were superb; how
could he ever have thought them dull?

His special friends were two young Norwegians. Johann
Halvorsen and Christian Sinding had come to Leipzig dazzled
by the same legends and had met the same disappointments in
their classes as Delius had. Now they pored over *Florida* with

him. They were startled and fascinated by the syncopation and the blue notes. The music of the future wouldn't be German, they agreed; it would be folk music wrought into new symphonic forms. *Florida* was heady stuff. They urged him to show it to Edvard Grieg when he visited Leipzig. Grieg had pioneered the use of Norwegian melodies; he would surely be fascinated with *Florida* and its Negro sources. Grieg had been a Conservatory student years before. Across his own exercises Salomon Jadassohn had scrawled "False!" Now he was famous as the composer of one of the most frequently played piano concertos in Europe. Halvorsen and Sinding both knew him well.

By the beginning of 1887, Delius had begun to cut most of his classes. Now he knew what Tom Ward had been too modest to admit; Ward was as capable as any German theorist. Delius worked tirelessly over his notebooks, missing meals when he was absorbed in counterpoint. Painfully he manipulated his scoring of the bass; if only he could hear in a concert hall what he had done. He knew some of the parts were stilted and didn't move properly. When *Florida* left him worn out, he turned to songwriting for relaxation: some German lyrics, an "Ave Maria" with German words. Perhaps remembering his Christmas in Danville, he wrote *Sleighride*, in which he felt he had begun to grasp orchestration at last. He also tried his hand at a *Marche Caprice* that turned out an ethereally stylized echo of a Jacksonville brass band. He showed Sinding and Halvorsen everything. They were amazed at his drive and output. By summer he needed a rest, they warned. Lack of sleep and his steady writing in a poorly lighted attic had given him eyestrain.

Sinding and Halvorsen couldn't go with him, but he left for Norway and a hiking tour of the jagged Stalheim district. Once more Norway stirred him. Everything was on the scale of giants: the dark firs, the rocky fjords. The boulder-littered paths he strode gave him a greedy appetite which maternal farmers' wives enjoyed satisfying with lamb and goat cheese. Rural families freely offered him their hospitality, smiling at the wandering young musician who would sit silently fishing in a mountain stream for hours and then suddenly begin to scribble in a copybook. One afternoon it rained. Marooned, he began to examine the library of the chalet where he was staying. An absent son was a university student in Christiania, Norway's capital, and had left some of his books behind him.

Delius's eye fell on a title by a German, Friedrich Nietzsche: *Thus Spoke Zarathustra*. It was a long poem, recited by an imaginary prophet named for a real one in ancient Persia. The images and ideas were dazzling. They were also heresy. The old civilization was dying, Zarathustra proclaimed. So was the old concept of God. Men must find a new one to take its place. What the world needed was a Superman who would guide the way to new beliefs compatible with the discoveries of science and the demands of an industrial age. Medieval Christianity wasn't enough. Superman was not a politician but an artist; he alone could reveal fresh truth in the collapse of Europe's traditions:

> I love the great despisers, for they are the great venerators . . . I love him who lives for knowledge . . . Behold the good and the just! Whom do they hate most? Him who smashes their tables of values, the breaker, the law-breaker—but he is the creator . . . Oh solitude of all givers! Oh silence of all light-givers!

In Nietzsche, Delius recognized a kindred spirit. Nietzsche, too, had had the experience of a mystic, a "state of illumination." He clamored for a new religion, a new reality. His language was a rich torrent. Delius read the book from cover to cover. What Nietzsche believed he believed. Men must say "Yes" to life, not deny it by thinking the human race was naturally evil. The artist must be true to himself, indifferent to praise or blame. He must also learn to be lonely forever. It was in loneliness he learned and created. The poetry of Nietzsche was a million leagues away from the world of Delius and Company, and it confirmed for Delius all his rebellion and his love of life and music. Nietzsche's Zarathustra echoed Wagner's Lohengrin and Ibsen's Brand: "A place where one can be wholly oneself—that is man's right, and I ask no more."

After his hiking trip, Delius went to France to visit his Uncle Théodor, who was staying in a Paris suburb. Ville d'Avray was full of graceful stone cottages and had a tiny lake. Uncle and nephew talked music. Once Théodor had turned the tide for him, and Delius was grateful. When he returned to Leipzig, Sinding and Halvorsen told him excitedly that Grieg had arrived. He and his wife, Fru Nina, wanted to meet Delius and see *Florida*.

"Children of the month of May," a Norwegian poet had once called the Griegs. "Children of opening leaves and rising life." Grieg was a tiny man with a mane of blond hair and a drooping moustache. Fru Nina was dainty and pretty and wore her fair hair cropped short and curly. She had a clear soprano voice and sang her husband's songs in concert. Audiences smiled at her quaint high-necked dark gowns and Norwegian silver filigree necklaces. She wore no stage makeup and was indifferent to the crows' feet laughter had etched at the corners of her eyes. Most men fell a little in love with Nina Grieg; Halvorsen and Sinding had, and so did Delius. The Griegs had lost their only child. For Fru Nina, young composers were to be mothered and encouraged. Grieg was a father to whom they could turn for help and advice. On Christmas Eve, 1887, Grieg planned to give a party. He would invite most of the Gewandhaus orchestra, which would play one composition each by Sinding, Halvorsen, and Delius.

Delius came with *Sleighride*. The Griegs' flat was decked with fir branches and mistletoe, and around the candle-studded Christmas tree the guests gathered to drink Norwegian punch. The punch was powerful—so powerful that after a few cups the orchestra declared itself incapable of playing a note, and the three young men went home on Christmas morning with their masterpieces unheard. But Grieg asked Delius to show him everything he had written. Tense with anticipation, Delius brought him a package of manuscripts. Grieg smiled. "When I came to Leipzig I too was a parcel stuffed with dreams." Delius told him about Bradford, Solano Grove, and Danville. In the coming April his term at the Conservatory would be over. His father wanted him to go back to America and he couldn't. Should he take a job? How could he manage? Did Grieg think he had ability—not only ability, but what was more necessary still: genius?

When a letter arrived from Grieg, he tore it open. Wonderful words leapt at him from the page: Grieg had found his work brilliant, full of resourcefulness. He must continue to compose at all costs; his future depended on a European environment close to major orchestras. "Follow your own true nature," Grieg emphasized. Some day Delius would be recognized; Grieg had no doubt of it. Genius, yes; Grieg had seen it in Delius's scores. He would watch his career from henceforth with keen attention.

It was a formal document, formally written and signed with Grieg's full name. It was to be Delius's weapon in Bradford after graduation. Grieg had understood. He would be an ally in the coming showdown. So, Delius knew, would his Uncle Théodor.

In March, 1888, Leipzig was caught in the grip of a hard frost which covered the river Pleisse with ice. Skaters gathered in moonlight parties and students haunted the cafés. Hans Sitt made a proposal. At the Restaurant Rosenthal he would assemble musicians from the Gewandhaus orchestra. If Delius would buy them a barrel of beer, Sitt would conduct them in *Florida*, which they were sure to play as a favor. Excitedly Delius borrowed enough money to buy the beer. Grieg came with Sinding and Halvorsen. For two hours Sitt rehearsed sixty players in the rhythms of *Florida*'s sections "Daybreak," "On the River," "Sunset Near the Plantation," and "Night." The players were baffled by some of the innovations, but they were enthusiastic over the music and the beer alike. When they had played *Florida* through, they applauded as loudly as Grieg himself. Delius was drunk, but not on beer. The sound of his own creation had transported him back to Solano Grove and the St. Johns River. It was all there. He had managed to recreate it. Sobering afterwards, he knew he had made mistakes in the scoring. He would have to do some revision. But the Restaurant Rosenthal had nevertheless echoed the spirituals and dances of Solano Grove. One of the dances he christened "La Calinda." It was based on the Fanti chanting he had heard:

But *Florida* had done more than copy folk tunes. It had expressed the mixed gaiety and melancholy of Negroes like Elbert Anderson, whose spirit had briefly been transported to the edge of a Leipzig park.

In April, Delius took his examinations. He was confident of passing, for he had learned in the Gewandhaus and Chamber Music Hall and in his garret what he hadn't been taught in class. He wouldn't know the result for some weeks, however. On the 11th, armed with Grieg's letter, he left Leipzig for

Bradford to face his father. Immediately Julius asked him when he planned to go back to America. Delius broke his news: He didn't plan to go back at all. His father's reaction was a predictable spluttering in anger. What had Leipzig been for? What were the results? All very well for the famous Grieg to say "genius," but what did geniuses live on besides their future glory?

A continued allowance, Delius answered. An expression of faith in his talent until he could support himself by composing. If Julius would put up half the money, he would ask Uncle Théodor for the other half. In time he was bound to succeed. When Julius's scorn was withering, Delius persisted. Only to Grieg did he confide his discouragement: he had to get out of Bradford. Its atmosphere had plunged him into gloom.

Grieg was scheduled to give a series of London concerts in May. He answered sympathetically that he could tell Delius felt low. Was he able to work? For composition a musician needed the right environment.

Julius continued to refuse Delius help. Homesick for Leipzig and the Griegs, Delius poured out to them his discouragement. He was coming to London; he hoped the Griegs could dine with him. But he was not going to London alone. Julius had Delius and Company business there. Julius finally agreed to meet the Griegs; it was a concession, but he would make it. On the evening of May 4, the Griegs arrived at his London hotel. The four had a lavish meal: beefsteak and chicken and fresh asparagus, French pastries, Italian cherries, and ices. After dinner Grieg began telling Julius that it was his duty to help his son because that son might well be one of the greatest musicians England had ever produced.

Julius stared. Here was a celebrated musical authority telling him in person more than he had said in that preposterously optimistic letter. Fritz a great musician? Julius couldn't believe it. But Grieg repeated the words. London had heard the

Griegs and was at their feet; Julius had seen it in every newspaper. Fru Nina had been cheered in St. James Hall in an
unprecedented demonstration by the normally reserved British
public. Might there be something after all in what the Griegs
said? And mightn't Fritz disappear as in Danville if he were
refused money indefinitely? When the evening was over, Julius
was stunned as he listened to himself promising the Griegs to
give Fritz two pounds a week. Théodor would have to provide
two more. It would be just enough for food and lodging—and
in Paris, doubtless, where Théodor had fled long ago. But
Théodor was no genius. Fritz, incredibly, had supporters to
say he was.

"Nothing of consequence will come of this," Julius muttered. The next morning when he left for Bradford he wondered how he had ever permitted the two Norwegians to talk
him into such an outrageous fantasy. "No son of mine is a
composer!" he stormed. Better to think of him merely as an
idler. Well, Julius was two pounds a week poorer, but at least
he could settle one thing to his satisfaction. If he said Fritz
wasn't a composer, he wasn't, and he wouldn't ever be. For
Julius Delius firmly believed he had never in all his sixty-six
years made a mistake.

8 ❧ Young Man About Paris

By the middle of May Delius was installed in Uncle Théodor's Paris flat. Lindens were rustling fresh leaves along the boulevards. Temporarily the two men would keep a bachelors' establishment; then Delius would find lodgings of his own. Meanwhile, when Théodor was paying afternoon calls, Fritz could be alone to work. In the evenings uncle and nephew entertained. Théodor's friend André Messager, a composer of operettas, came often. Society hostesses were fond of Théodor's gossip, especially young Princess Marie Léonie of Cystria. Princess Marie Léonie was the daughter of a French duke, the wife of a rich Italian. Pretty and in her twenties, she held musical gatherings in the drawing room of her mansion in the Rue Hamelin. She also invited chosen friends to spend occasional weekends at her chateau on the river Seine. Théodor and Fritz Delius were included.

Théodor and his world seemed to belong more to the graceful eighteenth century than the hardheaded nineteenth. Théodor's clothes were splendidly cut, his shirts frilled and kept immaculate by his valet Isidore. Théodor bowed rigid courtly bows from the waist. When he sang to himself, it was usually a quaint German song about a maiden's blue eyes. He was considerate and discreet, asking no questions. What his nephew did with his free time was his nephew's business, he made it understood. His housekeeper Mrs. Harding was also discreet. Mrs. Harding, according to Paris rumors, had several children with auburn hair, deep blue eyes, and very long noses. Fritz knew his own stubbornness in getting his way about music amused Théodor. All the Deliuses were apt to have "steely, inflexible wills." Julius's had seldom been broken, except by his brother and his son, who were now together in their revolt.

At first Paris was perfect. Fritz wrote the Griegs that he loved it. He felt a new sense of freedom; Paris streets were alive and gay. Paris orchestras played better than the Gewandhaus orchestra because the musicians sacrificed individual virtuosity for ensemble. He went to every concert he could, talked composition with André Messager and Princess Marie Léonie, and worked at a fresh sheaf of songs. He began, too, what he called a melodrama, a tone poem which was also a tenor setting of Henrik Ibsen's poem "On the Heights." Florida pulled him one way, Scandinavia the other. Sometimes he was unaware of the oddity of the results. "La Calinda" turned up in the middle of his *On the Heights* music, and the Norwegian folksongs he used were often tinged with suggestions of Florida blues. He was composing now by sticking one idea onto the next, cutting sections out of one part of the score and pasting them into another. What began as page four might turn out to be page ten, and page ten might be a mixture of Wagner, Norway, the Seminoles, and hot nights on the St. Johns.

When Théodor took a trip to London, Delius spent eighteen days working without a break. At last *On the Heights* was finished. It had filled him with memories of Norway's mountains. Yes, Paris was exciting and lovely, he decided, but he wouldn't stay in it forever. The wilderness of Norway had strength and majesty that Paris, for him, did not. French art was graceful, yet often shallow. But he could study it in the meantime, and his personal liberty was intoxicating.

His freedom extended even to Bradford, where he dutifully visited his parents in late summer but ran up a formidable tailor's bill in his efforts to keep pace with the nattiness of

Uncle Théodor. Julius raged, but paid. Julius himself was more fastidious than ever. When a particularly ugly woman friend of Elise's was coming to dinner, he would warn: "Put roses in the center of the table so I can't see her!"

From Bradford, Delius went hiking in Brittany. The bared rockiness of the northern French coast was enlivened by vivid colors in the peasants' costumes. Breton men wore embroidered jackets; the girls' bonnets were wide and starched. Perching on the cliffs he sketched out several new songs. Some were dedicated to Grieg, some to Fru Nina, and one to Princess Marie Léonie. When he returned to Paris and Uncle Théodor, he found a letter from Grieg warning him that he was combining strange elements. Mixing Wagner with Norwegian folksongs was questionable at best, said Grieg. Soon came another letter: Grieg had looked at the songs again and now they seemed fresh and daring. They were full of emotion which convinced, and that was the main thing. Delius felt the same way. Music reached the listener, or failed to reach him, by its emotion alone. "Music is a cry from the soul," he said. "It is a revelation, a thing to be reverenced."

The clangor of Paris began to get on his nerves. It was hard to compose when he had to listen endlessly to street vendors, the hammering of carpenters, and the singing lessons of prosperous but wheezy middle-aged housewives who kept their dormer windows open. Late in the autumn he moved to Ville d'Avray with its lake and marble fountains and a small house picturesquely named the Chalet of the Lilacs. In the adjoining forest he walked thinking out new musical themes. Villagers winked at each other. "The young man who goes about the woods singing," they said. But Ville d'Avray was used to eccentrics. For years it had been a haunt of painters. Delius experimented with a beard, settled for a moustache, and began revising the orchestration of *Florida*. At last he was getting somewhere. He was producing the tonal effects he wanted. As in Leipzig, he slept in snatches, eating only when he remembered to. From Leipzig soon came disturbing news: Herr Delius had done well in his examinations, said the Conservatory authorities, and was "a nice kind gentleman of high moral character." Nevertheless since he had cut so many classes, they felt themselves unable to issue a diploma.

Fortunately Christian Sinding remained at the Conservatory. Delius asked him to see what he could do to persuade the faculty to change its mind. Some day a Leipzig diploma might mean a job if he had to take one before he conquered concert halls. Sinding missed him very much, he answered, promising to help. Sinding and Grieg both began to warn him about his health again. Was he overworking? He ignored their questions. He had to finish the new version of *Florida* because there was a chance of its being presented in England. The conductor of a London concert series had been impressed with the manuscript Delius had hopefully sent him. But no sooner had the conductor received the final score than he decided it was really too revolutionary. Safer, he thought, to stay with Beethoven and Haydn. Delius's defiant reaction was to write an orchestral rhapsody called *The Quadroon*. He had to compose his own way, nobody else's. He would make no concessions. If he wanted to use rags, blues, Norwegian folksongs and Wagner all at once, he would.

Summer brought temptations to make day trips back to Paris. The Exposition of 1889, a celebration of the 100th anniversary of the French Revolution, had just opened on a lavish scale. An engineer named Eiffel had built an immense metal tower overlooking the Exposition grounds. There was a Palace of Machines, and a gigantic café-art gallery filled with the paintings of the once radical Impressionists, artists who tried not to copy nature but to interpret their impressions of it. To Delius the main attraction of the Exposition was the Javanese Village, where gilded dancers made strange contortions with their arms to the music of an instrument called the *gamelang*. Never before had he heard the shrill pipings of oriental music. When he wasn't listening to the *gamelang* orchestra, he was in the African Pavilion watching *vodun* drummers. Back at Ville d'Avray he relived all the exotic chants and beats. Conventional concerts lost their attraction. Even the Paris opera seemed stale. After hours at the Exposition he would roam darkening streets, careful to wear not his expensive Bradford suits but shabbier clothes that wouldn't invite robbery. Several times he strayed into the Montmartre district's morgue, staring down in mute pity at its anonymous corpses. All of life, not parts of it, must be put into music. Without compassion music was dead too.

For diversion he went to café concerts, the outdoor entertainments given by singers and dancers from Paris opera houses and ballets. They performed in pagoda-topped pavilions gleaming with gaslight. Outside, beneath thick chestnuts, torches flickered over the tables of the patrons. The women in the audience ranged from nobility to grisettes. Summer nights meant laughter and flirtation. Days at Ville d'Avray were for more interpretations of what he had seen. He began to set French verses for his songs, and he delved into French literature.

When Christian Sinding wrote him that the Leipzig Conservatory was sending his diploma at last, he was relieved and amused. The Conservatory, having examined a pile of manuscripts he had forwarded at Sinding's request, had decided that only because of its faculty had he been able to turn out such a quantity of them. Surely without Reinecke's and Jadassohn's help his labor would have been impossible. When the diploma arrived, it praised his industry and his "agreeable disposition." The last was an important trait for a potential music master. Sinding had been a diplomat. The questions of Julius and Uncle Théodor about the certificate could now be answered. Leipzig had actually called Fritz Delius diligent; his father and uncle were informed of the tribute. But he must continue living on his four pounds a week, they both warned. A bargain was a bargain.

The four pounds went farther in rural Norway, where in July, 1889, he took a vacation with Sinding and Grieg. They led him to a mountain range he had never seen, the Jotunheim. Giants' Home: it was well named. The three scaled the highest peaks together and explored the vastly glittering ice of a glacier. In Delius's love of the scenery he forgot Paris night life. Instead he listened to Grieg and Sinding during evenings when they told Norwegian folk tales: the loves of princesses and princes, the adventures of trolls and warriors and thieves. Jutta Bell had once told him the same tales in Florida. He had thought Florida was home then. Now, at twenty-seven, he thought Norway might be. Where did he really belong? In Paris, with the café concerts he loved, or Ville d'Avray with its stately little houses? In the Germany of Wagner, or the Java of the *gamelang* players, or the Africa of *vodun* drummers? Was it possible to belong to all these places and people? He didn't know.

His groping music showed that he didn't. It jerked and shifted from one mood to another. The tone poem *Summer Evening* he wrote after the trip to Norway was a blend of Grieg and America. He was still unsatisfied with *On the Heights*. He had seen true heights in the Jotunheim. His first version of Ibsen's poem wouldn't do.

When his lease was up at Ville d'Avray, he moved to the northeastern suburb of Croissy, green-shuttered and full of vegetable carts. Here he found another and cheaper house with a private garden on a silent street. As at Ville d'Avray he could write in peace. He polished *On the Heights* and began a piano concerto based on a Florida spiritual. Fitfully he worked on settings for Norwegian myths. He searched for a libretto to which he could write an opera but found none to his liking. Could he do his own, perhaps? The thought struck him to combine two Scandinavian tales: *Irmelin*, the story of a princess who turned away all her suitors until she fell in love with a wandering troubadour, and a tale about a prince living in the forest disguised as a swineherd while he searched for a magic river, the Silver Stream. The result was an opera to be called *Irmelin*. To Delius, Irmelin was no woman he knew or had ever known. She was perfect, unattainable. He would never find her because love and marriage had no place in his career. Irmelin demanded nothing, took nothing. She was innocence itself, and the only words she spoke were the words he gave her.

"I have at last arranged my life according to my own nature and truth," he confided to the Griegs while he was writing *Irmelin*. "World joy instead of world sorrow." In the summer of 1890, he revisited Leipzig, where he took with him everything he had composed and spent most of his money paying the Gewandhaus players to rehearse his manuscripts: *Florida, The Quadroon, Irmelin, Summer Evening, On the Heights,* his songs. He needed to listen, to sift, to cut. Through Grieg he met a Norwegian conductor, Iver Holter, and when Holter asked to see *On the Heights* he tightened it and sent it as an overture. Afterwards he waited. Would Holter actually play *On the Heights* at a Christiania concert? Was Delius the composer to have his debut at last?

9 ❦ Apprenticeship

"I have a very good impression," Holter answered guardedly. "The overture sounds well and is also interesting in its contents and is beautiful." However—it was becoming a familiar word—Christiania's concerts in 1890-91 were all settled. Could Holter keep *On the Heights* to think about it for the following season? Resignedly, back in France, Delius agreed. All the world said he was interesting and then put him off, he complained to Théodor. As usual Théodor listened, and promised to sound out his friend Messager on exactly how an unknown musician could get started.

Once more money became a problem. Delius couldn't enjoy the quiet of a suburb like Croissy and pay for German rehearsals at the same time. Yet he needed to hear his own music more than he needed Croissy. If he had to, he would compose nights and sleep days in Paris. In a quarter of the city called Petit Montrouge, near a shaded park and an inexpensive restaurant, he found a flat in the Rue Ducouëdic. It was a few small rooms in an old house. For a reasonable price the landlord promised to knock out a wall and make a larger studio. There would be a tiny bedroom off it, and a cooking alcove. Into the flat Delius moved a rented piano and a table and a chair. A red carpet had been provided. In the bedroom there was a cot, and the kitchen alcove housed a wood stove. From henceforth, the Rue Ducouëdic would be home.

To André Messager he showed parts of *Irmelin*. An interesting and delightful opera, said Messager briefly. It would be nice to hear it—sometime. Then in the autumn of 1891, Iver

Holter announced he would conduct *On the Heights* at Christiania in October. Delius was jubilant. He gave up eating meat to pay for the trip to Norway. Holter put *On the Heights* at the end of the program, after Grieg and Wagner. The spot was at once good and bad, Delius worried; late enough to leave an impression, but also an anticlimax after masters. As he watched the orchestra begin his nerves were taut. This time his audience was real and paying. Buxom Norwegian matrons and their whiskered husbands rustled programs and read Ibsen's lines which prefaced *On the Heights* as a mood setting:

> Now with steel strength I follow my fate:
> The high hills willingly traverse;
> My lowland life forever dead.
> Here is God, and dawn's light,
> While below in shadow the others stumble.

But echoes of "La Calinda" stumbled too. Next morning Christiania newspapers announced no new musical master. The debut of Fritz Delius had passed unnoticed except for the listing of his name.

In January, 1892, he spent a depressed thirtieth birthday. He had battled so hard to lead this life, to be able to climb to his own high hills. And where was it getting him? Even Théodor was beginning to make sly references to musicians who turned out unplayable operas and unsold songs. Now Delius felt his inspiration running dry. In a fit of impatience he burned several of his most recent manuscripts. "Passage work!" he told himself contemptuously. "Fillings!"

Perhaps the thing to do was to frequent the salons of the rich more often. Influential friends might speak to important conductors who wouldn't return his manuscripts with the comments "Illegible" and "Impossible" as some had done. When he began to accept more invitations to mansions like

Princess Marie Léonie's the women found him handsome, "Byronic," full of "Delian charm," and the men were amused at the monkish life he had been leading. He decided to learn to cast horoscopes for entertainment. When he guilelessly asked Parisiennes for their birth dates they were flustered. A reigning prima donna wanted her fortune told, but when she confided her age she begged: "Don't repeat it!" André Messager introduced him to his new fiancée, an Englishwoman who wrote songs. Her success in getting them published, she said, was due to the fact that they were sentimental ballads. What Delius had been writing had no popular appeal. Who wanted discords and complicated poetry? Who cared about American quadroons and Scandinavian princesses? Couldn't he turn out pretty trifles novices could sing in their parlors?

At the house of Messager's fiancée he met another operetta composer, Isidore de Lara. De Lara flattered beauties and danced attendance in particular on the Princess of Monaco, who had been born in New Orleans. Perhaps Her Serene Highness would be interested in some of Delius's music. De Lara promised to sound her out. Delius asked him to dinner in the Rue Ducouëdic and de Lara was shocked to find that the dinner consisted of one egg apiece. "I'm hard up," Delius explained. De Lara told the story everywhere. A two-egg repast! How unworldly Delius was, even though he was trying to establish useful connections. Why didn't he ply the rich with elegant compliments? It was a pity that princesses, to interest him, had to be musical as well as bejeweled.

De Lara's haunts soon sickened Delius. Boring parties were too high a price to pay for a will-o'-the-wisp chance of success. Instead, he began to spend free evenings with a couple who lived near him in the Petit Montrouge quarter and were as poor as he was. William Molard was a dilettante composer who worked by day as a clerk in the Ministry of Agriculture. His wife Ida, a bluff Swede, was a sculptress. Ida, like Ethel

Smyth in Leipzig, smoked cigars and preached about women's rights. She towered over the mousy Molard, who wore a fur hat and a shabby coat indoors because his flat was hard to heat.

The Molards were the center of a circle Delius found bizarre and fascinating. Here were people with ideas, people with dreams like his own making sacrifices like his own. August Strindberg, a Swedish playwright already a success in Europe, often dropped in to harangue the Molards' guests about his efforts to make test tube gold. Why had he given up writing for chemistry, Delius wondered? Strindberg was a veteran of two tormented marriages. He hated women and raged against them as he and Delius took walks together in the Paris zoo and visited a Norwegian painter Strindberg knew, Edvard Munch. Strindberg amused both Delius and Munch, but they pitied him too. They thought he was half crazy. Once they called on him in the dingy room where he lived by choice and watched him poring over his potions. He made excited conversation about his experiments and then said a friendly good-by. Next day Delius and Munch received post cards: "Your efforts to assassinate me by the Muller-Schmidt method have failed! Thank you so much." Delius and Munch stared at each other in bewilderment. What was the Muller-Schmidt method? They never found out, for Strindberg went back to Sweden in a spell of sanity and began to write plays again.

The Molards also knew an ex-stockbroker, Paul Gauguin. He was a hulk of a man with almond-shaped eyes, a crooked nose, and a twisted mouth. After deserting his family to go to Tahiti and paint he had returned to Paris absorbed in strongly colored canvases of Tahitian women and flowers nobody wanted to buy. He had a flat near the Molards'; the walls of it were bright yellow and over the door he had painted a Tahitian motto, *Te Faruru*: "This is an abode of love." He enjoyed dressing up in the feathers of South Seas chiefs. He and Delius often talked art and music over red wine in a nearby café, Charlotte's. The proprietor would accept paintings in lieu of ready cash and her walls were hung with Gauguins. Benignly, encased in a mountain of flesh, Charlotte would smile at her patrons. They would all come to something, she told them—Gauguin, Munch, Delius, the absent Strindberg. Meanwhile they needed her. They called her Mother Charlotte, and when Delius's allowance ran low she gave him credit even if she couldn't hang up his operas.

He had begun a new one, *The Magic Fountain*. It told of the search for the Fountain of Youth in Florida by a Spaniard named Solano. Solano would fall in love with an Indian princess, Watawa, who would guide him to the Everglades, where both would perish together. It was to be a Seminole tragedy.

Gauguin and Edvard Munch and the Molards were fascinated. What an odd story! American—really? But didn't Americans merely make steam engines? By the light of dawn Delius composed in the Rue Ducouëdic. Then he slept, and early in the evening he visited the Molards to watch Ida sculpt and hear William play. William would bang out favorite chords several times. Then he would shout: "That's beautiful, that is!" His young stepdaughter developed a crush on Gauguin. William had adopted her, but she wasn't grateful. When Gauguin painted him, she sniffed: "It seems to me Gauguin's idea was to paint a blissful imbecile."

Gauguin didn't paint Delius; he wasn't attracted to handsome men as subjects. But his friend and agent Daniel de Monfreid was and persuaded Delius to sit for him at the piano playing *Irmelin*. What de Monfreid caught was not Delius's attractiveness but his nightmare of failure. The pastel was a sad little study of a wistful, moustached young man with slightly receding hair who was staring down at his hands. Their wandering over the keyboard looked aimless.

In February, 1893, Isidore de Lara's efforts to interest Princess Alice of Monaco in Delius's music were successful. *On the Heights*, further revised, was performed at a Monte Carlo concert. The audience clapped enthusiastically. Next day Princess Alice wrote to tell Delius he had great talent. But there were no reviews, no stirrings in European musical circles. Wryly Delius smiled at the Princess's congratulations and compliments. They were an old story. Music publishers continued to return everything he sent them. Well, sneered Gauguin, it was a rotten world. You did the best with what was in you and nobody cared. The wilderness of the South Seas was better than the bourgeois bad taste of Paris. Delius only smiled. Once, he said, he too had been in the wilderness. What he had heard there nobody understood. Doubtless the fate of *The Magic Fountain* would be oblivion. But he went on working at it, because an artist was lost if he stopped. You had to plod ahead, no matter what.

In the fall he received a disturbing letter from Bradford. It was signed by the Secretary of Delius and Company. Delius knew recent American tariff laws had cut his father's volume of business. Max, still a subordinate since Julius refused to make him a partner, had been concerned; the firm had begun to lose ten thousand pounds a year. But Julius Delius was rich; there had been no talk of an immediate crisis. The Secretary announced one. Max still had no financial interest in the concern and no authority. Julius was sending insulting letters to his clients, and when Max went to mollify them they refused to listen to him. Unless Julius relinquished his control, his employees' felt not a single customer worth having would be left in half a year. Julius, said the rest of Delius and Company, was not in step with the times. Worse news followed. Max Delius had left Bradford and disappeared.

Delius was powerless. When his father announced his allowance was to be cut in half, he understood why. Clare, thank God, had recently married a Yorkshire squire, John Allan-Black. Though her parents had forced her to give up a concert career, she seemed happy enough living in an old stone manor house at the edge of the moors. She played and sang for her husband. Clare was safe. But Ernest had vacated Solano Grove and was missing; now Max was missing too, and Delius and Company was tumbling into wreckage. The empire Julius Delius had built he was himself destroying. No longer would the resources of Delius and Company stand between an obscure composer and starvation. There was only Uncle Théodor, who had invested his money independently and prudently. But Théodor was beginning to grow testy. When Delius urged him to buy all Gauguin's paintings for sale, he laughed outright. Why didn't anybody else want them? If Fritz was such a nine-day wonder, why didn't people print or play his music? A far-off concert room in Christiania and a Monte Carlo gambling palace were hardly the Gewandhaus or London's St. James Hall. "You ought to return to America," Théodor prodded. Gauguin ought to get a job. To crown everything, *The Magic Fountain* began to go badly. The libretto wasn't right.

When Jutta Bell appeared unexpectedly in Paris, she came like an angel of deliverance. In Florida the Bells' grove had been frozen out. Now she was living in London and giving singing lessons at what she called the Bell-Ranske Institute. When he handed her *The Magic Fountain*, she began telling him what was wrong with the characters' motives. She would collaborate with him. He needed an operatic apprenticeship; he had no literary style.

Together they began to rework *The Magic Fountain*. Sometimes they argued fiercely, but he began to make changes. As he made them, the opera improved. He joined forces, too, with a French critic to write a handbook on orchestration. It would bring in a little money. A German opera house inquired about

Irmelin, though nothing came of it. The Griegs were still faithfully propagandizing.

Finally *The Magic Fountain* was done. Now the language flowed more easily. Delius scratched in the last note and made a copy of the manuscript. Was it really the best he could do? Had he captured the dignity of the Seminoles, the dank extravagance of Florida swamps? He began to doubt it. But he sent off the copy to Eduard Lassen, director of one of Germany's most famous opera houses, Weimar. He had little hope of acceptance. When he heard nothing, not even a rejection, he wasn't surprised.

Living on eggs, salad, bread, and an unsatisfied longing to write the opera that would truly capture America not in literal realism but in the fantasy of suggestion, he devoured books by American authors. Uncle Théodor urged him to forsake American literature for American money—the kind Danville had paid. Delius ignored the advice. One mild evening by lamplight as he sat at his table he was gripped by excitement. The novel in his hands was George Washington Cable's *The Grandissimes*, set in New Orleans. Part of the novel retold the legend of Bras-Coupé, a captured African prince. But that was the same legend Delius himself had so often heard in Florida! Bras-Coupé's African name, said Cable, was Koanga, of the Congo. Plantations, groves, canefields . . . it was a world he knew because he had shared it. Already he had worked enough with Negro music to know how to use it. Banjos, fiddles, bones . . . a Negro opera, the first ever written . . . planters and their overseers and sheltered daughters, and in slave quarters captives who hated and loved as white men did . . . This time there would be no failure, no superficiality. *Koanga* would be years out of his own experience.

10 ✌ Koanga

When Théodor heard about *Koanga* he was astonished and shocked. What a subject! The thing was doomed from the start. Negroes! What self-respecting conductor would play the work? Go back to America, Théodor pressed. Perhaps Americans would be interested. Nobody else would. When Delius refused, Théodor bridled. The more he thought about his ne'er-do-well nephew the angrier he got. He had promised to help until Delius was recognized. Well, he never would be! That was becoming clearer by the day. Théodor demanded a decision. Either Delius left for the new world, or he would cut off his allowance.

For Delius, whose brain was crowded with ideas he longed to work at undisturbed, the blow was hard. He could sell his violin to gain time. But then was *Koanga* to be sacrificed for a job teaching *Hearts and Flowers* to American debutantes? Never, he swore. Home in the Rue Ducouëdic he decided to appeal to the only person left to help him. Aunt Albertine Delius Krönig in Germany was his godparent. Once she had believed in him. Would she gamble now on *Koanga?* He sent her a fragment of the score, and waited for her answer. Meanwhile he spent all his nights composing. During the day a neighboring ironmonger banged too hard at pots and pans to allow any concentration. In addition to *Koanga* he began a fantasy of the Yorkshire moors, *Over the Hills and Far Away.* Its austerity was a refreshing change from *Koanga*'s Southern richness.

One evening in January, 1896, just before his thirty-fourth

birthday, he took time out to go to dinner in the Petit Montrouge flat of a friend. At first he paid little attention to a plain girl opposite him. She was talking about modern art. Her full, tall figure verged on plumpness. She had twisted her light blond hair into an unbecoming figure-eight bun on the top of her head, and her gown was badly designed. It made her look even plumper than she was. She seemed shy. Her name was Helen Sophie Emilie Rosen. For two years she had had a studio in Petit Montrouge. She painted in tiny dots of color, a technique called "pointillism." Everything an artist saw could be broken down into light fragments. Art could become an exact science.

She stammered a little as she tried to explain all this in her uncertain English, strongly accented with German. Delius raised his brows when his host murmured that Miss Rosen had been invited to exhibit her work in the Independents' Salon when she was only seventeen. She was twenty-eight now, deadly serious about making her mark. Yet from time to time she laughed gently. Her favorite author was Nietzsche, she said. She loved the poetry and independence of *Thus Spoke Zarathustra.*

"I know the book too." Delius leaned forward. "I admire it very much." Then he gave her a more appraising glance. What a pity she didn't make more of her good features: the pale blue eyes, the pointed chin. Miss Rosen was also an amateur musician. After dinner she offered to play and sing two songs of Grieg's. Her voice was a tiny soprano. As a performer she had no talent, but there was something fresh about her. She even resembled someone he knew. Who? He told her about Grieg's friendship. Soon he was talking about *Koanga* and its use of banjos and she was listening intently. Might he come to her studio to play her some of his own songs? Perhaps she could give him an opinion of them. They had been written for modest home performers like herself, though no publisher was interested except a neighborhood music shop or two.

Miss Rosen said she would be delighted. She had little technical knowledge of music, but her grandfather had played the piano, and her widowed mother, his daughter, with whom she lived, enjoyed listening to after-dinner songs.

By the time Miss Rosen had left the party, she and Delius had made a date. She was the first prodigy he had ever known and he was surprised she wasn't conceited. Seventeen-year-olds weren't often asked for their paintings by Paris salons. Well, but her whole family was talented, his host explained. Her father, the late Professor Rosen, had been an authority on European folklore. He had also been a diplomat. In spite of the fact that he was a Jew, the Prussian government had made him its consul in Belgrade; Jews weren't often trusted with official posts. Professor Rosen had written scores of books on language. One of Miss Rosen's brothers was an artist. Another had married into the family of the English novelist Dickens. Yet it was her mother's father who had been really famous.

Who had he been, Delius asked?

"Ignaz Moscheles."

Good lord! The grandfather who "had played the piano"! Delius was chagrined. He had been condescending, almost paternal. The girl had grown up on traditions of Moscheles and Mendelssohn and Schumann, and he had talked to her about himself! Of course she looked familiar; she had the high forehead, broad nose, and light eyes of old Moscheles himself, and every Leipzig student had passed Moscheles's portrait daily in the conservatory. But perhaps she might understand his own plight. She had grown up among musicians, artists, writers. She might even have suggestions about music to study, conductors to try, publishers to contact.

Two days later he brought her twelve of his favorite songs and sang them all. She listened, in complete silence, to the

restlessness of "Twilight Fancies" in which a girl cried out
suddenly:

> "What is it I long for?
> God help me!" . . .
> And the sun went down;
> And the sun went down.

Miss Rosen was transfixed. When he had finished, she
finally breathed: "What a glorious revelation!" She had heard
nothing to match this, she said. He was a pathfinder. He had
to continue at all costs. Every note was spellbinding. Her
praise came low and impassioned. He must play her *Koanga*.
She would do anything she could for him. She would talk
about his music, sing it. She wanted to hear every note. And
her close friends called her by her childhood name, Jelka;
"Yelka," she pronounced it. She hoped he would call her
Jelka too.

He was elated. Jelka and her mother were sophisticated
critics. Madame Rosen was charming. She liked him as much
as Jelka did, but she was self-effacing. Most of the time when
he came to Jelka's large studio, he played for her alone: all of
Irmelin, parts of *Koanga, Over the Hills and Far Away,* a set
of variations he was composing called *Appalachia.* It was "the
old Indian name for North America," he said. He had used
"Dixie" and "Yankee Doodle" and Cracker folksongs in it.
Jelka was fascinated. But she loved the melodies of the
Negroes in *Koanga* more. "They are delightful, delightful!"
she repeated, looking across at him with wide-eyed enthusiasm. She also showed him her paintings. Candidly he criticized their weakness; she used too much rose and pink. She
answered that he was the first man she had ever known who
treated her with the honest respect she longed for as a professional.

She was soon in love although Delius wasn't. Love was out

of the question, he still believed. He knew many women, some beautiful, and most he found amusing. But he never permitted himself to become serious. To live on a wife's money would be degrading. He had none of his own. It was that simple. For him the attraction of Jelka Rosen was her quietness, her faith in his future, and the atmosphere of rest she created whenever he was with her.

Jelka was far from feeling any rest herself. She fell so blindly in love she counted the hours and days they were apart. Had it started to happen as he sang "Twilight Fancies" to her? Her greatest fear was that she would be like the girl who watched the sun go down in the song. Delius would tire of her; he wouldn't find enough in her to interest him; then he would leave her, and the world would be a blank, "the sun gone down forever." Whenever he played "Twilight Fancies," she felt a chill of terror. It was only too clear he was completely indifferent to her as a woman. She could keep him merely as a friend. Every time he came to see her she fought with her emotion and had to pretend a casualness she knew she could never enjoy again.

On the other hand, Delius decided Jelka Rosen had brought him luck. His life took a turn for the better. Aunt Albertine Krönig promised to help him and stepped into the gap the quarrel with Uncle Théodor had left. She had shown his music to some German friends, who had praised it. She herself liked it in spite of its difficult harmony. Delius could count on her. Hadn't he proved he could work doggedly? Then the Prague Opera wrote him unexpectedly to ask for *The Magic Fountain*. Its unusual story of American Indians had interested them in a lavish production; they had heard of its existence from several musicians. They were prepared to give it a run of weeks.

The offer was exciting, but the German one that came next was more exciting still. Eduard Lassen, director of the Weimar

Opera, had had time to read *The Magic Fountain* and now he wanted to stage it. In Delius's mind there was no hesitation. At Prague the work might be ignored by the rest of Europe. If it made its debut at Weimar it would be talked about everywhere. He wrote to Lassen, confident that his bad days were coming to an end. Then he went back to *Koanga*.

Soon he asked for Jelka Rosen's advice about it. She was no writer herself, but she knew an English writer, Charles Keary, who might want to work on *Koanga*'s libretto. She agreed the exaggerated dialect of George Washington Cable had to go. No European would be able to make head or tail of New Orleans Créoles and Negroes.

Together Delius and Jelka began taking the afternoon train out to Paris suburbs. There they walked in the woods. Sometimes they talked, but at other times they hardly spoke. In her silence, he could think. At the end of the day he asked her to have supper with him in the Rue Ducouëdic. Thanks to Aunt Albertine he could now buy an occasional beefsteak. This he served with an egg and some watercress. He did all the cooking himself. "I learned that in my Florida days," he told her. He played. After dinner she let him work. She always sensed the exact moment he wanted to start. She went home alone, telling him not to bother escorting her. He must get on with his task.

When Jutta Bell wrote him she wouldn't be able to give him further help with *Koanga*, he was hardly disappointed. Jelka's friend Keary was after all a professional writer.

Keary was staying in a little village about forty miles south of Paris: Bourron. Jelka and Madame Rosen usually spent their summers in the hamlet next to it, Grez, on the winding and serene Loing river. At Grez there was an abandoned house with a garden Jelka liked to paint in. When she introduced Delius to Keary, he proceeded to change most of Jutta Bell's lines. Delius saw the result and was annoyed. Now the words were too high-flown. What Negro ever said: "The dawn begins to gild the east; each cabin door opens to greet the strident call; the world resumes again its old unchanging round"? Really!

But it would sing well, Keary insisted. An opera needed extravagant arias. Nevertheless Delius put in more believable interludes: overseers yelling "Come out, nigger!" as they had on the St. Johns, slaves afraid of the whip, women's chants to African gods: "Aie! Voo*doo!*" The plot he and Keary settled on was simple. Koanga, or Bras-Coupé, refused to work in Louisiana cane fields because he was a captured prince. Impatient overseers set a quadroon girl Palmyra to try to lure him into work when the whip failed. But the overseers hadn't counted on Palmyra's respect for Koanga's African past. He awakened her pride in being a Negro. "Africa!" she affirmed, "Land of my fathers." She would marry Koanga on her master's plantation. He promised to work for her sake because he loved her. At the wedding a white man seized Palmyra for himself and Koanga killed him. Then he fled to the depths of nearby bayous. Calling to African gods for revenge he lured many slaves into the freedom of the swamps. When a posse was sent out to capture him, its hunt continued until he was found, dragged to the plantation, and whipped to death. Palmyra, watching, killed herself in love and bitterness. She would no longer degrade herself in slavery. She would "rise to Koanga's estate" of freedom, and so, one day, would all her race.

The opera's proud music was impressive, and Delius knew it. La Calinda had turned wild and exuberant. *Koanga* was better than anything he had ever done. It was unique. Every page had power and fire. Beside it *The Magic Fountain* was nothing. Reluctantly he decided there was only one course to take. He couldn't make his operatic debut with something he now saw as inferior. Doubtless Aunt Albertine would throw up her hands in horror at his folly, but he had to withdraw *The Magic Fountain* from production. Jelka, when he told her, understood. *Koanga* must be the first Delius opera. Nothing less would do. An artist had to be ruthlessly critical of himself.

One summer day she asked him to take her boating on the river Loing. It was as smooth and sparkling as an opal. Tall poplars and willows bordered it. She wanted to show him her garden. The bright blue of the sky dazzled them both as they looked up at fleeting clouds. Their boat drifted on, past the gray pile of a ruined tower. Queen Blanche's tower, it was called. Once a queen of France had waited in it for her absent king during the Crusades. Near the tower and the old gray stone village church several houses were clustered. All of them were weathered.

"They breathe tranquility and content, don't they?" Jelka smiled. The one whose garden she knew best loomed empty and shuttered. She and Delius moored their boat at the dock and she led him onto overgrown paths. Roses grew wild all around them. Columbines and marigolds bloomed untended among the weeds. The fragrance of summer lilies drifted over a faint breeze. How strange that the owner, the Marquis de Carzeaux, never spent any time here. A wide stone terrace had been paved near the wall. It was open only to the eyes of the priest who lived next door. Locusts hummed in tall lindens. Perhaps the Marquis de Carzeaux had no taste for remoteness.

"I could really work here," Delius told her. "Everything is so quiet and unspoiled. I'd like to live in a house like this, wouldn't you?" Slowly then he drew Jelka back to the boat. Both looked behind them a last time. He was thinking of writing music in the empty mansion, and she was thinking of being married to him there. Of Grez and the tall shuttered house on the river each had a dream.

But the dreams were hopelessly different.

11 ✑ Return to Florida

Late in that summer of 1896, he took his usual hike in Norway. This time he met a fellow-vagabond in a wandering violinist, Halfdan Jebe, short and swarthy and keen-eyed. Jebe lived entirely by what he earned playing in small towns, and he played with verve, although he admitted he was incapable of the discipline concert artists had to have. He preferred being a nomad, taking up his violin only when the mood struck him. Witty and cynical about women, Jebe preferred the company of men, who could climb the tallest crags with him and could leap the widest chasms. He planned to come to Paris later in the year and promised to look up Delius in the Rue Ducouëdic to renew their friendship.

On his way back, Delius paid a strained visit to his parents in Bradford. "Danville!" Elise Delius jeered. "The only time you made a living for yourself. But you will have to do something. Go back to America. Even Théodor told you." The subjects of Ernest and Max, both unheard from, were avoided. Delius had tried to trace Max on his own but had had no luck. Julius. had grown more difficult than ever. He was curtly formal. Delius breathed a sigh of relief when he left. His parents wanted to hear nothing of his music. Julius still said he wasn't a composer, and so he wasn't. That was that.

From Bradford he went over the moors to visit Clare and her husband at their country house, Stonegappe. Once Charlotte Brontë had been a governess there and had written her novel *Jane Eyre* in the servants' quarters. Clare showed him the drawing-room view she loved as Charlotte Brontë had:

gray-purple moors stretching away in the distance, the misted bulk of the Pennines. She picked him heather and bilberry sprigs and day after day rode over the turf with him to the places they had known as children: Withens and Ilkley and Skipton, stony crags and steep rocks. Their two horses she had named Moonlight and Starlight. She had children of her own now, the ages she and Delius had been when they had first seen Skipton Castle. In the nursery he amused her brood by the hour, crawling on all fours in a circus game of menagerie. "But first," he would shake his finger at them. "Eat your porridge!"

In her home and her family Clare had been able to make peace with herself. She still sang. Sometimes, she admitted, her longing for a career in music had been so great it was almost unbearable. On a trip to London she had heard a prima donna. After the concert Clare had gone to a party attended by critics. She had sung for them herself. "But your voice is better!" several had exclaimed. Why did she do nothing with it? Clare had only smiled and shaken her head. Now at Stonegappe she sang for Delius the songs he had brought with him. One of her favorites was "Homeward Journey," the journey he was making now:

> I see again the hills and valleys
> That once I knew in happy childhood's day;
> The same fresh breeze blows cool upon my forehead,
> And gold lies on the snow as once it lay.

All of the songs might have been created for Clare; perhaps they had been. He had written nearly forty of them. Only a few had been sold to small French music stores. He had recently sent some to a concert agent in New York.

He also played her *Koanga*. When he had finished, there were tears in her eyes. How moving the African melodies sounded in her house on the moor! The opera would be performed soon and when it was, she would come to the premiere. He hadn't realized how much he had missed Clare. They had shared a lot of visions together. Hers, she said, would have to be realized in his own success.

Success? He smiled a little thinly. At Weimar he had had to throw success away with *The Magic Fountain*, and if he weren't successful at thirty-four, pray, when did she think he would be?

"I believe and I'll always believe!" she countered.

Back in Paris he found the city especially beguiling that autumn, full of overblown roses and browning plane trees and sparkling theatres. He began a nocturne for orchestra in which he would convey the city's moods. He also took up his piano concerto. It needed shortening. But something in the Florida spirituals he was using in it eluded him. Perhaps he had been away from Florida too long. Perhaps he had exhausted the vein of Negro melody in *Koanga*. He was restless, unable to concentrate. When he saw Jelka Rosen she was disturbed at "the entire lack of color in your face."

In this mood of dissatisfaction he received a letter from the New York concert agent. He hadn't been able to place any of his compositions. The story was always the same: the harmony was too involved, there were too many discords, the tunes weren't catchy. But the agent had been traveling and had recently found himself in Florida. Knowing something of Solano Grove from correspondence with Delius, he had found his way to it from St. Augustine. On the St. Johns he had discovered grove after grove abandoned. Repeated freezes had destroyed most of the orange and grapefruit trees. But now Florida farmers were talking of growing tobacco. The soil on the St. Johns was said to be especially suitable for cigarette tobacco. Had Delius ever thought of leasing Solano Grove to tenants who knew tobacco-growing? He and his tenants could all make a tidy profit. He could continue to live in France, but would get a regular income.

To Delius the idea was strongly appealing. Suppose he got his father to sign over Solano Grove to him entirely? Julius wouldn't have to send his pound a week then, for his son would have something to count on. Might Solano Grove mean independence after all? Surely in England or Germany it would be possible to find a young man who wanted to emigrate to America? Solano Grove would be made to order for such a person.

The more Delius thought about the agent's suggestion the more taken with it he was. When Halfdan Jebe visited him, he asked Jebe what he thought. Capital! said Jebe. Why didn't they both go to Florida and look the place over? Delius could work on his piano concerto at Solano Grove among his Negro friends and Jebe would pay his way by violin-playing. It would be a lark.

Delius was still firm about living permanently in France, but he wanted a change of scene. His father's reaction to the scheme was one of relief. He was happy to part with a useless orange grove. By Christmas Delius and Jebe had bought their steamship tickets. To celebrate their coming trip, they invited Jelka Rosen to dinner in the Rue Ducouëdic and announced what they were up to.

Somehow—she never knew quite how—she managed to get through the evening without showing "the terrible fear that clutched at my heart." This was the end of Delius in her life. She knew it. He would forget her. America was full of beautiful women. Why hadn't she gone to a better dressmaker, experimented with a new hairstyle, tried to be as chic as other women her age? Until Delius, her painting had been the main thing in her life. Now it wasn't enough. She hated Jebe! She hated his rough country accent and his raucous jokes and his bohemianism. He would be sneering at her behind her back all the way to Florida. Why had he had this miserable idea of visiting the United States? Already her mother had begun to question her about Delius. Madame Rosen's friends had been dropping sly hints about the look in Jelka's eyes as she sang Delius songs. But Delius didn't want her to sing them for him. His sister Clare's voice was magnificent, he merely informed her. He needed Jelka for nothing; Florida meant the grave of her happiness. And he had spoiled her for any other man in the world.

Jebe found Delius's unawareness of Jelka Rosen's worship vastly amusing. Here was a fellow who could win half a dozen Paris heiresses and he took no advantage of the chance. Even plain Jelka Rosen was head over ears in love with him and he didn't know it. Instead he pursued vague ideas of musical experimentation, lived on a pittance, and took favors from nobody unless you counted pocket change from a rich aunt who never missed it. It bordered on the ridiculous.

At sea the ridiculous actually happened. One of the passengers, a young man, began to follow Delius and Jebe closely. On a blustery evening the young man hid in their stateroom. When Delius came in alone, the young man shouted, "Here I am!" and removed his hat. "He" was a woman Delius had met at several Petit Montrouge parties. She had determined he would fall conquered at her feet. They must never be separated, she declared. She would follow him to the ends of the earth. "What are you going to do about it?" she taunted with a grin.

He was stupefied. His face reddened. "You must get out," he stammered. She refused. He tried to reason with her about her reputation. She said she didn't care. Finally he seized her shoulders, opened the door, and pushed her out.

When Jebe heard about the incident he was convulsed. "You pushed her?"

Delius shot him a look of triumph. "I *booted* her!" After a pause, he added sedately, "With a very brotherly kick."

The men got her a room. She refused to give her name and so, as a gentleman, did Delius. But there she was, and they were six days out of New York. To call her presence on the ship awkward was an understatement.

There was nothing to do but to brazen out the situation. Delius couldn't abandon her in a strange country. What nuisances women could be! Now he was saddled; he would have to explain her all along the way, through Danville where he planned to visit the Phifers down to Solano Grove itself. How could he introduce her? Simple, Jebe answered. Musicians were perpetually "on tour," weren't they? He himself would play the part of a mad Russian violinist, and she could be passed off as a singing Russian princess. Russians were expected to be exotic and unconventional. Jebe had even thought of a name: Lemonoff, in honor of the Florida citrus industry.

The unlikely team of Monsieur Lemonoff and The Russian Princess duly made their concert debut in Danville performing the music of Delius at what had been the Roanoke Female College. Now it was a branch of the Randolph-Macon Institute, but its girls were as sheltered as before. Lemonoff and The Russian Princess were a dazzling event in their musical lives. Robert Phifer was delighted Delius had brought performers with him, though Willa Phifer, now a young woman, thought The Princess's feet were too big. Her contralto voice wasn't much to brag about, either. But Monsieur Lemonoff told a lot of jokes, and what a glorious time her father and Delius and he were having playing together! The Phifers asked guests every evening, and the three men went through Phifer's piles of chamber music. When The Russian Princess wasn't singing, she was rather silent, Willa thought.

Delius was told Virginia Ann Watkins had married and was living nearby; he didn't see her. He felt as if the episode had happened to someone else, a guileless boy and not the man he was.

In Jacksonville he hoped his companions could shift for themselves. At Bay Street, with mounting excitement, he boarded a DeBary steamer for Solano Grove. He turned to look back; Jacksonville had changed almost beyond recognition. Streets were paved, oaks and palms had been cut down, tall buildings were now silhouetted against the shimmering sky. Camellias and early azaleas were in bloom. Not orange blossoms, people told him. Hardly an orange tree was left on the river. But from the steamer deck he saw the same deep green jungle, the same twisting vines. If anything, the St. Johns was wilder than it had been ten years before. He passed the deserted grove of the Bells. Charles Douglas, he heard, had sold out after the last freeze for five hundred dollars.

At Solano Grove he strode down the dock until he came to the house. It was still standing, still badly in need of paint, but sound. Then he found Elbert and Eliza Anderson in their own little shack in the pines. Eliza's sister Julia was a young woman now, married to a farm worker. The Andersons were overjoyed. Their real master, the "funny gentleman" they had never stopped talking about, had come back. Yes, said Anderson, the piano was still in the cottage. Merryday and Payne's had never come to collect it. When Delius had arranged for a tuner, he set to work on his concerto. Miraculously it began to come right. At night, as so long ago, he listened to the Andersons singing. The moss hung down from the oaks, and a scattering of orange trees still lived and bloomed in a sheltered patch. Frogs were croaking on the shore of the St. Johns. The Negroes still danced by firelight. La Calinda was real; so were the river chants and the work songs of *Koanga*. It was good to be in the wilderness again. It was what he had needed. Paris was wrong for him. He had missed nature. He realized that now. If only there were a Solano Grove in Europe.

He stayed for five months. Anderson was certain the land would grow tobacco. If Delius found someone to come to America, Anderson would work with him faithfully. Anderson had even learned to write a little; he could report in letters about the crop. What surprised Delius was that not only did the piano concerto improve in the setting of Solano Grove but so did his nocturne *Paris*. He seldom went even to Jacksonville. Only two things were lacking. He had sought in vain another "moment of illumination" like the only one he had ever had— the long-ago evening on the cottage porch. And he had no-body to talk to who really understood his work. He rather hoped Jelka Rosen, back in France, wouldn't hear of the dis-appearance of the woman he had had to turn into a Russian princess.

When the idyll at Solano Grove came to an end, he realized that this time the parting was permanent. Solano Grove had taught him he must find solitude somewhere in France. He couldn't keep crossing the ocean—not on his few francs. Alone, he must keep trying to recapture that moment of illumination in his music. Finally in Jacksonville he met Jebe and The Princess, and they took the train back to New York. Florida, the golden land, was behind him. He must make another Florida somewhere else.

His flat in the Rue Ducouëdic was waiting. It was damp, and it looked shabby, tiny and cramped. The Princess ac-cepted his indifference and dropped swiftly out of his life. Halfdan Jebe went back to Norway. Uncle Théodor still refused to see him. He visited Gauguin's friend de Monfreid who had painted him, and he walked restlessly in the park. When he called at the Rosens' one afternoon late in June, a maid told him Madame was away and Mademoiselle no longer lived in the city. Mademoiselle and two other young ladies had bought an empty house in the village of Grez, on the river Loing. They had all moved into it a month ago.

Was it possible? He dashed off a hurried postcard, packed a small suitcase, and took the train. He hardly knew why he was doing what he did; he simply wanted to see Jelka Rosen very soon. Alone he trudged down the dusty lane into Grez toward the house of the Marquis de Carzeaux. That would be Jelka's house. He was sure of it. She had managed to buy her garden. At the tall double blue door in front he rapped the knocker. When she came at last, he said casually, "I suppose you can put me up?" and walked inside. Could she give him some afternoon tea?

Jelka's friends Ida Gerhardi and Julia Wolfthorn were both German and both painters. They had heard of him from Jelka. Jelka was flustered as she brought out refreshments. The Marquis de Carzeaux had put his property up for sale, she explained. She had been in despair. What would she do without her garden to paint in? For days she had begged her mother to advance the purchase price. From her father she had inherited the other half. Everything she owned had been sunk into this place. Poor Madame Rosen had clutched her purse full of savings all the way to the town house of the Marquis de Carzeaux. Jelka smiled affectionately at the memory. "I *had* to buy it," she repeated breathlessly. There was little furniture. Ida and Julia had each brought a few chairs and tables. They had gotten a piano, though—an Ibach grand, really quite a good one. They had decided to settle in Grez and do nothing but paint and have little at all to do with Paris or their old friends. He of course was different. They had a cook, Marie. They had all done a great deal of work.

But they couldn't put him up. The priest next door would be scandalized. Instead he must find a room. He could use the girls' piano during the day while he stayed in Grez and rent cheap lodgings at the nearby Inn of the Pool of Water. When he finally departed to see the innkeeper, Jelka closed the door after him and leaned against it. "Oh!" she moaned to Ida and Julia. "Is all the old anxiety to begin again?" And then she added, "How heavenly it is!"

He remained in Grez all summer. There were flowers everywhere. Water lilies bloomed above their green pads on the Loing. Fishermen dawdled on the stone bridge. The meadows were dotted with daisies. In luminous, clear air, fruit began to ripen on the trees and bushes: peaches, plums, gooseberries, currants. Jelka's cook, Marie Blandel, grew vegetables and fed him delicious meals. Jelka and Julia and Ida knew painters staying in neighboring towns. At night they all came for Marie's dinners to argue art, music, poetry, and philosophy, while twilight fell on the Loing and cuckoos flew up to the treetops and fireflies flickered. Marie hovered like a mother hen. Ida Gerhardi said she knew a farmer in Germany she thought might want to go out to Florida to grow tobacco. She promised Delius to find him. In August Julius Delius formally signed over Solano Grove. Now Delius had only his few marks from Aunt Albertine to count on. But living was cheap at Grez. Marie worried that he wasn't eating properly when she didn't feed him. From time to time he left Grez to visit German conductors with his scores. Some began to show interest. Others reminded him of Weimar and his withdrawal of *The Magic Fountain*. None made any promises. He always came back poor.

But it was stupid that he should be paying the inn rent! Marie exclaimed one day. She was a thrifty peasant from Brittany, and it galled her to think of a Grez landlord collecting money for a cot in a garret. Monsieur must surely move into the vacant wing of the house! When Jelka and Ida and Julia shook their heads, she assured them Madame Rosen would be pleased to put them in her charge. Was she not trustworthy? As for the priest next door, he would be the first to understand. Marie was a daily communicant at his morning mass, and she would be acting as a parent. The Lord knew that Monsieur needed a parent too; ah, how that wretch of an innkeeper was overcharging him! When Madame Rosen came down, she was consulted and made no objection. With Marie's presence there would be no question of impropriety. The two wings of the house were separated.

By autumn Delius was installed in his new quarters. He kept the flat in the Rue Ducouëdic and made frequent trips to Paris, but he found he worked best in Grez. In September he was visited by a friend of Grieg's, a Norwegian playwright named Gunnar Heiberg. Heiberg intended to present his political satire *The Council of the People* in Christiania. Would Delius write the background music? It was a certain opportunity of production. Who knew? The newspapers might even give Delius a paragraph or two.

Delius began, confident of success. He also began to set parts of Nietzsche's *Thus Spoke Zarathustra*. The "Night Song" section especially haunted him. When he had sketched out the music he called in Marie and the girls one evening to listen to him play it. There was only one candle in the room. There was only one chair. In it Marie presided, her hands folded in her ample lap. The girls sat on the floor. Through an open casement drifted the smell of phlox. Thin curtains fluttered in the wind. At the piano he lost himself in the deepest and most sonorous chords he had ever made. There was no other sound. The night song was a tribute to stars and leaping fountains and wide black skies. Night was eternal, sang Zarathustra, but so was dawn. Eternity was a renewing.

"As I listened," Jelka whispered afterwards, "it was so beautiful I thought my heart would break."

Jutta Bell-Ranske

Virginia Ann Watkins

A card party at Leipzig. Left to Right: Fru Nina Grieg, Grieg, Halvorsen, Delius, and Sinding.

Delius, by Daniel de Monfreid

Jelka

Stonegappe, where Delius played *Koanga* to Clare.

Clare and Hugh

Delius at the time of his marriage

12 &ℓ Premières

He finished his *Norwegian Suite* for Gunnar Heiberg in record time. Since *The Council of the People* was so consistently mocking, Delius made the music mocking too. Heiberg had given him no leeway for poetic mysticism. The drama was a broad lampoon on the Norwegian parliament and on Norwegian official pomp. Most of the scenes consisted of lawgivers making themselves ridiculous in debate by comic antics and wild proposals. The parliament might have been a flock of angry chickens. With huge enjoyment Delius had indulged in biting dissonances and garish instrumentation with circus-like touches in the brass. At the end of October, 1897, he left Grez for Christiania, and when he arrived Heiberg told him quite a bit of interest had already been shown in the play. Tickets were hard to come by. Reporters had actually been making inquiries. Norwegians were fond of political scraps. The people of Christiania were less moved by the simple, dreaming temperament of a nature-loving Grieg than by the social and urban consciousness of such writers as Henrik Ibsen and Heiberg himself.

Delius found Christiania's weather frigid. Already snow lay piled in the streets, and he was reminded as his booted feet crunched over it of ancient Norse legends in which warrior kings skied from town to steep town to recruit their troops. Chimneys were smoking from the high pointed roofs he passed, and chestnut sellers warmed their gloved hands over the tiny fires on their pushcarts.

He was nervous, not because he doubted his own music but

because he would be conducting it. For several days he had been practicing waving his arms in front of the mirror in his hotel room. Was that how you went about leading an orchestra? He was afraid he would start listening to his music critically and forget to guide the players in its interpretation. He hadn't expected to conduct, but the theater's budget was short. On opening night he peered out from behind the heavy velvet curtains onstage and was startled by the extreme youth of the audience. Surely most of them were university students, he exclaimed to Heiberg. Heiberg, with a grin, answered that they were. "It may be a lively reception."

When Delius descended into the orchestra pit, there was polite applause. The announcement had been made that he was the composer, but few of the students knew much about him. Half a decade had passed since Iver Holter had presented *On the Heights.* Some of the middle-aged couples present vaguely remembered having heard of Delius somewhere, but the students had just emerged from childhood. The emotion they all shared was a violent patriotism, a hatred of Sweden under whose rule Norway was imprisoned, and a fervent belief that Norwegian writers and statesmen were going to lead them into the sunlight of independence.

As the play progressed and Delius haltingly conducted his numbers, he was aware of restless noises behind the podium. Was the audience bored? Why wouldn't they stop talking? Soon he understood the voices were far from bored. They were muttering, at first, and then amid hisses and catcalls they were shouting down curses on Gunnar Heiberg for his blasphemy of the Norwegian state. Delius struggled to raise the orchestra's volume; but how did you do that? He flailed his arms until he had gotten the brasses pitched to a blare. Just at this moment they blew out his minor-keyed parody of the Norwegian national anthem, "Yes, We Love This Land." In the theater there was a huge, shuddering gasp, then Delius heard the stamping of feet, cries of "Traitor!" and when in the pandemonium he turned, he saw the undergraduates rushing toward the stage and the orchestra pit. In one of the youngsters' hands a silvered pistol flashed in the gaslight and then cracked out a shot.

Good God! They were firing at his head! He threw down his baton, leaped up to the stage and rushed to the rear exit. Heiberg plunged after him. With the roar of the mob and the fire of its guns in their ears, they dashed out into freezing weather. Next door stood the ancient Grand Hotel. If they could reach its lobby perhaps the mob would stop short of storming it. By the time they had both raced in, the shouting had grown so loud they could hear it even behind thick walls. The hotel's clerk and porters stared, baffled as Delius and Heiberg fled to the hotel restaurant. When they had shut themselves in, they leaned against its tall glass doors in relief. A riot was happening out there. Only the police could stop it. Meanwhile Delius and Heiberg were confronted by a bewildered stare from a very old gentleman with bushy white side-whiskers who was sipping his evening toddy.

Delius stammered out an explanation. The old gentleman smiled, then answered courteously, "I am sorry for the affront Norway has offered a distinguished visitor, Herr Delius. You must remember we are barbarians up here. Allow me to apologize. I am Henrik Ibsen." The noise in the street outside grew deafening. But Ibsen reassured Heiberg and Delius the rioters would never attack the Grand Hotel. Fortunately, Ibsen was one of their heroes, and they knew he lived here. "All the same," he chuckled, "I didn't think the young devils had it in them."

Hours later, after the crowd had rampaged through Christiania shouting and shooting, the police broke it up. Muffled in his heavy overcoat, Delius hurried back to his own hotel. When he got there the manager was waiting. He must get out.

His satire on the national anthem was unpardonable! The hotel could risk no violence and damage to its furnishings by harboring him. Hastily Delius packed. The sky beyond the window began to lighten with the first red streaks of dawn. The Grand Hotel would have to take him in. He buried his face in scarves and found his way back to Ibsen's haven and threw himself on the management's mercies. Because they had no wish to offend Ibsen, they reluctantly gave him a room, and when he had wakened from a nap he sent down for the Christiania newspapers.

There were headlines. The play and its music had touched off hysteria. Delius was an Englishman; he had dared to accept Norway's hospitality and then mock its ideals. He was pernicious, a menace to society. The students of Norway had risen up to defend sacred national traditions. Also, the theater was extending the play's run to six weeks. Apparently some of the reporters must have gotten to Iver Holter, perhaps to Ibsen himself. There were accounts of Delius's Leipzig studies and of *On The Heights*. Prominent Christiania citizens were asked their opinions. Generally they favored having the play continued, but they were horrified by the violence it had begotten and they demanded troops to restrain the students. For a few nights the play had better not be given at all. Tempers must cool.

Finally the students themselves were abashed. What, they asked themselves in a Christiania University council, had they done? They had fired blank cartridges, they reassured the city. But were not speech and music to be free in the new, revitalized Norway? Had they betrayed their own dream? After heated harangues pro- and anti-Delius, they passed a resolution. They could never approve of the sacrilege he had committed, but the riot and the shooting had been in bad taste. Therefore they were censuring themselves.

For the time being Delius had had enough of conducting.

From Christiania he traveled to the German town of Elberfeld armed with a letter of introduction from Ida Gerhardi to the municipal conductor, Dr. Hans Haym. Elberfeld was a mixture of crooked medieval streets and vast factories. These produced splendid musical instruments and Elberfeld was said to be receptive to musical innovation. Dr. Haym himself was warm and welcoming. To his horror Delius learned from Haym that the Christiania riot had made not only the newspapers of Norway and France and England but those of Germany too. Yet Haym was amused. He wanted to conduct *Over the Hills and Far Away*. He had heard glowing reports of it from Miss Ida Gerhardi. Could scores be procured, and would Delius stay for the performance? All this notoriety might be turned to the piece's advantage. People would be curious. Dr. Haym believed thoroughly in Elberfeld's progressiveness.

But Elberfeld wasn't progressive enough for *Over the Hills and Far Away*. The audience chattered during the entire performance and afterwards they hardly applauded. The next morning Elberfeld's music critics demanded an investigation. How had Dr. Haym dared to "inflict upon us such a specimen of musical modernity"? The town council was therefore considering Haym's dismissal. Delius was a revolutionary. The stalwart youth of Norway had seen him for what he was. He was "scandalous and outrageous." It took hard persuasion on the part of Haym to keep his own job. He must not repeat such an offense, the burghers of Elberfeld warned him.

Two members of the audience disagreed. A professor of music at Düsseldorf demanded to meet Delius. What could he do? he asked. He would work hard to obtain Delius performances in his own city. The other visitor was a conductor, Alfred Hertz, who frequently staged operas in Elberfeld. He wanted details of *Koanga*. When all the scandal over the *Norwegian Suite* and *Over the Hills and Far Away* had died down, he wanted to stage the Negro opera. Elberfeld, and

Germany, must be made to learn that musical time could not stand still. The professor, Haym, and Hertz were allies of crucial importance. Back at Grez, Delius regaled Jelka Rosen and Julia Wolfthorn and Ida Gerhardi and Marie with the news both good and bad. Jelka paled when he told them about the shooting.

She herself hadn't been idle. She had managed to arrange a Paris performance of his piano concerto in a version for two pianos. It wouldn't be a concert, only a drawing-room "musical evening." But a German pianist, a friend of hers, had promised to play one piano if Delius could manage the other with the simpler part of the arrangement.

He was dubious. Already he knew he wasn't much of a conductor. But he was willing to try himself as a pianist. Would she come with him? He would feel better about the affair. Glowing, she promised. Both were disappointed. Delius did what he could with his part, but the performance of the German pianist was hopelessly dry and mechanical. Jelka was furious. She was also not quite happy with the way things were working out between herself and the other two girls at Grez. It had become plain to her that Ida and Julia were also falling in love with Delius. Julia was making increasingly frequent visits to Germany when he was away, but at Grez she and Ida were setting their caps for him. Small good it would do them, Jelka reflected sadly. But she wanted to share him with no one. If she meant nothing to him as a woman, she knew she was coming to mean more and more to him as a confidante and fellow-artist. If that was the way it had to be, it was better than nothing.

Ida Gerhardi had not only turned up Dr. Hans Haym of Elberfeld. She had other resources. Early in 1898, she produced a young German who wanted to grow tobacco at Solano Grove and eagerly Delius signed a contract with him. The German departed with fervent promises that they would all be hearing from him and he would prosper greatly in Florida. When no one ever heard a word and Elbert Anderson wrote he had never arrived, Ida wasn't daunted. She knew a pair of brothers who also wanted to go to America. She promised to find them as soon as she could.

On a brief visit to the Rue Ducouëdic, Delius had a surprise. A note was waiting for him in the handwriting of Uncle Théodor. When he answered it with a visit, his uncle was emotional. Their quarrel had been folly, Théodor now declared. Two such men, aristocrats and followers of the arts as they were, ought to stick together. Théodor had heard about the shooting in Christiania. Delius must be more careful of himself. As Delius faced Théodor he was shocked to find his uncle had become old. He was nearly eighty. But always he had been dapper, fastidious, well-preserved. Now he was thinner and bonier. His shirt frills were as elegant as ever, but there was a new distance, almost an otherworldliness, in his blue eyes. His face had turned paper-white. Théodor was lonely, Delius realized. But for himself there was Grez; he couldn't endure any city for long any more. Théodor understood. Yet he would once more be there to help if Delius needed it. He also asked a favor. "When I die, I wish to wear my evening clothes and I wish my body to be dressed by a Delius." Isidore the valet was of inferior social rank. This had been worrying Théodor. Restraining a smile, Delius promised. Uncle Théodor would go to his grave in his dinner jacket, prepared by the hands of his nephew and nobody else.

All that spring and summer in his wing at Grez, Delius worked. Jelka was away with her mother. Julia Wolfthorn was in Germany. Ida Gerhardi was visiting friends. While Marie fed him delicious meals, he pored over a revision of his tone poem *Appalachia*. It was too unsubtle, he decided. Out went "Dixie" and "Yankee Doodle." He used instead a simple Negro hymn, "No Trouble in that Land Where I'm Bound," and proceeded to construct a series of variations on it, hoping to capture the Negro's tragedy and also the spiritual nobility of men like Elbert Anderson. At one point a chorus entered singing Anderson's old song: "Oh, Honey, I am Going Down the River in the Morning." Whenever Delius felt himself going stale on *Appalachia*, he turned back to his nocturne *Paris*. He wrote most of a *Dance of Life*. His touch was becoming surer with each of his compositions. If only he could hear more of them! The years were passing; he was now 36.

One morning in the garden he noticed a large black jackdaw in one of the trees. The bird seemed unusually tame. When he brought it crumbs, it ate them only a few feet away. He was amused and fascinated. He took to feeding the bird daily until it began to perch on his shoulder. He had acquired a pet. He named it Koanga, and soon Koanga was flying in and out of the house and following him even to his music room. Solicitously he and Marie pampered it until it stopped relying on the garden for its food altogether and virtually moved in. When a Paris woman wrote Delius a coquettish letter, Koanga picked it up in his beak and flew away with it.

"There, what would you!" exclaimed Marie. "See how wise he is! He knows that Monsieur is now not interested and must devote himself to his work." When Delius dropped one of his cufflinks in the garden, Koanga found it and retrieved it. Jelka was touched when she returned. Delius was positively childish over the bird's devotion. The more she saw of his eagerness and unworldliness the more she began to resent the Delius family. Why did his parents refuse to help him? Koanga became a fixture. Delius had a Grez carpenter make him a cage for traveling. The first time Delius packed for Paris, Koanga hopped into the cage. Thereafter, whenever Koanga saw a suitcase, he would peck open the cage's door himself.

On a quiet, misty night in October a telegram arrived at Grez. It was from Isidore the valet. Théodor Delius had suddenly collapsed. Delius hurried to Paris by train and when he reached his uncle's flat, Théodor was unconscious. Hours later, on silken sheets, Théodor slipped quietly out of life. Remembering his promise, Delius began a task he found "macabre." Isidore stood at his side with Théodor's clothes. When Delius had managed to get the clothes on the rapidly stiffening body, Isidore handed him the decorations of the noble orders Théodor had belonged to. At last Théodor was ready. This strange old man: how much had he ever really known of him? Théodor had been a rebel, yet in the end he had clung to the conventions. When he was committed to earth in a brief Protestant service, it was Delius alone of his family who mourned him. Standing over the grave in the cemetery of Père Lachaise, he asked himself what Théodor had really wanted of life. Had he gotten it? Delius knew now he would never understand.

He was not prepared for the visit of Théodor's lawyer. Théodor had done two startling things in his will. He had commended the children of his onetime housekeeper to the care of his brother Julius in Bradford. Julius would be floored. So was Delius when he learned Théodor had left him a thousand pounds. It would be more than enough for a concert! He could pay the musicians, hire the hall, perhaps even convince his parents he had accomplished something if the concert were held in London. He couldn't live on the thousand pounds forever, anyway, so he might as well enjoy them. And he could realize another wish. Paul Gauguin's agent, Daniel de Monfreid, was holding an exhibition of Gauguin's works. Gauguin was back in Tahiti painting furiously. When Delius went to de Monfreid's house, he saw a picture he immediately knew he wanted more than any other. It showed a silent and dreaming Polynesian girl stretched out on a couch. In the background whispered two women; at a window a raven was perched, watching.

"I do not know if I am mistaken," Gauguin had written de Monfreid, "but I think that it is good. I wanted to suggest

by means of a simple nude a certain long-lost and barbaric
luxury. The whole is drowned in colors that are purposely
somber and sad; it is neither the silk, nor the velvet, nor the
cambric, nor the gold that makes this luxury, but simply matter that has become enriched by the hand of the artist . . .
As a title, 'Nevermore'; it is not by any means the raven of
Edgar Poe, but the bird of the devil, that is watching." Poor
Gauguin. He was obsessed by life's transience and by the
threat civilization posed to his wilderness. But he had reason
to be. Everything beautiful in the modern world had to fight
for its very existence, and every man knew the reality of the
death that lay ahead of him, whatever he believed about it.
Delius paid twenty pounds for the canvas. The price was steep,
but he loved *Nevermore* and he wanted it with him at Grez
to remind him of the transience of his own life, the necessity
to give always his best while he could.

Maestro Alfred Hertz was enthusiastic about conducting a
Delius concert in London when Delius approached him. He
promised to assemble an orchestra. Backed by Hertz, Delius
was able to enlist a London concert agency, and Halfdan Jebe
promised he would come from Norway to lead the violin
section. The concert agent was soon alarmed at what he had
done. But a Negro opera would be an attention-getter. There
were some lovely lyrics, too, to be sung—one for instance
about a princess called Irmelin. Delius had written an opera,
Irmelin, but this appeared to be a separate song to some unattainable woman or other:

> Irmelin rose,
> Irmelin sun,
> Irmelin loveliest of all.

The song was very recent. Delius's agent began writing frantic
business letters to Grez while Delius tried to work to the
last moment.

Their negotiations were complex. Concert hall managers

started to fight with the agent over rents. Players were hard
to find, and when they were unearthed they charged astro-
nomic rehearsal fees. English music was also suffering under
what was called the deputy system. If a player didn't feel in
the mood for a rehearsal, he could send a substitute. Hence
on the first night of the concert the man playing, for instance,
the oboe might never himself have rehearsed with the orchestra. The results were often disaster. *Koanga* required many
singers in the chorus; Delius's agent had to recruit them from
nonprofessional volunteers. It was fortunate Uncle Théodor's
money had been prompt in coming, for the agent demanded
continual advances.

In May, 1899, Delius left Grez with Koanga, the jackdaw,
for London. He bought new evening clothes to celebrate the
concert. But when he attended it, he was weary of its mechanics. Alfred Hertz led the orchestra with a sensitivity he
was grateful for, but all during the first part of the program
he was conscious of glaring errors of judgment in his scoring.
Over the Hills and Far Away went well enough, but he was
dissatisfied with his songs and *A Dance of Life.* The *Night
Song* of Zarathustra could stand revision too. When the last
note of *Koanga* died away, he was astonished to hear the
audience clamoring for its composer. He had no instinct for
taking bows. But his agent implored him to go on stage, and
as he looked out at the crowd he felt a sudden amusement.
How could they think he was important as a man? It was only
his music that mattered. But he bowed, smiling a whimsical
smile, and as soon as he decently could he melted into the
throng. He felt only a longing to return to Grez and work.
Party invitations poured in. Most of them he refused. He
waited in vain for a message from Yorkshire. Clare hadn't
been able to leave her young family, he knew, but apparently
his mother and father were choosing to ignore the concert
totally. He wasn't really surprised. It was, merely, a little odd

to have newspapers calling him great and his parents refusing to call him anything at all. He held a few conferences with librettists. He walked in green London parks. Then he crossed the Channel and went back to Grez. Shortly after he got there he was presented with bills from his agent which were far above what the agent had estimated. But the concert had enhanced his reputation. There were continental reviews, and they were good.

After some weeks of composition he longed to go to the Norwegian mountains. He wrote Edvard Munch asking if he were too busy painting or if he would like to go too. But Munch was preparing for a future exhibition Delius had promised to help him with in Paris. He liked Munch. And Munch liked both him and his music; they toyed with the idea of giving a joint exhibition and recital, though they never managed to work out the details. Munch was a dreamer too, half mystic and half satirist. Some of his canvases were lyrics, and some were dark with a menace critics called suicidal. Munch's suns blazed relentlessly; his melancholies were black. It was his northern mists that were as softly clinging and haunting as Delius's northern songs.

That autumn Ida Gerhardi came with her pair of Germans. As her other prospects had, they announced glowing hopes for tobacco at Solano Grove and they promised to work. When they arrived in Florida they found themselves short of money. The letters Delius got were begging letters. When he told them he couldn't help them, one left for Wisconsin and the other vanished into the prairies of the American west. Solano Grove was vacant again. Ida produced another set of Germans. One was young and wanted to get away from his family. He had a friend who knew farming. They both put up 250 pounds to become Solano Grove's half-owners, and they sailed determined to succeed.

It looked, in the beginning, as if they might. The house was in good shape, they reported. Elbert Anderson was "a tower of strength." They had planted tobacco in moist corners of the land. The place was tangled, but they thought they could clear thirty acres a year. It was lonely, though. There didn't seem to be any people nearby. They were considering the purchase of a motor boat because Solano Grove was so cut off from everything.

In a few months their letters turned to laments. A tropical deluge had wiped out their tobacco. They had planted new seeds and nothing had come up. Summer had found them hacking at tough brush and wishing they were at the North Pole. How hot it was in Florida! When their first winter arrived with a hard freeze they announced Florida was not too hot but too cold. One would stay for a while until he received instructions about selling Solano Grove, but the other had already departed. Elbert Anderson wanted to buy the place yet had little money. What should be done?

Nothing, Delius wrote curtly. Clearly the dream of making a living from Solano Grove was doomed. Let it go back to its jungle; the battle of reclaiming it was hopeless. Besides, he wanted to write another opera. Jelka's friend Charles Keary promised to help him with the libretto, and Jelka rather thought she could work on it a little too. He was surprised; she was a painter. But she asked him to let her translate the words of one of his songs from Swedish into English and German. When she finished, he was delighted. Jelka had an easy, graceful feeling for language he had never guessed from her shy conversation. The song bore the title:

"Black Roses"
Translated from the Swedish by Jelka Rosen.

As Jelka smiled at the heading Delius found she was almost pretty. She had her own friends and he had his; but he had been noticing that she was away from Grez more often. It was rumored that in Paris she actually had a small circle of admirers, among them the sculptor Auguste Rodin. Several letters came to Grez from Auguste Rodin, and Jelka was proud of the aging artist's admiration for her work. Julia Wolfthorn no longer lived in Grez. For some reason or other she had departed; Delius couldn't imagine why. Ida Gerhardi, too, was finding diversions in Germany and seldom returned. It was all quite puzzling. But now he had work to do, and what did he care about the possibility of Auguste Rodin introducing Jelka to new men and new interests?

The garden at Grez, when she was away and he couldn't hear her soft laughter and her humming as she painted in it, was curiously depressing.

13 ✃ Jelka

The text he had chosen for his new opera was a tale by the Swiss writer Gottfried Keller. Long ago Keller had seen a newspaper item in his native town:

> A youth of nineteen and a girl of seventeen fell in love. They were children of poor parents who having long been bitter enemies refused their consent to the lovers' marriage. On August 15 the two young people went to an inn where the poor folk of the neighborhood were making merry, and stayed dancing there till one in the morning, after which they left together. The following day their bodies were found in a nearby meadow.

From this clipping Keller had constructed his fragile, poetic story *A Village Romeo and Juliet*. The boy he called Salomon or Sali, and the girl Verena or, for short, Vreli. He made the cause of the parents' quarrel a strip of wild land each wanted to buy. The wild land was being claimed to no avail by its former owner's grandson, a vagabond who played his fiddle at village weddings but had never been baptized and so could own no property. The Dark Fiddler, everyone called him. In the village inn, which Keller gave the name Paradise Garden, the Dark Fiddler played to a troupe of fellow-roamers. When Sali and Vreli at last left the inn they went to a river barge. As it floated away, Keller decided, Sali would pull the plug. In each other's arms, the lovers would be drowned. No love on earth could be perfect, Keller was saying. There was perfection only when man was lost in the infinite, in the eternal.

Don't set this story, Delius's musical friends in England had advised him; you need to write an opera with "heaps of dancing and a happy ending" because London critics had called him gloomy. But he didn't listen. In *A Village Romeo and Juliet* he intended to dispense with acts altogether. He didn't need melodrama here. He wanted a series of scenes, "pictures," that would convey strong emotional impressions with a minimum of realism. The emotion would carry the work. It would stand or fall by its music. He was waiting eagerly for Keary's version of the libretto. To Keller's tale he himself added an ethereal sequence in which the lovers dreamed they were being married in the village church.

When Keary's libretto came, it was more verbose than *Koanga*'s had been. It was in fact impossible, ludicrous, unusable. Delius stormed in with it to Jelka in her studio and demanded she read the fantastic thing through. When she had finished, she agreed with him. He would have to forget Keary entirely. He and she could surely do the work themselves. People were beginning to expect high standards from him. His nocturne *Paris* was to be performed by Dr. Haym at Elberfeld and a pianist had asked to see his concerto. Jelka was positive they could both puzzle out a good text for *A Village Romeo and Juliet* together if she worked at sections alone and then showed him what she had done. He was pleased, and when she brought him the first part, he found writing the music for it as natural as breathing. For months they slaved together over a plot that could have moved the most unromantic of hearts. She wrote a wedding hymn for the dream sequence. He filled a carnival scene with the hectic clamors he had known at Leipzig fairs. The characters Sali and Vreli emerged as all that was good and innocent. The Dark Fiddler was a wandering soul who sang to a wandering wind. Bargemen on the river echoed choruses like those Delius had heard long ago in Stroud and in Fernandina and on the St. Johns. All his past life was coming back in a rush. His days were hardly long enough to fill the tall pages of score paper on his desk.

After the Elberfeld performance of *Paris* Dr. Haym announced that this time the audience had responded with enthusiasm. Was not Fritz Delius of German blood? It would never do for England alone to call him a genius. Dr. Haym felt positive there would be a Delius vogue in Germany because the people who were frightened of his discords were even more strongly repelled by the discords of another new composer, Richard Strauss. An anti-Straussian would become a Delian by default.

Delius had every reason to be happy. He was doing good work. Success was coming at last. There ought, he knew, to have been a new spring in his step, a new zest for life. But something was happening to him he hadn't planned, and he didn't like it. He wanted to depend on no one, and he knew he depended on Jelka Rosen. Marriage was impossible for him because he had no money. But it was Jelka he wanted to be with in his free time, Jelka he wanted to hear in the garden, Jelka he wanted to listen with him to the performances of his music. If this was love, he was perilously close to it. And it must not happen. He would have to leave Grez if it did. He couldn't propose to Jelka because he couldn't support her. He still had to wait for Aunt Albertine Krönig's checks as a schoolboy might wait for money from home. No woman could be asked to put up with such a situation. Had he thought Jelka plain? Her eyes were clear and deep. She was fair, winsome, generous. He was amused at her refusing to call him Fritz. He was English, she said, so he was Fred. These days she told enchanting stories of Grez villagers. She had compassion; new wit was emerging in her. But mostly he wanted to hear her laughter floating up to the window of his studio—

the studio he had because of her—and to share with her his work. To care for Jelka was impossible, but it was happening all the same, and he fought it by leaving her for the Rue Ducouëdic without notice time after time to pace Paris streets. *A Village Romeo and Juliet* was finished at last. It hadn't been a wise choice of operas in his predicament. From it had flowered not only the love of his characters Sali and Vreli, but an involvement he wanted no part of—his own. He and Jelka had even written a wedding scene. It was ironic.

September, 1901, was a warm month heavy with the tang of ripening grainfields. Slowly Grez's kerchiefed peasant women bent over their harvests. Apples were turning red and the sharpness of fresh-pressed cider permeated Grez lanes. He stayed on in his wing, edgy and withdrawn. Only when a telegram arrived did he tear himself away from the paradise he now found tormenting. Julius Delius, it read simply, was dead. The funeral would be in Bradford.

From Clare, in the hushed solemnity of a Claremont whose shades were drawn and whose tall front door was hung with black crepe, he learned of his father's last days. A stroke had paralyzed him. Julius the feared man of iron had become a mute figure in his bed, staring at his family with a look of puzzlement. Clare shuddered. It was almost as if he had known he had their respect but not their love. His glazed eyes had seemed to be begging for understanding. Had Julius Delius been human? Had he treated his children as he had because he had been trying to do what was best for them? If so, his tragedy had been that they had never known it. They had given him no love while he was alive. Now he was gone, and Delius and Company would be gone too. There was enough money for an ample widow's allowance for Elise. There was some money for his daughters. But of his sons, two had disappeared and the third had done worse; he had become a musician. For Fritz there were about 500 pounds. The remainder of Julius's investment in a son's career had been washed down the St. Johns river to the blue Florida sea.

Delius felt himself completely alone. Clare, the "dearest girl" he so often wrote to, had her own life and her "bonnie children." The faint hope that his father might some day understand the compulsion that had driven him was now gone. His mother was coldly silent. What was left of Théodor's money plus the 500 pounds were all that stood between him and "extreme poverty." Solano Grove was a complete fiasco. He ought to marry Jelka Rosen because he needed her, but he couldn't do it. The knowledge of all this drove him inward, away from human contacts. When he returned to Paris, his friends there noticed a change in him. He laughed less often, he was preoccupied. Sometimes his jaw was set in a stern, rigid line. "You're aloof," they told him. The only thing to do was to throw himself into music once more. The English writer Oscar Wilde's play about Salome and St. John the Baptist appealed to him. Then he learned Richard Strauss was going to compose a version of *Salome*. Maybe he ought to attempt an Italian type of opera, full of drama, and try to win a paying prize with it in Rome. He chose a French tale of love and murder, *Margot La Rouge*, and set to work. There would be sustained melodies, arias, duets. He finished it and then went to the premiere of Claude Debussy's opera *Pelléas and Mélisande*. Ah, but that was opera, the same kind of opera *A Village Romeo* was. It was delicate and fantastic. He had never heard any of Debussy's music before. Debussy was a Paris critic, all the fashion. He was arrogant and opinionated, people said.

Margot La Rouge won no prizes. Disgusted with his failure, Delius put the manuscript in his files. It had a few good moments and many bad ones. Perhaps later he could salvage some of it. Jelka was not at Grez when he came back. Madame Rosen, said Marie, was ill. She was in fact dying, and Jelka wanted to be with her.

When Jelka rejoined him, she came an orphan. Madame Rosen had given her the house at Grez free and clear. Jelka's brothers lived far away. Her friends Julia and Ida had gone for good. She didn't feel like attending the parties of Auguste Rodin at the nearby village of Meudon, arguing art and sculpture in Rodin's huge studio peopled not only by his friends but by his massively vital statues. Jelka was soon remote and preoccupied herself. She read a lot when her painting had tired her.

Then Delius learned *Paris* was to be conducted in Berlin by Ferruccio Busoni, a much-discussed virtuoso. He knew he wanted Jelka with him to hear it. The idea was mad. He would be fonder of her than ever. But she promised to go.

As a pianist Ferruccio Busoni had been a prodigy; he had made his debut at the age of seven. Now he was writing music of his own and was working at transcriptions of Bach. Dark, fiery, and unpredictable, he said he often conversed with invisible spirits in his garden. When Delius and Jelka reached Berlin, Busoni welcomed them. Christian Sinding was there too. Sinding had recently married. Busoni and his wife gave a dinner for all of them, and in the middle of it Busoni exclaimed, "Well! And here we are, three great composers! And each of the ladies is thinking, 'My man is the greatest of all!' " Delius was embarrassed. Afterwards he told Jelka, "That's not the sort of thing one should say, you know!" And in what sort of position was he putting her?

On the night of the performance he expected great things of Busoni. To his horror he found Busoni didn't know the score. He was murdering *Paris*. Mistakes jangled and clashed, the rhythms were wrong, the orchestra couldn't come in together. Delius went white with rage; he turned to Jelka and snapped, "Let's get back to Grez." All the way home on the train he hardly gave her a word. She was afraid to talk to him. When they arrived, she took refuge in her books. She had discovered an American, Walt Whitman. There was a poem about a pair of birds, "Out of the Cradle Endlessly Rocking." One of the birds disappeared and the remaining one mourned its mate while a small boy watched. Jelka sent the poem to Delius without comment. For days she didn't see him. When he finally emerged from his wing of the house, he told her briefly that he was writing a setting for the Whitman poem, and thanked her.

On a chilly spring morning they went walking together in the nearby Forest of Fontainebleau. The buds on its gnarled and spreading beech trees had begun to swell. Tiny streams swirled among ancient mossy rocks. Abruptly he made an announcement. He had no right to marry, but he must. Could she stand the humiliation of his poverty, his dependence on relatives, his not providing a home for her but living on her bounty? He hadn't meant it to be like this. No artist had a right to marry. His work was the only thing in life that mattered to him. But Jelka was part and parcel of it. Her faith now made it possible.

To Jelka, who had loved him for so long and so obsessively that the days of her life before him were unreal, his proposal based as it was on her sharing his music was nevertheless a surprise. He cared for her and she hadn't known. His love was hardly wild, but he wanted her with him always and she hadn't had a clue. Yes! she told him breathlessly. What did she care where their tiny household budget came from? It was stupid even to think of it. So it didn't matter about the "women of exceeding beauty" he had known in Paris! Her plain gown didn't matter, nor her outdated hairstyle, nor the fact that she was thirty-five. He was forty-one. Their lives were already enmeshed. He made a confession; he hadn't gone to Florida with Halfdan Jebe alone. When he told her about the girl in his stateroom, she laughed in delight. Everyone had wanted him; but he had chosen her! His denseness about women was one of the things that appealed to the mother in her.

Aunt Albertine Krönig was not enthusiastic about their engagement, but she would continue to help him. There were endless complications with French authorities. Jelka was a German national and he was English. They had to begin a tiresome series of negotiations with their consulates. He would have to produce his father's death certificate and Jelka would have to procure the death certificates of both her parents. They must prove their own ages. And who would be their witnesses? Marie offered but she could not write her name; therefore Jelka must locate one more witness. In the midst of the confusion Edvard Munch came down to Grez wanting to paint. He appeared to regard the coming marriage as a vast relief to all their friends. He was actually amused. They went back with him to Paris where they searched for more documents and wrote an endless chain of inquiries. The flat in the Rue Ducouëdic Delius found dingy. He negotiated with his landlord about giving it up forever. What did he need Paris for when he had Grez and Jelka? A hot summer dragged on; Delius was busy helping Munch arrange an exhibit of his paintings. Munch had no business sense and he himself had little, but he could drive a harder bargain with gallery-owners than Munch could, he thought.

On a warm Sunday afternoon in Grez, Delius and Jelka went walking in the Forest of Fontainebleau once more. The date was September 23, 1903. On their way back they stopped at the tiny Grez village hall. Their papers were ready at last. The Grez schoolmaster and Marie appeared for Jelka, and Delius had asked Grez's carpenter and his brother, a gardener, to appear for himself. The Mayor of Grez was away, but his assistant was ready to perform the civil ceremony. While the twilight gathered beyond a narrow window he read them Chapter Six of the French Civil Code, "Concerning Marriage."

"Do you wish to take each other as man and wife?"

"We do." The leaves on the trees outside rustled in a faint wind.

"I therefore declare in the name of the law that Monsieur Fritz Théodor Albert Delius and Mademoiselle Helen Sophie Emilie Rosen are united in marriage."

The witnesses scratched out their signatures; Marie made a mark. She had to admit her age, fifty-six. When the little ceremony was over she left her charges alone. There would be no honeymoon; they couldn't afford it. The connecting passage between the house's two wings was opened, and Delius and Jelka settled down to a life the entire village of Grez—the priest next door included—thought they should have been living long before. Grez, too, was amused and vastly relieved.

In the first letters Delius wrote after his marriage he made an announcement: his name was now Frederick, not Fritz. Grieg teased him about the change and said he wanted to meet the woman who had caused it. As for Jelka, she turned radiant. Wherever she walked, said the villagers, there was sunlight. Every morning she was up at dawn to churn the butter herself because Delius had mentioned that he liked it fresh for breakfast. She made lists of his favorite foods, and she was careful to find out what he hated. At market she inspected each vegetable. Then too she found his correspondence helter-skelter. Gradually she began to take it over; it wasn't right that he should be bothered with the mechanics of performances when he had to compose. She was painting less; but he didn't notice. He only knew it was glorious to be alive, to have his work and a wife who understood it, to live in the midst of the beauty of Grez.

When Delius had finished the Whitman poem, which he had retitled *Sea Drift* and in the last section of which he had reused the Everglades music of *The Magic Fountain*, he began a composition that would be the most ambitious he had ever done. It was to be called *A Mass of Life*. Into it he would pour all his gratitude for being in this noonday of his years on earth. The text would come from Jelka's copy of Nietzsche's

Thus Spoke Zarathustra. He would incorporate in it the "Night Song" he had written and played to her. And the *Mass* would end with words he could now believe because he was experiencing their reality:

> All joy wants eternity,
> Wants deep, profound eternity.

He had come into the sunlight himself.

14 ❦ Years of Fulfillment

He was surprised when a reporter from a British musical journal arrived at Grez asking for an interview. It was true that publishers in Germany were now beginning to show renewed interest in his music, though few had printed any. Alfred Hertz was going to stage *Koanga* at Elberfeld, and Dr. Hans Haym planned to give *Appalachia* there in the spring. Performances of *A Dance of Life* were scheduled at Dusseldorf and of *Paris* at Brussels. His piano concerto was on Elberfeld's autumn list. But why should the public be interested in him personally? Nevertheless he granted the reporter's request.

"He is a pale man," the reporter wrote, "ascetic and monkish; a man with a waspish wit, a man who allows his wit to run away with him so far that he is tempted to express opinions that he does not really hold. He is a man who pursues a path of his own, indifferent to criticism, and perhaps indifferent to indifference. Decidedly a man of most distinguished intellect, and a quick, eager, but not responsive personality . . . He is about 40 years of age, taller than one at first thinks, lean, wiry, strenuous in every movement, a fine face with piercing eyes. Every movement he makes is rapid, decisive; he is a prodigious walker, bicyclist, and swimmer."

He and Jelka swam in the Loing. They bought a small white rowboat, and in their spare time they worked on their knees in the garden planting hundreds of bulbs, clearing out flower beds, grafting young apple and pear trees, pouring heavy bags of gravel on the paths. The garden must be flawless. When-

ever they could afford to, they gave dinners on the terrace for
their Paris friends, and the laughter of the guests echoed down
Grez streets under white-gold stars. Here and there they found
furniture: overstuffed chairs, a sofa, a sideboard for the dining
room, a wicker table for the garden. They bought English
flags to fly from the steeples on their roof. Inside they hung
Jelka's paintings and photographs of Strindberg and Ibsen
and Nietzsche and Edvard Munch and the Griegs. Gauguin's
Nevermore had the place of honor in the music room over the
Ibach piano.

They were sad when Marie wanted to leave. They didn't
need her now, Marie said. She was going back to Brittany.
After an emotional farewell in which she begged her Catholic
God to bless them, they felt forlorn. But Jelka began a careful
search for the ideal cook to help her and finally settled on a
young widow, Madame Gréspier, who moved into Marie's
bedroom and then was treated to a lecture by Jelka on exactly
how she was to cook each morsel of food that might tempt
Frederick Delius. Appearance was as important as taste. Every
cherry must be plump and ripe. Peaches must be unbruised.
Delius merely thought it a marvelous stroke of luck that
Madame Gréspier cooked and cleaned so diligently. He looked
forward to late afternoons with Jelka in the garden, when
Madame Gréspier would bring out a tray full of hot tea in a
silver pot, and freshly made biscuits. He was beginning to enjoy being pampered.

"Have you brewed the tea four minutes, Madame Gréspier?"

"Certainly, Monsieur Delius."

"Are you sure that it is really four minutes?"

"But naturally. Four, even five minutes, Monsieur Delius."

"No, no. It must be only four." And Jelka would make a
mental note. The four minutes must be timed by herself each
day. The only cloud on her horizon was that when she would

puzzle out loud over a domestic detail he would ask her mildly, "Why don't you do what Clare does?"

She had never met the fabulous Clare, but she had heard of her—too often. Delius's friends had a thousand stories about Clare's beauty—"the lily of the north," they called her. They raved over Clare's voice. She had been known to lure a roomful of bridge-players into a hotel music room when she had been singing there during a vacation. She was artistic. She now had, Delius's friends said, a drawing room decorated in ivory, pink, and black. You might paint pictures with those colors, but you didn't use them in houses. Clare's children were models of good behavior. Clare could charm the most difficult people—ferocious professors of music, stylish yachtsmen who had been everywhere and seen everything. Clare was brilliant. It was to Clare that Delius wrote his longest letters, Jelka knew. He always told her everything of importance, he said. Jelka did not enjoy sharing his confidences. When she learned Clare was coming to the premiere of *Koanga* in Elberfeld in March, her feelings were mixed. True, because of Clare's intervention Elise Delius had sent them a wedding check for twenty-five pounds. But the Delius family as a whole, in Jelka's eyes, was only a vast and solid barrier which had tried to prevent her Fred from working out his destiny. Clare was a Delius too. Therefore Jelka did not appreciate his suggestions to follow her example.

Jelka herself had designed the sets for *Koanga*'s debut at Elberfeld. She had painted white-pillared houses, luxuriant palms. When she and Delius arrived for the rehearsals, they were delighted by the skill of the cast, though the leading baritone protested his skin was sore from having to make himself black every evening and afterwards wash off the paint. Negro singers weren't available in Germany.

When the day came for Clare's arrival, Jelka was apprehensive. The moment they met she realized her nerves had been justified, and she felt new stabs of jealousy. Clare was everything people said. Her figure was perfect. She had finely chiseled features and shining auburn hair and a striking warmth. Immediately she embraced Jelka and told her she knew she was a perfect choice for her brother. Once, in Clare's presence, he asked Jelka to "find out how Clare does it." Clare got him aside soon afterwards and protested: "You must never say that!" But he kept on, and Jelka didn't "know the way men were" as Clare had hoped she would.

Koanga wasn't a wild success. It was interesting, critics agreed, and America must certainly be a strange place, but was mere Negro music a fitting basis for an opera? An English musician expressed a fear that if more of this sort of thing were forthcoming "the Congo would flow into the Thames" and European music would be tainted. Delius's answer was to comment that Germans, Englishmen, and white Americans "went on stolidly creating dead works" which were imitative instead of being original. The more he composed the more he thought American folk music and American literature had to give an old world that in many ways had tired and gone stale. He worshiped Walt Whitman. He began to read Mark Twain. He played Florida songs. America and Scandinavia: these would be the founts of the vital music of the approaching twentieth century. The French were too superficial.

Part of his bias against French musicians was based on an airy review of some of his songs by Claude Debussy in a Paris magazine. They were intended, said Debussy, to be sung in rich neighborhoods for elderly convalescents trying to sleep. Delius didn't take the comment lying down. For his part, he replied, Debussy's music tended to be "palely lascivious." *Pelléas and Mélisande* was a great opera; but could Debussy write another?

At Elberfeld, Delius and Jelka had been immediately drawn

to the conductor who at the last minute had replaced a touring Alfred Hertz. Fritz Cassirer and his wife were young Berliners, and Cassirer had displayed an understanding of Negro music Delius found admirable. Mrs. Cassirer and Jelka had even hastily made several costumes in an effort to meet the performance deadline. The Cassirers enjoyed the company of the Deliuses too, though Mrs. Cassirer was privately amused at Delius's behavior when he dined out in German houses. Germans could cook better than they could talk, he informed her. He hated to listen to the prattling of frivolous women. His wife and sister never prattled. At table he would answer his female partners with "Yes, oh, yes," at suitable intervals, and Mrs. Cassirer could see he was "occupying his mind elsewhere."

When Delius and Jelka invited the Cassirers to Grez, they came and fell in love with the house and the village, the trembling ivy on the old stone walls of Queen Blanche's tower next door, the antics of Koanga the jackdaw. Mrs. Cassirer noted Delius's "extraordinary passion for nature"; it seemed second only to his music. Most of each day he spent secluded in his study, though occasionally the two couples took river picnics together on the Loing. One morning Mrs. Cassirer was awakened by the squawking of a hen being slaughtered by Madame Gréspier. At lunch Jelka served chicken.

"I couldn't touch a mouthful of that poor hen!"

Delius leaned forward gravely. "My dear Mrs. Cassirer, every chicken you have ever eaten was once alive."

Cassirer's belief in Delius's music bordered on fanaticism. He announced his intention to conduct as much of it as he could. *Koanga, Appalachia, Sea Drift*—these American pieces were "the music of the future." He helped Delius make extractions from Nietzsche for *A Mass of Life*. Together the Deliuses and the Cassirers went to Brittany, and Delius made Mrs. Cassirer and Jelka laugh with his "racy comments" on

the peasants and their bright costumes. He and Cassirer bi-
cycled every day; then they would discuss the *Mass*. Cassirer
promised to give *A Village Romeo and Juliet* in Berlin. The
Cassirers had brought their small daughter. Delius spent hours
playing with the child, absorbed with her in mysterious games.

The Brussels performance of *Paris* in December, 1904, drew
critical raves. Only the voice of Richard Strauss was raised
in protest. He called it "a not quite successful imitation of
Charpentier," the composer who had written the opera *Louise*,
with its Paris street cries. Delius replied that he had written
Paris first; it was he who had first known—as he wrote with
bad spelling—that they were "very caracteristic." At Grez he
labored over the *Mass of Life*. The strong choruses resounded
in his brain. Nietzsche's own adoration of life came to renewed
life on score paper. There were sections of tranquil meditation,
of exaltation. "Arise, mid-day!" The *Mass* was the greatest
thing he had done, he believed, and Jelka had made it possible.

Whenever he traveled with her to hear the increasingly
frequent performances of his music in Europe, people smiled
at them. For one thing, they traveled with a tame jackdaw in
a wooden cage. For another, they were so absorbed in his
work. "Perfect at-one-ness," was the verdict. "To see them
together listening to his music is to be present at a kind of
sacrament."

Only one tragedy dimmed their happiness. Delius had never
stopped trying to find his brother Max. He had traced him
across England, then to Canada. At last he got a letter from
an official of the Canadian Pacific Railway. Max was dead of
cancer in Canada. He had died poor, in pain, in exile. The
waste of it filled Delius with new bitterness toward his parents. He began writing a series of choral pieces, *Songs of
Sunset*, which dealt with winter and death. They were a direct
contrast to the *Mass of Life*. Max was dead, Ernest was lost,
he alone remained. But he had Jelka. He had at least stopped

being a fool about his pride. When he took her to Norway to meet the Griegs, they fell in love with her. But Grieg was growing feeble. He had difficulty breathing when he walked. "I cannot compose in my bodily misery although I feel that I have still got the stuff in me. That's what makes life so unbearable." Grieg too was near the end of his journey. Emphysema was slowly killing him. Delius shivered; how horrible, still to want to compose and not to be able to because you were sick. Hardly even to be able to walk! He couldn't imagine anything worse.

The year 1906 turned out to be momentous. At last he found a publisher. The Berlin firm of Harmonie, run by a relative of Salomon Jadassohn, bought everything he had written. Performances of his work were now so numerous he couldn't get to them all. The piano concerto was performed and so was *Sea Drift*. He was the rage. Cassirer was planning a *Village Romeo* production in Berlin. When Ferruccio Busoni heard *Appalachia* performed, he burst into tears and his wife had to comfort him. He was weeping for the abuse of American slaves, he said, and had evidently forgotten his abuse of *Paris*. When Cassirer reported difficulties in the mechanics of staging *A Village Romeo*, Delius wrote a musical interlude for him. As the hero and heroine made their way to the inn they needed time. *The Walk to the Paradise Garden* would give it to them, and could be performed separately since it was purely orchestral.

On Grieg's introduction the Deliuses met a young Australian pianist named Percy Grainger. He was a vegetarian with a luxuriant head of pale curly hair and energy that was maniacal. Grainger never walked; he bounded. Before he played he had to beat his hands on his knees furiously for thirty seconds. "I can't play unless I'm excited." He was crazy over English folksongs. When he sang one of them on a visit to Grez, Delius asked him if he could use it for a rhapsody.

Grainger agreed, and Delius began writing a piece to be called *Brigg Fair.* "Jelka, stuff Percy well with oatmeal!" he instructed her. "We know better, don't we?" Percy Grainger was young and reverent. His parents were far away in Australia. He needed others. The Deliuses realized now they would never have any children of their own. They didn't talk of it much, but to Delius the knowledge he would have no son made him want to help young men as he himself had once needed help. He gave Percy fatherly advice on his compositions and praised his playing. Percy was awed. To think the stylish Delius had time for him!

Delius gave advice to other composers too. Some of it was brutally frank:

> You complain that you rarely get a second hearing of your works. You ought to be thankful you get a first! Consider the position in Germany. There's a society with headquarters in Berlin for the encouragement of new music. . . . Well now, last year it had 280 new symphonies sent to it. It was able to arrange performances for six of them. Think of the years spent in composing the other 274! Don't ever dream of becoming a professional composer unless you have private means. If you're sure of your three meals a day, good. In that case write individualistic music to your heart's content. You can afford to wait for recognition. . . . Of course, there are always shop ballads. In England you can earn your living by writing stuff that wouldn't be listened to in Germany.

Oh? Mr. Delius was pro-German, then? Of course he *was* German when you came down to it, said the English. But lately the Germans had been swaggering and diplomatically aggressive, and they were growing less popular.

Life at Grez had settled into a routine which had filled Delius with creative energy. He was soon put to a test of his powers of concentration, for one morning Jelka received a letter from a woman friend who had had a love affair with a German prince. The prince now refused to marry her, and she was expecting a child. Her family had turned her out. She had no money, nowhere to go.

"She must come to us," Delius said without hesitation. Somehow they would contrive to pay her medical bills. They had the space; they would feed her and care for both her and the child when it arrived. When the woman came, Jelka put her in a cheerful room upstairs, and after the baby was born Delius insisted on giving it its first solid food. This must be German cereal, he pronounced. Day after day he fed the growing baby, a girl, himself. "Eat your porridge!" For more than a year the woman and her baby lived in the tall shuttered house on the Loing, and when at last she found a job that would enable her to bring up the child, Delius knew he would miss it. "Send me her picture," he said wistfully.

It had been eight years since Alfred Hertz's London concert of his works. In Berlin *A Village Romeo* played to a packed house. Only England was backward about performing Delius compositions. At last London made amends. His piano concerto was presented at a series of Promenade Concerts early in 1907; one of the critics wrote that his emotions had been so stirred by the middle section he could hear none of the rest. He was so "carried away" he could hardly write his review. Cassirer was going to conduct *Appalachia* in London and musicians were full of speculation over hearing another exotic American work by Frederick Delius. Delius himself crossed the Channel; he wanted to find a decent orchestra for Cassirer to lead. Without his intervention the deputy system might wreck *Appalachia*. He had also been asked to serve in an organization of British composers, the League of Music. He hated paper and committee work, but he had consented. Composers needed to stick together. Heaven knew it was a melancholy enough struggle on the way up.

His eye was caught by a concert announcement at Queen's Hall. A program of modern French and English music? And who was the conductor, Thomas Beecham? The only association Delius had with the name Beecham was the one all England had. Sir Joseph Beecham was a rich Lancashire manufacturer who turned out Beecham's Little Liver Pills. Every English schoolchild knew a ditty about them:

> Hark! The herald angels sing:
> "Beecham's pills are just the thing!
> Two for man and one for child,
> Peace on earth and mercy mild."

When Delius was told Thomas Beecham was Sir Joseph's son, he was surprised. Sir Joseph was reported to be so devoted to his product that all the newel-posts on the stairways of his house were triumphantly carved into the shape of liver pills. An artist had come from that? But a composer had come from Delius and Company. After the concert Delius strode backstage. It had been electrifying. He had to meet young Beecham and tell him how much he admired him.

Beecham—his intimates nicknamed him Tommy or sometimes, simply, The Boy—was a tiny dynamo. Grave dark eyes looked out from a pale face; he wore a short goatee. He was a perfectionist. He had opinions on anything and everything and never hesitated to express them: "Wisconsin, U. S.A., is one of the great cultural deserts of the world." Beecham was startled at the tall figure in the caped coat who began speaking to him in an exotic blend of accents, a "polyglot mish-mash" (Yorkshire? French? German?): "This is the only city in the world," Delius told him, "where a first class band can appear many times in the year without the knowledge of those whose business is to write about such things." Delius's laughter was rich and mellow, Beecham thought, his presence commanding. "The man is at least a bishop in mufti," Beecham said to himself. Delius asked him if Fritz Cassirer could have his orchestra for *Appalachia*. Beecham agreed, and looked forward to hearing it.

When the night of the Cassirer concert arrived, Beecham, like the rest of the audience, was spellbound. As the last echo of Elbert Anderson's slave song died away, the audience rose to its feet and cheered. When Delius came on stage to bow, he looked surprised. What music! Beecham made an immediate decision that for the rest of his life he himself would champion it, play it, use the Beecham fortune to finance its performances, and stuff it down the throats of any misguided souls who didn't happen to like it. In this opinion he was joined by a composer of light operas, Norman O'Neill. O'Neill was Irish, gay and whimsical. He and Beecham both soon became intimate friends of Delius and were asked to Grez.

They were enchanted. Beecham found his high opinion of Delius fully shared by Mrs. Delius—so much so she had gotten to the point where she could enjoy almost no other composers. She was glowing with news of fresh Delius performances: Switzerland, Birmingham, Liverpool, Munich, Sheffield, Elberfeld, Hereford . . . The world was waking up. Beecham was treated to the antics of Koanga. He examined manuscripts. To himself he noted the reason for their difficulty: Delius gave performers too few directions. This could be remedied by careful editing, and Beecham resolved to do it. He wanted *Appalachia* to be the first Delius work he conducted. Delius was delighted with his suggestions for it.

Delius hadn't given up entirely the idea of conducting himself. He made arrangements to lead *Appalachia* at Hanley, a Liverpool suburb, with the Hallé Orchestra in the spring of 1908. When he arrived from Grez he was fascinated by the tall ships in the nearby River Mersey, and half the time the performers didn't know where to find him. He was on the docks, enthralled. When he did rehearse he had no idea of how to control the players. And when he learned some of them hadn't shown up at one rehearsal he grew furious. *He* had shown up, and he thought he had the flu. "Call yourself an *orchester?*" he shouted, his teeth chattering from a chill. "Why, you're nothing but a bloody village band!" And then he added: "The trouble with the English is that they know nothing of organization. My God, if this country ever went to war with Germany, what a hiding it would get!" The words were noted, and were not forgotten.

The performance was generally agreed to be bad. Beecham's in London late that April was flawless. Delius had to admit it. Here was the one man above all others who knew what he was driving at. Soon Beecham began studying *A Mass of Life.* It was more elusive than *Appalachia* had been, but Beecham resolved to blue-pencil the score until there could be no possible doubt of the composer's intentions. He also agreed to join Delius on a summer tour in the Norwegian mountains.

They went to the Jotunheim. As they climbed, Delius told him about Florida and the Negroes and hummed their songs. He and Beecham inched their way over glaciers, and whenever they came to mountain streams Delius would fish, sitting for hours without a word. At other times he talked of Whitman, Nietzsche, French painting, his composition. His hiking pace on dry ground was so strenuous mountain farmers stared: "Look at the Englishman who runs!" Beecham's version of the trip when he returned to London was that he had kept up with "Delius's arduous exertions." To Jelka, Delius wrote the truth one evening: "Beecham seemed quite done up and faint and I thought we should have to turn back. He pulled together, however, very pluckily. I carried his rucksack and the guide carried mine. . . . Ultimately Beecham could scarcely walk any more. We had to wade a stream which took me almost up to the waist. The man carried Beecham across."

Beecham recovered sufficiently in England to begin terrorizing his performers into greatness. Once he was conducting Wagner's *Die Meistersinger,* and he disapproved of the tenor in the part of the hero, Walther. He was supposed to be wooing Eva, the heroine.

"Have you ever made love, Mr. X?"

"Yes, sir," answered Mr. X, blushingly.

"Do you consider yours is a suitable way of making love to Eva?"

"Well, there are different ways, sir."

"Observing your grave, deliberate motions I was reminded of that inestimable quadruped, the hedgehog."

Beecham's interpretation of Delius's tone poem *Sea Drift* both the Deliuses found "thrilling." One of the reviewers was a sportswriter filling in for an absent music critic. "Mr. Delius," he pronounced, "seems to have exhausted the whole gamut of aquatic emotion."

At Grez, Delius began a new opera. *Fennimore and Gerda* was based on a novel by a Danish writer. It concerned the quest of a modern young man, Niels Lyhne, for happiness. He became involved with a neurotic woman, Fennimore. Finally he freed himself from her and, in the pastoral surroundings of his ancestral estate, found the young girl Gerda who would permit his own gift of writing to flower undisturbed. Delius used a minimum of dialogue. For a scene on a fjord he wrote an intermezzo which had echoes of *Appalachia* in it, not because Negroes were concerned but because separation was. It was a tragedy he always associated with them.

He also composed *In a Summer Garden*—his own. "Roses, lilies, and a thousand sweet-scented flowers," he prefaced the score. "Bright butterflies flitting from petal to petal, and golden-brown bees murmuring in the warm, quivering summer air. Beneath the shade of the old trees flows a quiet river with water-lilies. In a boat, almost hidden, two people. A thrush is singing—in the distance." When it was finished he laid it on Jelka's desk without a word. Later she found it there with its inscription:

> To my wife Jelka Rosen
> All are my blooms, and all sweet blooms of love
> To thee I gave while spring and summer sang.

The quotation was from an English poet, Rossetti.

Twice in 1909, *A Mass of Life*'s brilliant choruses echoed in concert halls. Audiences cried for more. Beecham was dissatisfied with his version in London and resolved to try again. In Elberfeld, the *Mass,* conducted by Dr. Hans Haym, galvanized the same people who twelve years earlier had ridiculed its creator for *Over the Hills and Far Away.* In gratitude to Dr. Haym, Delius decided to give him title to Solano Grove. The conductor had a young relative with plenty of money dying to go to Florida. It was the least Delius could do for the man who had championed him during his struggle to be heard. Jelka agreed. If Haym's relative had money he could manage the place. It was the best fate Solano Grove could have.

Delius himself made a few more stabs at conducting. In England he led his latest piece, *A Dance Rhapsody*, in the cathedral town of Hereford. The score called for a bass oboe, an instrument few performers could handle passably and almost none well. Delius's bass oboist was particularly unlucky. He sounded, said one of the spectators, "like a mother duck trying to lay an abnormally large egg." Later, in London, Delius tried conducting *In a Summer Garden.* Afterwards he hurried to his friend Norman O'Neill waving his check and he demanded to be taken instantly to a bank. He was earning real money as a performer, he told O'Neill and his darkly pretty Swiss wife, Adine. Wasn't that splendid? Both the O'Neills were astonished. Could a check mean so much to Delius?

When he and Jelka came to London for the English premiere of *A Village Romeo and Juliet* under Beecham on February 22, 1910, the rehearsal schedule beforehand was strenuous. Delius ate little and slept less. Everything must be right. He began to feel queasy. His back started to bother him. Frequently he had violent headaches. Jelka tried to keep him in bed and couldn't. At the theater Beecham warned him he was overdoing; his nerves were obviously in a state. Jelka brought doctors who advised complete rest. It was "a severe bilious attack"—brought on, Delius quipped, by "associating with the better class of people in England." Because he could eat so little he got thinner until his look, to Jelka, was actually haggard. "Oh!" she told the O'Neills. "I am so anxious for him!"

When the opera had been performed, critics were lukewarm: "The composer as yet does not quite know how to keep alive the interest of the scene during the theme's development, and there are a good many unnecessary waits while nothing is happening. . . . Mr. Delius seems to have remarkably little sense of dramatic writing for the voice. But his healthy desire for originality of form and expression marks him as one of the factors to be reckoned with, and if he has not as yet proved very conclusively that the new forms are more inspiring than the old, he has still shown that he has something to say on his own account." One reviewer made jokes: "The audience, or some of them, may regret that the lovers were not more effectually separated . . . The Dark Fiddler's main function seems to be to make faces at them."

The music was lovely, people said, but was the piece an opera at all? Where were the acts and the spectacles? Delius tried to ignore all these comments, but he brooded about them. Real love like Sali's and Vreli's was never violent and stagey; couldn't the critics see that? Jelka managed to get him back to Grez, where he worked fitfully on *Fennimore and Gerda* when he could. Most of the time he was wretchedly sick, exhausted, and bewildered by the first real illness he had known since his far-off childhood accidents. Both he and Jelka had small regard for orthodox medicine. Neither had ever needed it. Now they were persuaded to try a homeopathic doctor, who believed in curing a disease by giving as its remedy a drug that would produce symptoms of the same disease in a healthy person. The trouble was that most of such doctors couldn't pinpoint exactly what disease they needed to treat.

Late in the autumn of 1910, Jelka took him to a sanitarium at Dresden. He got no better. Angry at its staff for doing nothing to help, she suggested a transfer to Wiesbaden, one of the most famous health resorts in Germany. Its immense Kurhaus overlooked acres of misted green park. Patients were required to take therapeutic hot baths. Delius was put on a schedule of baths, a diet, and sleep. He was paying for all his years of struggle, Jelka believed. Beecham, in England, believed the same thing. He wrote anxious letters to Wiesbaden. But Delius began to improve, and when he longed to be back at Grez he left the sanitarium with Jelka for more rest in their own house and, on balmier winter days, their garden and the Forest of Fontainebleau.

"Fred is very much better but still needs constant care and looking after," she wrote Norman and Adine O'Neill. Adine was becoming her intimate friend. "Everybody thinks he looks very well now. He is working again and we take nice walks. He had quite overrated his nerves." He wrote a few new songs. He began a tone poem of the Norwegian mountains, *A Song of the High Hills*. When Percy Grainger came to visit him they talked of forthcoming Delius performances, so many Delius was losing track. It was Jelka who attended to the mechanics, he told Percy. And yet he could wish for more performances still, though he preferred quality to quantity. He needed money, as usual.

"Why don't you write something for a small ensemble amateur musical societies could provide?" Percy asked. "Most of your works call for large choruses and a massive orchestra. They're expensive to produce. Try a miniature."

Delius made a few jottings in his notebook. Something, perhaps, based on sounds of nature . . . something in Yorkshire, or Grez . . . the coming of spring. Always when he thought of spring he thought of the first cuckoo's cry he heard each year. It was spring's official opening for him. He had loved listening for it ever since his days with Clare and Max on Rombald's Moor. *On Hearing the First Cuckoo in Spring* wouldn't be program music. He detested music that represented other things. Music's job was to express what couldn't be expressed any other way. "Otherwise," he would say with a shrug, "you might just as well write a piece called 'Good morning, it's a fine day.'" *On Hearing the First Cuckoo in Spring* would faintly echo the bird's call, but mostly it would mirror his own feelings toward the English and French countryside. When he had finished he was delighted with it. It wasn't a major composition, but a few people might find it pleasant. To go with it he wrote another simple tone poem, *Summer Night on the River*. Perhaps the river was the Loing, perhaps the St. Johns; perhaps it was all rivers in summer under the stars.

Spring came to Grez in a cloud of pear and apple blossoms. One afternoon an acquaintance from a nearby village, an English painter, turned up unexpectedly with his gangling young nephew. Philip Heseltine was seventeen, a pupil at Eton, shy and gawky and at first tongue-tied. "Oh, Mr. D-delius!" he stammered. What was the matter with him? Delius asked him to stay to tea. He tried to reassure him with a kindly smile. Was something bothering the boy?

Philip blurted out that he had heard a Delius song. A chorus near Eton had performed it. "It was a veritable revelation!"

It was "wonder music." Philip had to hear all the rest of Delius's works. He wanted to be a musician himself, though his family intended him for the Civil Service. That is, his mother did. His father was dead, and his mother had remarried. He had come to France to see his uncle, and imagine what he had felt when he had learned the great Mr. Delius actually lived in Grez! To be able to see him and thank him, to ask his advice on how to play some of the vocal scores of his operas: it was the greatest thing that had ever happened to Philip. If he could help by copying orchestral scores, correcting proofs, doing just anything at all, he would be honored.

Delius looked more closely at the boy. The Civil Service? He sounded more like a developing artist. His worship was a little embarrassing, but there could be no question of its sincerity. Delius asked him to come back. He came. He was hungry for advice. He listened to Delius play. He began to confide in him about girls. It was not long until Delius understood the boy longed for a father he didn't have. Philip knew music; he knew it technically as well as emotionally. When he went back to Eton for classes he began to write long letters. If ever Delius came to Eton "in Mr. Beecham's motor" Philip would be transported, overjoyed. The last evening at Grez had been "the most glorious evening I have ever spent." And how kind dear Mrs. Delius was! Philip dashed hither and yon to Delius performances. Richard Strauss's music only "filled him with disgust." He himself was trying to write a little. It was "poor stuff," he knew it was, but if Mr. Delius would actually pay him the compliment of looking it over . . .

In this vein Philip's letters continued until Delius felt personally responsible for him. Philip sent his songs and Delius found high promise in them. Philip must never feel he was imposing. Delius even imagined he knew when Philip was playing his music. The other night he had had a compulsion

to play *Brigg Fair* for no reason at all; had Philip been thinking of it? Philip had. This convinced them both that destiny
had taken a hand in their affairs. Jelka was fond of Philip too.
She found it so easy to agree with his opinions.

Delius told Philip he must never hesitate to confide his
problems. Sometimes Delius's answers would be late, because
he found it tiring to write letters when he was composing. But
he would always tell Philip exactly what he thought. Few
people dared to be frank. Above all, Philip mustn't waste his
life doing something he hated. To waste life was criminal.

Grieg, Delius remembered, had listened to Delius himself
when he had been young and tormented. Now Grieg was gone,
and Fru Nina lived in seclusion in Norway. Philip needed
guiding. He needed to develop his gift. He too would live for
art. Delius would help him, and so repay a debt he could
never repay to Grieg.

Toward Clare these days he was less understanding, though
he was always hers with "ever so much love." When a London
producer who had heard her sing approached her with a plan
for her to give a concert of her brother's songs, she was enthusiastic. She had always longed to do it; so many of the
songs had been written for her, and the producer felt she
alone could do them justice. In her delight she wrote to Grez.
The letter she received in return made her stare. It was from a
Fred she couldn't recognize. She must not try to "coin change"
for them both by singing his old songs. He would never for-
give her if she did. Then her "affectionate Fred" told her it
was "the sort of *réclame* I loathe." *Réclame*? Advertisement?
But what was any concert but an advertisement of the composer? What had happened to Fred? Not until later did she
understand that it was Jelka who didn't want her to sing
Delius songs. They belonged to Jelka now.

Delius's life at Grez was remote from everything but composition. He and Jelka read newspapers occasiónally, but they
never bothered much about the outside world. Jelka still

painted in the garden when she had time, which was seldom. When they went to performances together they were caught up in a fever of excitement and acclaim. Even America had heard Delius works. A young conductor in Boston named Fiedler had presented *Paris*, and another had done *Brigg Fair* in New York. Critics had found both works "strained and distressing." "Mr. Delius stands at the extreme left among present-day composers." He "follows the stormy paths of modern harmony." He was "very dour." Only one found him "possessed of delectable freshness and tenderness."

He was nearly fifty. His hair was thinning. Long ago he had given up his moustache. He carried himself as straight as a rod; his step was as quick as ever. He forgot the mysterious illness he had had. Jelka was plumper now; always, though, she was soft and feminine. She loved wearing huge chains of amber beads. Some days she chose the ivory and jade she had inherited from her mother. He hated women like Ethel Smyth in London when they shouted about women's rights. It had been amusing in Leipzig in his student days; now it was growing ludicrous. Ethel Smyth was a successful composer, and what business did she have to be marching in parades for women's votes? But she had been aggressive in Leipzig too. Perhaps parades were a way of life for her. Jelka was serene, reserved, everything a woman ought to be. He knew she had organized his life for him, and he was grateful. Because of her he had been spending years of creation and he knew they had been good ones.

In 1912, he took a trip to England, and while he was there he decided to visit his mother. She received him stonily. She had never heard a note of his music and she never would, she said. Her husband had decreed he wasn't a composer. When Delius saw Clare and she asked him how the visit had gone, he admitted he had "funked it."

The time he spent with Clare brought back his childhood.

He had been rather short with her about the songs, he supposed. Clare had grown older, yet she never really changed. She had the same dreaming eyes. And did he remember the Pennines? Spring sweeping across them and down into West Riding dales? In a mood of nostalgia he conceived the idea for a series of *North Country Sketches*. One of them he would call "The March of Spring," and it would mirror all the moorland springs he had shared with Clare.

Just before he left England for Grez, he attended for the first time a performance of a troup of dancers who had become almost overnight a theatrical sensation. The Russian Ballet was flamboyant, exotic. Its music Delius found strange and jarring but exciting too. When he went backstage with Thomas Beecham, Beecham introduced him to a short, pale Russian composer, Igor Stravinsky. Stravinsky had written the score for the ballet *Petrushka* which Delius and Beecham had just seen. Stravinsky spoke no English; he understood French. Delius's own French was halting and heavily accented, but he managed to make Stravinsky understand his admiration for him. Later Stravinsky made inquiries about Delius, none of whose compositions he had ever heard. The man had a peculiar history, he was told. He had actually been trained on an orange grove in Florida. When at last Stravinsky heard a Delius performance, he decided it would be interesting one day to see Solano Grove for himself. What had gone into the making of those heavily-shaded Delius harmonies? Years were to pass before Stravinsky stood under tall pines on the shore of the St. Johns river, but, eventually, he did.

When Delius's Aunt Albertine Krönig died in 1913, she left him several hundred pounds' worth of German investments, though other relatives had managed to get even larger shares of her fortune. Dear Aunt Albertine; well, Delius thought with satisfaction, she had lived to see him famous in her country.

The German Kaiser, Wilhelm II, was an idiotic little fellow blustering about national might. Some people were quietly removing their investments from German banks, but Delius saw no reason to worry. Clare, he said, must leave her own share of Aunt Albertine's legacy in Germany as he was leaving his there. Why, he added, the Kaiser wasn't a real Kaiser at all; he was a "café concert Kaiser" with a "too numerous family." He knew, though, that his mother still had Bismarck's picture over her bed.

The summer of 1913, Jelka persuaded him not to spend hiking in cold Norwegian mountains, as he usually did, but in the warmth of Italy. They compromised by going first to the Alps, then down to Venice. They rode along narrow canals in gondolas together and listened to street songs. Everywhere their company was courted. He had money this time to buy her little souvenirs. It was a magic interlude, and the hot Italian sun blazed down like the sun of Florida, while blue waters sparkled in chains of tiny diamonds. Soon, however, he and Jelka were homesick for Grez. They had a stiff schedule of performances coming up. Everywhere—in Germany especially—audiences were clamoring for his music. His publishers demanded fresh material. He wanted to go back to work, and Jelka longed to help Madame Gréspier in the garden.

The garden was beautiful all year. Even a harsh dry winter couldn't dim its splendor forever. In the late spring of 1914, daffodils gave way to roses. The vines had climbed to the bedrooms on the house's second story and they were freighted with crimson blooms. The tall window of Jelka's studio reflected a red-gold afternoon sun. Delius's letters to Philip Heseltine from Grez reflected his own tranquility. He was forgetting his past. He told Philip that any man could succeed at work he loved. Developing genius was like exercising one's muscles. Before a dedicated man was fifty he would know fulfillment.

On June 28, 1914, an Austrian archduke was murdered in
Serbia. Austria was an ally of Germany, and both countries
now despised not only Serbian killers but Englishmen and
Frenchmen. When Frederick and Jelka Delius were finally
made to awaken from their trance, the world had gone to war,
and the café concert Kaiser's troops were goose-stepping their
way down through Belgium toward France and the village of
Grez on the river Loing.

15 ❧ "This Fearful Carnage"

When cannons began to thunder and whole fields of ripening Grez grain lay unharvested because farmers had been called to the front, Delius was still dazed. War was not possible! His generation had never known a war that was anything more than skirmishing in far-off colonies. The English and their subjects the South African Dutch had had a family quarrel at the turn of the century, but the tramping of infantry had not been heard on European soil since Prussian troops had taken Paris in 1870. He had been a child then, hearing of it only in distant Bradford. It had meant nothing to him at eight. England and Germany had been friends for time uncounted, hadn't they? Yet now the Germans were crying, "God punish England!" because England had dared to protest their invasion of Belgium. German crowds were cheering spike-helmeted generals pushing toward Paris in a series of conquests that would surely lead to London itself. The war might be unbelievable, but it was washing across northeastern France in a scarlet tide.

The music of Delius, born Fritz but long since called Frederick by his own and Jelka's choice, was immediately forbidden within Germany's borders. He had denied his German ancestry; let him suffer for it. Officials seized his and Jelka's bank funds and stopped the royalties from his German publishers. The only really sure income they both had was cut off.

"The war is a madness destroying beauty!" he raged. Some of his friends were amused. Did he think he was the only person affected? On the house at Grez shining flagpoles still flew the English flags he and Jelka had first raised there years before. Now he refused to take them down. He was a Yorkshireman born, and a Yorkshireman he remained in spite of his exile. The villagers begged him to reconsider. The Kaiser's troops were rapidly advancing toward the Marne river, and soon they would lay Grez waste if they found defiance in it.

He turned a deaf ear. The flags would continue flying and he would continue writing music. Life would go on as it always had. His English royalties would have to buy the food and pay Madame Gréspier.

Underneath his resistance he felt a numbing shock. For more than a decade he had lived with Jelka in a world she had created especially for him. Every day of his life during these years, he had listened to her telling him he was one of the greatest musicians the world had ever known. She had answered the letters he was too busy to read. She had supervised his wine cellar. She had ordered his books. She had been the guardian of his working hours and had arranged the quiet for his sleep. She had helped him choose the words he set to music and she had translated them even when she was faced with fitting Walt Whitman's American exuberance into singable German. As she and Delius had walked beside the amethyst-colored heather and yellow-green undergrowth in the shade of the Forest of Fontainebleau's massive beeches she had listened to him as he tried to articulate his musical ideas. Her husband and his compositions were the most important things in the universe. Whatever else mattered?

It was not surprising, after all this time, that he had begun to share her opinion of his work even while he still smiled at her idea of his personal glory. It was to Jelka that the war was really a blasphemy. The intensity of her love had never wavered. Whenever they were photographed together her hand was possessively on his, or her arm was on the chair he sat in; always she faced him instead of the camera. When printers made errors in his scores, she wrote them what she called "thunder letters." But armies didn't respond to thunder letters. The danger of invasion was real and present. She might try to forget it but she couldn't.

The sound of the guns began to echo closer. *Boum-bon-bon-boum!* Delius heard them the last week in August, when panic started to spread. By the first of September he couldn't concentrate on a note. He and Jelka were drawn to the Fontainebleau road, the main highway south from Paris. Dazed, they watched together as a terrified stream of humanity rushed past: Belgians with carts piled high with their shabby furniture; peasants from the north of France, some of them old women staggering along in ragged skirts and worn-out shoes. Once-stylish Parisian matrons swathed in all the furs they owned sat hunched in the back seats of their motor cars while frightened chauffeurs honked powerlessly at the refugees to clear the road ahead. Farmers trudged with burlap sacks slung over their shoulders, their faces furrowed and grim in the hot sunlight. Children whined, and their haggard mothers clung to their hands. Sometimes cars full of French officers stirred up dust going in the opposite direction, north, all of them shouting for passage room. Day after day the Deliuses saw southbound army trucks loaded with wounded men whose cries echoed afterwards in their dreams. Mixed with the nutty tang of the grain ripening untouched in the fields they both smelled blood and death. But still the English flags flew over their house at Grez.

When the British army marched from the coast into Fontainebleau to stop the Kaiser's legions, the blasting of the cannons on both sides grew louder. There would be a battle on the Marne river. If the French and English lost, Grez was bound to fall.

"*Nevermore,*" Jelka said tight-lipped. Now their Gauguin painting was the only financial security they had, for Gauguin, who had died in 1903, was now famous. They would have to leave, and take *Nevermore* with them.

The flags rippled overhead as they began burying in the garden what silverware they owned. Delius's back began to ache, but he hacked at tough soil while Jelka and Madame Gréspier tried to disguise the caches he had made. They carried wine bottles into the depths of the cellar and cluttered the stairway leading up from it with piles of firewood. The Germans, if they came, might ignore what they would think was a woodshed. Jelka and Delius climbed rickety ladders to take down the paintings which filled the house: not only *Nevermore* but her own and the ones Edvard Munch had given them. A statue Auguste Rodin had sent they would have to leave where it was. It was too heavy to lift. Deftly they stripped canvases from their frames; then they rolled the canvases and began packing them in suitcases. *Nevermore*, nearly as tall as Jelka, she would carry herself while Delius managed with the rest of the luggage. Koanga the jackdaw would have to be left behind.

On the morning of Saturday, September 5, 1914, they hauled down their English flags at last. "My dear, it's time to get." Delius smiled ruefully. "That's what the Americans would say." Madame Gréspier chose to remain in Grez. The Deliuses planned to reach the port city of Nantes and then travel by boat to England. They began their journey by train, but at the town of Bourron they were ordered off by French officers and herded with other refugees into a luggage van where they stood jammed and faint with the heat. Jelka was clasping *Nevermore* as tightly as she could. Hours later she and Delius were pushed from the van into what had been a cattle truck. The floor reeked with droppings. They both fought nausea and exhaustion as they sat hunched on their luggage jostled by sixty frightened people bound with them for the coast. The truck arrived at the stopover of Orléans in the middle of the night. There were no hotel rooms. He and Jelka managed to walk to the railway station with their burdens and found its floor thick with refugees' mattresses. There was no space for them even there. Jelka couldn't endure much more, he knew. Finally he found an empty park bench where she fell asleep with her head on his shoulder, her blond hair coming loose from its pins.

He and Jelka were only civilians. They were among the lucky. What about the men on the front where he was now, at fifty-two, too old to go? What really mattered to any man was life itself and the right to keep it. Life was more necessary than music. It would be difficult, understanding this as he understood it now, to resume a remote, perhaps even selfish, existence of composing.

In the morning he took Jelka to the main Orléans hotel, where he begged for the first room that would become vacant. The manager brought them coffee, then the welcome news that there would be a place for them to spend the night because people were leaving for the port of Nantes as fast as they could. The Deliuses couldn't. Now they were too tired to move.

"We'll stay," he told her quietly. "This time we'll stay until we're bombarded out."

At mealtime they ate with French officers who rustled dispatches from the front. Orléans was filling with hundreds of thousands of Allied soldiers. Troop trains were rumbling shakily through on their way to the Marne river, and the poplar-lined Orléans road was thick with a crawling cavalcade of supply trucks. Some of the trains were coming back. Delius walked among their wounded, trying to hear their pleadings as he bent down to comfort them.

"At Charleroi there were fifteen hundred of us," a young private whispered; he had a bullet through his elbow and shrapnel in his heel. "Only fifty came out." Boys of school age lay dying on stretchers; some had become double amputees. Clare's only son Hugh was the same age; would he try to enlist? The thought was tormenting. Day after day Delius moved down the long rows, straining to catch last words. One man he saw was a German spy, still bound hand and foot. His eyes were dead already. This was the real war; not battles. This was the waste of it. And Philip Heseltine . . . would Philip be wasted too? The shock of the casualties was wrenching Delius at last from Jelka's shelter, and he was torn with compassion and fresh anger. Had he been fool enough to think he had no part in any of it? Because of these young ghosts, his music would never be the same again.

At the end of the week Orléans was cheering an Allied victory on the Marne. Streets turned alive with shouts and cheers. But there were no military bands. Instead, stony-faced lines of soldiers proceeded northeast, the pounding of their boots echoing roughly on cobbled avenues. The Allies had made a good stand at the Marne against the German military machine of organization. "If only they can smash the Germans once for all and end this fearful carnage!" Delius exclaimed. Once more, surely, Grez was safe. He and Jelka knew they wanted to be back in it as soon as they could.

They found a half-empty train to take them north toward home. So few people wanted to go north, closer to the front lines. In their garden they began digging up their silver. Koanga flew down to them from their plum trees. They left the barricade on their wine cellar without admitting why to each other. The danger really remained; but they didn't want to put it into words.

Often, in other years, Delius had sat at the Ibach piano in the music room trying to recapture his youth: the Negroes he had loved, America, Norway, Yorkshire, all the distant lands. Now his emotion was different. He was impelled to begin composing in a heat of outrage. He would write a *Requiem* "to the memory of all young artists fallen in the war"—boys like his nephew Hugh Allan-Black, who was beginning to write poetry; Philip Heseltine, who dreamed of music; Percy Grainger, who had gone to America to train military bands in case America entered the conflict and they would be needed. Hugh and Philip and Percy were still alive, but they could all be killed, even Percy, if he were sent to the front at last. In his *Requiem*, Delius began lashing savagely at a civilization of imperialists who attended their churches and then turned to maiming and killing each other. When life is gone it can never come back again! the text he wrote cried out. Don't drug yourselves with dreams of gold-paved streets in the sky while you slaughter on earth. Let the young have love and work. And if they have to die, let them go in dignity.

> I honor the man who can love life . . .
> The passing spirit sings this only:
> "Farewell. I loved you all."
> And the voices of nature answer him:
> "Thou art our brother."

The earth, the force of life, the "All-Being" Delius could not now bring himself to call God because he associated the concept with bigots, would endure. What he said was "All-Being" animated the universe and absorbed the lives of all men eventually, yet they deserved to live these lives first. "All-Being" was creation and hope:

> The woods and forests are full of coolness and silence . . .
> Eternal renewing; springtime again.

Orthodox believers would call this paganism. Let them. He knew "All-Being" from his own contemplative experience. "I do not think I have ever done better than this," he wrote to Philip Heseltine.

But he hadn't considered the mood of wartime Britain.

Britain was in love with the verses of soldier-poet Rupert
Brooke, who told his countrymen: "If I should die, think only
this of me: That there's some corner of a foreign field That
is for ever England." Delius preferred the poetry of more
mocking young writers like Charles Sorley:

> All the hills and vales along,
> Earth is bursting into song,
> And the singers are the chaps
> Who are going to die perhaps.

A few such writers dared to satirize Rupert Brooke. Edvard
Munch was daring to paint a huge war canvas, *Funeral March*.
With works like these would stand the *Requiem*, with its
doctrine that war was immoral and no victory was worth what
it cost and Christian clergymen who endorsed killing were
wrong and only human love could make the world endurable.
When Delius sent the *Requiem* to England, not a single conductor who saw it dared to play a note. Even Thomas
Beecham was horrified when he read the harsh, spare score
and Delius's text. "This is the most curious flight of futility
that ever misled the intelligence of a great artist." He frowned.
Why, the public wanted victory hymns!

By the time Delius had finished the *Requiem* his eyes were
bothering him: "I have rather tired them," he said in the
spring of 1915. It was as if he were trying to see through a
thin mist of shifting veils. Jelka told him he must go immediately to a London eye specialist—homeopathic, of course.
They must leave Grez after all. Beecham offered them the loan
of a house just outside the city's West End. There was a mill
wheel nearby. Delius would like its sound, and the ferny
garden, and the softness of English air. Delius and Jelka managed to get space on a Channel steamer. The priest next door
promised to look after Koanga.

When Delius visited the eye specialist, the doctor prescribed strong glasses. For the first time he had to wear thick rimless lenses, and he found it difficult to get used to them. But they helped. Soon he began to study his notebooks once more and pore over groups of improvised chords he had ringed as "good."

It was pleasant to be with Thomas Beecham again. Less pleasant were other experiences he and Jelka began to have. England had been gripped by a frenzy of German-hating. The name of the dead Prussian chancellor Bismarck now stood for all that was evil. Hadn't Bismarck begun Germany's imperial expansion? All German music written after his rule had begun was banned as an invention of the devil. By such logic Brahms's *Song of Destiny* was sublime and could be performed, but his Fourth Symphony was sinister and could not. London gossips began remembering interesting facts about the Delius family. Old Mrs. Julius Delius actually displayed Bismarck's portrait. She called him "dear Uncle Otto." One of her sisters was married to the Prussian general von Arnim. Jelka Delius herself was a hundred per cent German, and she spoke with a German accent. Delius had no English blood either, and he was openly berating the British war effort. The British were "inept fools," he said. The uncle of Philip Heseltine who had brought Philip to Delius at Grez now declared Delius was probably a German spy. Rumors circulated, too, about how Delius had shouted to the Hallé Orchestra years before that Germany would conquer England. "What a hiding you'll all get"—those were his exact words. He had always derided the English. Some English music, he had once told a group of composers, was "stuff that wouldn't be listened to in Germany." Every joke he had ever made about his fellow-Britons came back to haunt him. Even critics whispered and raised their brows. They found him "fresh and appealing" no longer. "You have to twist yourself into his moods," they began to say. And that offensive *Requiem*!

"It's a rotten time," Delius sighed to Norman O'Neill. "And I have to earn some money." Beecham, though he had been repelled by the *Requiem*, stepped in to help. He defended Delius's loyalty and pointed to the "essential Englishness" of such works as *On Hearing the First Cuckoo in Spring*. He enlisted the help of influential London hostesses. Recently *On Hearing the First Cuckoo in Spring* had been recorded under his baton and he distributed copies: "No truly cultured home should be without one." Some of the labels on the records were reversed. One willing lady won *"heaps* of Delius converts, dear Tommy!" with what had been marked as the *Cuckoo* and was actually a Polish dance by the composer Moszkowski. Delius didn't laugh when he heard about it. Moszkowski, he said, wrote trash.

Lady Cunard, the wife of the steamship magnate, invited the Deliuses to her luncheon parties although London hostesses privately agreed Mrs. Delius was "dumpy." Often Lady Cunard brought the Deliuses face to face with cabinet officials. Sometimes Delius amused them with carefully straight-faced discussions of orange-growing. He was an expert, he said. At other times Lady Cunard found him incredibly tactless. Was the man so absorbed in music he didn't realize what he was saying? Lady Cunard shuddered at the memory of one luncheon in particular.

"Why is it," Delius asked the table abruptly, "that the British public displays such abysmal ignorance of opera compared to other European countries?"

Beecham, who was present, rushed to the rescue. "Don't talk like that. Just you wait until I produce your *Village Romeo and Juliet* again. That will disprove what you say."

"Bah! The public here doesn't know a note of my operas and cares less."

A young politician smiled a sly smile. "Perhaps that's because they don't like them."

"Don't like 'em!" Delius turned. "Don't like 'em? Tell me what they *do* like!"

Lady Cunard broke in with a quick question for the politician about a radical cabinet member. Compared to Delius, radicals were positively safe.

Beecham also tried to find a buyer for *Nevermore*. Edvard Munch was making inquiries at galleries in Norway. But Delius had set his price for *Nevermore* at 3,000 pounds. It was the minimum that would see him and Jelka through the years to come until peace. Meanwhile she began painting a copy for him. Ah, the wretched Germans! she fumed. And the wretched English! How badly they, too, were treating her Fred. Could he help it if after all this time he "spoke with an un-English lilt," making the wrong emphasis on his words? Why did they say his carefully tailored clothes and wide-brimmed dark hats made him "look like an actor"? So few people in the world cared about the things she and Fred cared about. He had known great painters, recognizing them for what they were years before anyone else; no one was impressed. Jelka was always glad when Philip Heseltine came out to visit. He had failed his army physical examination. Fred needed Philip, who appreciated him as he ought to be appreciated.

Philip was usually in trouble over women these days. He also had a set of Bohemian friends—people like the novelist D. H. Lawrence. Lawrence had tuberculosis and wanted to go to Florida. Could Delius lend him Solano Grove?

It wasn't his to lend, he had to tell Philip. It belonged to a relative of Dr. Hans Haym. Haym, Cassirer . . . he heard nothing from them. All he knew was that Haym had two sons in the German army and was prohibited from playing Delius pieces. "California's a better climate anyhow," Delius told Philip. "Solano Grove is probably a wilderness of gigantic weeds and the house will have tumbled down. It's five miles from a store. There are nice little towns in California. To let Lawrence go to Florida would be sending him to disaster." For it had been disaster for Tom Ward's tuberculosis thirty years before. The only Florida friend Delius had left was Jutta Bell, who had forsaken London for good and gone back to Jacksonville to teach.

Philip had rekindled Florida memories. An *Air and Dance* Delius composed was full of tiny snatches of Negro blues. Yet when he tried English songs because Philip liked English poets, they turned out stiffly artificial. Once more his eyes were bothering him. He got stronger glasses. Then Jelka persuaded him to leave London and spend a summer with her in Norway. They stayed in a tourist hotel, Molmen's, in the Gudbrandsdal mountains, and they enjoyed fresh creamery butter and foamy pitchers of milk. "No end of good things to eat!" he said happily. She made sure he had everything he liked. If only they could build a little chalet of their own in Gudbrandsdal! Just a few rooms; a local carpenter could do the work. It would be cheap; perhaps if Beecham did well at the box office with his scheduled Delius concerts they could manage somehow from the royalties. Delius had an English publisher now.

Norway was neutral and remote. Delius found it a good place for composition, and he began a violin and piano sonata and also two concertos. The Molmen Hotel echoed with dissonant chords. It was impossible for him now to turn out the old tone poems of his youth, the luxuriant variations like *Appalachia*, with leisurely beginnings and endings and spontaneously rambling melodic lines. The war had changed him forever. Orléans and its rows of wounded had taken something from him: his exuberance, the elusive poetry of other years, his spontaneity itself. Now he wanted to work with form, in chamber music and in concertos. It would be more rigid form than variations had called for. He had no interest in symphonies, because they were on too large a scale and because often when they demanded the introduction of contrasting themes a composer had to do it not by instinct but by pre-ordained tradition. And he would always, he knew, be a composer of emotion rather than purely academic technique. Symphonies required sophisticated manipulations in which he had had no interest since his student days. The simpler demands of sonatas left him freer, and at the same time provided for him a challenge. He had always relied on chordal shading and vertical progressions. His piano concerto had once been criticized as "muddy" because of this. Now he would tackle the horizontal relationships between melodic lines in his chamber music. In his concertos the solo parts would allow him freedom because of their simplicity; the orchestral backing was secondary.

When the summer was over, he and Jelka returned to London. An American sculptor, Henry Clews, wanted to do a head of him and Delius spent long hours posing for it. Clare visited him and Jelka with the news that her son Hugh had lied to the army about his age. He had joined up as a private and was in the trenches in France. Clare tried not to show it, but she was frantic. "All men are needed," Hugh had told her. When Delius said the war was futile, Clare bridled. It *had* to be for something! He shook his head. The horror of it was that if Hugh died, he died for the greed of governments.

Delius began his *Double Concerto for Violin and Cello* with bell-like tolling: the slow, regular sound of Channel buoys, the sound of fate. Buoys had rung like that in Filey Bay . . . It was years since he had thought of the lads who had been drowned in Filey Bay. The violin and cello parts wove in and out of each other until their melodies climbed into a tramping march: the English infantry, French farmers, Hugh, Philip Heseltine's schoolmates. A climax of high chords merged slowly into a Florida hymn tune, "Sing to Mary," which became an elegy for the fallen. In the last movement the march rose one more time, to drop back to the tolling buoy bells and the hymn blended together. Though the Concerto's form was traditional, it was one of the most personal things Delius had ever written.

He grew miserable in London, hating its crowds and its traffic. He knew he belonged in Grez. The eye specialist had done what he could. What did it matter about risks at Grez? You took risks every day in London with motor cars you sometimes hardly saw until they honked at you in the street to get out of the way. He and Jelka went back and were elated to find the house intact. The flower beds would be a mess in the spring, full of weeds, but they could work in them. He wanted Grez blossoms again, the heavy fragrances of his summer garden.

Philip wrote him long confidences. D. H. Lawrence, Philip announced, was giving up writing. Delius replied that such a sacrifice was lunacy. Did Lawrence think he could fulfill himself by pottering about as a farmer? Nobody could know where genius came from, but when you had it you were obligated to use it. Philip himself should stop frittering away his time; he ought to turn exclusively to composition. There would be a receptive public. People would have suffered by the end of the war; they would realize politicians were stupid bumblers, and they would look for meaning in the arts. Especially Philip must believe in the young of Britain as he, Delius, did; he was being frank with Philip because he cared so much about what happened to him. But Philip went on hatching schemes for the promotion of Lawrence, though he began writing a book on Delius's music too.

Delius persevered. Philip ought to compose. He must express his own emotional nature; that was what music was. He mustn't copy other composers. He mustn't toy with arbitrary "systems." Look at the Austrian, Arnold Schönberg, with all his exercises in quarter tones. Exercises didn't move human souls.

"The twelve-tone system of Schönberg," Delius liked to say dryly, "is like going to church without any trousers on. Bound, you know, to attract a great deal of attention."

During 1916, and the early months of 1917, he and Jelka stayed in Grez. The war dragged on. They worked in their garden. But in a sudden bitter freeze the house's water pipes burst. All Grez's plumbers were at the front; he and Jelka tried to figure out patchy repairs of their own. "Our pump is the soul of our house!" she discovered. When they ran out of coal, he chopped wood. They couldn't keep the house warm, he wrote Norman O'Neill. In the nearby village of Meudon, both Auguste Rodin and his wife were dying of the cold, though neither Delius nor Jelka knew it until it had happened. Delius's fingers were always numb these days, but he tried to go on writing: more sonatas, a string quartet, a recreation of the Scandinavian tales Grieg and Sinding had told him long ago in the Jotunheim. Poor Sinding. Nobody ever played anything of his now but a trifle, "Rustles of Spring."

When Delius composed a fragile *Song Before Sunrise*, Beecham was enthusiastic. It was dedicated to Philip Heseltine and was based on a chapter with the same title in *Thus Spoke Zarathustra*. One day a telegram came to Grez: Hugh, Clare's son, was dead. He had been "blown to pieces" in the trenches. He would fight and write poems no more.

Still no conductor would touch the *Requiem*. With renewed determination Delius tried to have it produced and sent it from city to city in England and France. Everywhere he was refused. The death of Hugh made its performance more urgent than ever, he felt. America had at last been dragged into the conflict too, and had declared war on Germany in April, 1917. Perhaps Americans might be wiser about the *Requiem* because of their own Civil War. Florida and Virginia had been full of its graves. So were other states. Surely the *Requiem* wouldn't shock Americans. He decided to use what money he could scrape from his English royalties for a trip to America with

Jelka. They would take the *Requiem* with them to conductors in New York and in California, and they would personally persuade them to perform it. Then they would see Solano Grove. He asked Philip to go along. But Philip couldn't; he couldn't get a passport even though he had been rejected for military service. He was of draft age.

So the dream of traveling to America with Jelka and Philip too, of showing her Florida in company with the boy he now looked on as his son, was doomed. When he and Jelka were planning to sail by themselves in the summer of 1918, he was seized with a series of violent headaches. Again his vision blurred, and his hands were numb. Jelka, frightened, hurried him to the French Riviera. Someone would do the *Requiem*, she reassured him. Now he must get well. Soon the crocuses they had planted together would be up in Grez, and their chrysanthemums and late hydrangeas. They could spend fall afternoons together in their white boat on the Loing. Perhaps they could begin cutting back the overhanging willow branches fishermen had been complaining about near their dock. When the climate of the Riviera didn't help, she began telling him: "In Grez you will be well again. You will be able to use your eyes and hands as much as you want." But they lingered to savor the Mediterranean wind's salty freshness.

September, 1918, came to a France that was as strained and as hysterically anti-German as England had been. When a war-tormented Grez neighbor announced to the village at large that Delius had left for the Riviera because he was a German spy, many believed him. Monsieur Delius had always lived a peculiar sort of life—solitary, hermitlike. The lights had always burned late from his music room. Perhaps he had been signalling to other Germans with them. Perhaps his English flags had been a disguise. His name and his wife were German too. One humid night full of cicadas an angry Grez crowd marched on the house and shattered its windows with fistfuls of rocks. Afterwards a division of the French army commandeered it and proceeded to make themselves at home in what they were assured was the lair of a traitor. They tossed mud-stained boots on the furniture, they broke the dishes, and they finger-marked the woodwork, where for good measure they gouged holes with their pocket knives. Then they filled corners with trash they were too indifferent to remove even when the house began to be infested with roaches. Whenever the men found souvenirs they liked they took them: small pitchers, cut glass, silver, kitchenware, table ornaments. For several weeks the pillage went on until the army marched out again and turned the house back to a heartbroken Madame Gréspier. How could she face Monsieur and Madame when they came back?

When they arrived, they listened unbelieving to her story. Delius stared at his scattered papers and scores and torn rugs. "A barrack," he breathed. "A filthy barrack." With Jelka he walked slowly through one defaced room after the other: wisps of barnyard straw, poultry litter, gashes, floors scratched by hobnail boots, broken chairs and empty panes. The music room was a shambles, its walls stained by summer rains which had blown in. Only the Ibach piano had been left untouched, and its surface was thick with a coat of grime. This was what French soldiers and Grez had done to a man who had lived in it for more than twenty years. The house was too filthy to be cleaned. It was spoiled forever.

"Well." He cleared his throat. "We shall finish our lives somewhere else, Jelka."

When the Armistice came on November 11, 1918, they were cramped with Madame Gréspier in a tiny London flat in Belsize Park Gardens. What savings they had left were melting away. Still nobody wanted to buy *Nevermore* at their price. Friends were being kind enough: Beecham; gay, cheerful Norman O'Neill and his Adine; a rich musician named Balfour

Gardiner, who wanted to lend the Deliuses money. But victory had come too late, Jelka decided bitterly as she watched revelers milling in the street below on Armistice night. Her mind flew back to the afternoon she and Fred had stepped ashore from a boat on the Loing into the neglected garden paths of the Marquis de Carzeaux.

"I'd like to live in a house like this, wouldn't you?" She could see Fred's old whimsical smile again, his blue eyes bright without the thick round glasses he now had to wear. She could see him striding broadly down the tangled walks as if they had been bare. Those walks had become hers before the year was out. She had known even then she must give him anything she could. There had been a chance of his needing the house so she had bought it. In it their love had grown, and *A Mass of Life* had come from their happiness. She hadn't let anything hurt him until she could no longer stand against a war. Now Grez had hounded him out. In her powerlessness to make him another haven she thought of the final verses of a chorus she had written for *A Village Romeo and Juliet*:

> Halleo, halleo, in the woods the wind is sighing . . .
> Homesteads all around are scattered
> Where men live until they die.
> But our home is on the river:
> Travelers we—
> Passing by.

Delius during World War I

Delius, by Henry Clews

Høibagerli today

The blue door

Delius at the Ibach piano, under Jelka's copy of *Nevermore*. On the piano rests a statue by Rodin.

With Clare in the garden at Grez

Delius with Jelka and Percy Grainger

Margaret

16 ❧ Farewell to the High Hills

One of the consolations Delius had in London was being near the O'Neills and especially their little daughter, Yvonne. He had asked to be Yvonne's godfather, and when she was christened, he gave her a tiny necklace of gold and pearls he chose himself. When the O'Neills had to be away on tour— Norman often conducted his operettas and songs and Adine was a pianist—Delius always ended his letters to them, "A kiss for Yvonne!" He began thinking of writing piano solos for her to play. He hadn't composed much for the piano, but as Yvonne grew he wanted her to be able to share his music. That she was now only a toddler didn't dismay him. He would try to keep his pieces simple: "If anything is too wide stretched for her hands it can be arranged by giving it to the other hand." He also wrote a *Dance for Harpsichord*. Concert audiences' interest in the harpsichord had recently revived and he was curious to hear how his own chromatic music would sound on it. When Clare, still grieving for her son, came up to London in 1919, she brought her youngest daughter Margaret. Margaret was on her way to her first school, and Delius had asked to see her. He hadn't since her babyhood.

As Margaret and her mother waited at Stewart's Tea Rooms in Piccadilly Circus, Margaret was excited. What would her uncle the composer be like? Her brother Hugh's death on the front had upset him, she knew. He was fifty-seven now. She also knew her grandmother, Elise Delius, didn't like talking about him. Whenever anybody asked Granny about his music, Granny always turned off the question with "He was a very handsome child." That was all.

Above the roar of the Piccadilly traffic Margaret heard a quick deep voice: "Dearest Clare!" and Margaret saw coming toward them with long steps and a figure as erect as her mother's a very tall man with dark, receding hair and a high forehead and a warm smile. It was Uncle Fred, and he embraced her mother and then turned to her. She didn't feel nervous at all when she saw his eyes. He was nearsighted without his glasses, which he wasn't wearing, but his eyes were kind and direct, the darkest blue she had ever seen. He began treating her as he would have treated a grown-up, standing behind her chair for her, talking to her earnestly. "Have you been singing? Do you have your mother's glorious voice?" Her mother told him her voice was untrained but would be heard and judged at her school. Then they all talked about Yorkshire and the moors. Uncle Fred had last seen them on a trip north to hear some of his music. He asked her if she liked heather. Had she been to Skipton Castle? Did she know Filey Bay on the coast? He had often thought about making a Yorkshire opera out of Emily Brontë's *Wuthering Heights* but hadn't done it yet. He also talked a lot about cricket. He'd been very keen on it, he said, and he still followed newspaper reports of the matches Yorkshire teams played. Some day he would like Margaret to come and see him with her mother when he and Aunt Jelka were settled somewhere. He had had a beautiful house in France. As he talked of Grez, Margaret could see how homesick he was. Before he left she promised him she would stay with him when she could, and her last sight of him that afternoon was his slender figure walking rapidly toward the door. He turned to wave, and then was gone.

Many young composers visited Delius and Jelka in their London flat. It had a piano of sorts. The composers played their works hopefully and Delius gave them advice. "Don't waste your time with publishers and don't bind yourself to them for more than two years. Develop an individual style and stick to it." Richard Strauss's music he pronounced "clever"—a little witheringly, one apprentice thought. Another played Delius a Sea Symphony he had written. He had massive shoulders, liked forthright rustic English music, and had served in the war. His name was Ralph Vaughan-Williams. When he had finished his Sea Symphony Delius smiled very politely. "It is not"—he hesitated—"*mesquin.*" Why French? Then Vaughan-Williams remembered the word's meaning. So "not shabby" was the only verdict of Frederick Delius on his music! To a friend, Delius confided later: "I couldn't stand Vaughan-Williams's things." With another young composer he spent hours trying to teach him instrumentation and counterpoint. "Be yourself," he kept repeating. "Don't copy. Be as simple and natural as you can."

He and Jelka lived quietly in Belsize Park Gardens until the spring of 1919, when they left London for the village of Sennen in Cornwall. Sennen was only a few miles from Britain's southernmost point, Land's End. He and Jelka loved walking together on the cliffs, listening to the crash of the sea below. The air was like sparkling wine, tanged with mist and spume. They heard sea lions barking on the rocks and the fading tolls of Cornish church bells. But Sennen wasn't and couldn't be Grez.

Philip Heseltine was trying to start a music magazine in London. The project couldn't get off the ground, he complained to Delius. He hadn't enough money. Besides, people were beginning to laugh at his schemes. They teased him about his perpetual artistic Utopias. He simply had no luck at all. Delius promptly threw cold water on his self-pity. It wasn't a question of luck. Philip couldn't stick to anything; that was the real trouble. Delius wasn't giving him a sermon, but once again he had to offer the strongest advice he could: persevere. Philip could be a gifted composer. Delius had known it from the start, and because he cared so much about what happened to Philip he felt it was time to be stern.

Philip had submitted several songs to publishers, yet always they had been refused. Was it, Philip wondered, because nobody took him seriously? Was Delius right about putting everything into composition? Philip had an idea. He would take a pen name. He chose Peter Warlock; a warlock was a male witch in medieval horror tales, and the sinister joke delighted him. When Peter Warlock sent in his first songs they were promptly accepted. So he had at last launched a career! As Peter Warlock, then, he would submit his book on Delius; he would even begin behaving as anybody named Peter Warlock should, roughly and gaily and rowdily, not like shy, stammering Philip Heseltine. He would give himself up to music entirely—Peter Warlock's music. And as long as his new inspiration didn't fail him, he could forget the gawky, ridiculous Philip of the past completely. He began to study Elizabethan songs, savoring their bawdy vigor. What had the delicacy and quiet of Philip Heseltine ever done for him? Nothing. Again he began to listen to the music of Frederick Delius. And now he found that Peter Warlock didn't like it half as much as Philip Heseltine had.

Jelka was busy designing scenery for a forthcoming production of *A Village Romeo and Juliet* which Thomas Beecham planned. He was now Sir Thomas, having inherited the title an England grateful for Beecham's Pills had conferred on his father. To Jelka's delight the German town of Frankfort also wrote to announce a Delius opera, his *Fennimore and Gerda*. Ah, what scenes she would paint for that! So the Germans had forgiven Fred at last; it was about time. But first she would go to Grez alone. Was the house really so bad it couldn't be cleaned? Fred was miserable away from it and wasn't writing much. She had to get him back to it somehow.

In Grez she found a French army officer who listened to her

complaints with sympathy. He began rounding up several possessions she had thought lost. He directed the scrubbing and repairing of the house. Her spirits rose. Why, they could return to Grez after all! What did they care about the suspicion of the villagers? They would ignore them. She could hardly wait to tell Fred. The army even promised to pay for some of its damages. With the officer, Jelka scoured and swept and dug out dirt until she was convinced the house could be more perfect than ever. She and Madame Gréspier, who was looking after Fred's meals in Cornwall, could finish the job.

That summer the Deliuses returned to the small hotel they had liked in the Gudbrandsdal mountains of Norway while the redecorating at Grez was being finished. Then they went down to Frankfort, where *Fennimore and Gerda* delighted German critics. One said simply, "Delius is always right." Jelka found the performance "most thrilling." She loved describing for her husband the effects she had painted. Delius's nearsightedness was worse than ever, and though he had seen her sets of autumn forests and ice-frozen fjords backstage, she had to tell him how they looked from the audience. He couldn't make out any details from a distance.

When they returned at last to Grez, he began looking for Koanga. On her last trip Jelka had seen the jackdaw flying in the garden; now they both assumed he would come back to the house. But Koanga didn't remember them this time. Delius called to him and tried to coax him down with seeds and grains, but Koanga only cried raucously from the highest branches of a poplar. He had gone wild for good. He too had been changed by the war. He would no longer need his little traveling cage; sadly, Delius stored it away.

Edvard Munch came down from Norway to paint his portrait and Madame Gréspier served rich stews. She began to bring out the wines the French troops had never found in the cellar. Everything in the house had been freshly painted, and its new windowpanes sparkled in clear country light. Jelka's copy of *Nevermore* now hung in the music room; the original was still with a London gallery waiting to be sold. Jelka hoped it would be sold soon; inflation in Germany was making their resumed German royalties and even Aunt Albertine Krönig's legacy worthless. It now took forty-two billion German marks to buy a single American penny. Sir Thomas Beecham was pushing Delius music as hard as he could in London; so were other conductors. The *Double Concerto* and *Song of the High Hills* made successful debuts. But still there wasn't enough money for the rising prices in postwar France. An influx of rich Americans raised prices still further. "How shall we *live?*" Jelka asked herself. Food, clothing, tickets to distant cities to hear Delius concerts—everything was costing more and more. When Delius got a letter one morning from London, Jelka was relieved. Basil Dean was an impresario noted for his spectaculars. He never did anything in a small way. Now he intended to stage a play that needed incidental music which was exotic and compelling. He had thought of the rich harmonies of Frederick Delius.

Hassan, or the Golden Journey to Samarkand was a tale of the near east. It had the flavor of *The Arabian Nights*. The author was James Elroy Flecker, a poet who had died poor, but whose works were now fashionable. *Hassan*'s hero was a beggar who rose to be adviser to a corrupt sultan. Other characters in the play had color and charm: Ishak, the philosopher in pursuit of a dream of perfection; a pair of lovers who went to the executioner rather than give each other up; a rough crowd of robbers who reveled in streets crowded with oriental merchants peddling their wares. The play ended with Hassan bound for a haven in Samarkand. Samarkand was an ancient and shining city, one of Asia's and civilization's oldest. It symbolized human longings for beauty and peace. The road to Samarkand had been the road of the biblical Wise Men to

Bethlehem. It was modern man's pilgrimage in search of his own soul.

Basil Dean wanted a stunning production. An early scene called for a serenade under starlight beside a fountain. When Delius read the play, he knew he could write the kind of themes Dean required, and he was excited, too, because Dean intended later to stage *Hassan* in America. To have a hit play in London and New York! It was the answer to every money problem he and Jelka had ever had. He must put out of his mind the newest symptoms which had begun to plague him: the thicker clouds before his eyes, the lack of feeling in his hands, occasional pains in his back. He could see doctors later. Now *Hassan* must be made to glitter. He must put everything he had into it. If *Hassan* became a triumph somebody would be sure to risk the *Requiem*, and that hope spurred him on.

When he signed Basil Dean's contract, the fingers of his right hand were stiff. He hoped no one could tell. He and Dean conferred over all the episodes which would need accompaniment. Already he had ideas for the serenade and for the finale, the procession of pilgrims to Samarkand. He could hear the bells of the pilgrims' camels, the distant harps and the muted voices he would use. In his mind he could see the robed procession moving into the distance. Basil Dean told him the orchestra must be kept small, but he knew he had the technical skill now to make the most of every player. And the theater people he met on brief trips to London from Grez to consult with Dean were delightful. They gave supper parties for him. Dean paid him a large advance. The cares of the war were receding. He and Jelka could have their Norwegian chalet. He had seen the very spot he wanted; it was near Overli Farm in the Gudbrandsdal valley just outside the tiny mountain village of Lesjaskog. He and Jelka designed the plans: a huge living room-music room combination with a fireplace in the center, four small bedrooms flanking it, and a kitchen in back. How marvelous to have such a place in hot Augusts when Grez air shimmered under a strong sun and made him sleepily unambitious. Often lately he felt so listless. He needed mountain air. When he sent specifications for the hut to a Lesjaskog carpenter, the carpenter promised to begin work immediately. Delius also ordered a wide oaken front veranda.

One morning in Grez he went as usual to his piano in the music room. Drafts of *Hassan* were laid out on his desk nearby. He was working on the lovers' duet, and he squinted to see what he had written the day before. Then he set out a blank page. First he went over the melody in his mind. When he knew exactly what he wanted, he reached with his right hand for his pen. The pen fell from his fingers with a harshly final clack to the wood floor.

He stared. He tried to flex his fingers and couldn't. He had no control over them at all. He tried to move the fingers of his left hand. Clumsily he managed to use them to pick up the fallen pen and lay it on his desk. Again he tried to hold the pen in his right hand. It was impossible. Stunned, he leaned back in his chair. He must get Jelka. She would know what to do. What was happening to him? Even his legs felt weak when he finally got up to go to her for help.

They had no telephone at Grez. He had always refused to have one installed because he wanted privacy. The doctor would have to be sent for. He was a homeopath, and said it was "a lameness that would pass off." Delius must rest. But that was impossible! He had to finish *Hassan*. Afterwards he would submit to all the coddling Jelka wanted, but first he had to earn the money to pay for his convalescence and for the hut in Norway. When the trouble had gone away, they would be glad for their tiny northern retreat. While he had this weakness she must help him compose. Did she think she could take down the notes as he called them out? He would show her how to correct the score. *Hassan* was their security, their salvation. She mustn't fail him.

When Clare came to Grez for a visit, she gave a quick gasp. What was the matter? She had never seen her brother look this way—tired, pale. Even his walk was halting. By day he dictated to Jelka and at night Clare played and sang. Whenever she saw him from the corner of her eye, she was frightened. He sat so still in his chair; and he had never been still. Clare's visit was followed by one from Sir Thomas Beecham. "You're not yet sixty," Beecham told him bluntly. "You have no business to be looking the way you do." Beecham begged him to consult regular physicians immediately. He got Jelka aside and she admitted Delius was always tired, couldn't use his right hand, and was having eye trouble.

"If he won't get a decent doctor, I'm going to send one!" Beecham exclaimed. But Jelka thought ordinary doctors knew nothing. Her belief in homeopathy was complete.

At last *Hassan* was finished. The final days of dictation had been terrible; Jelka knew little about orchestration. Delius had had to explain to her about divided strings, time rests, the C-clefs, instead of treble and bass, which instruments like the viola had to have. She had made mistake after mistake and the score was covered with erasures. But they had managed. When they sent it to Basil Dean, he coolly informed them the play had been put off. It was splendid, of course, that Mr. Delius had been so prompt. But one could never tell in the theater, could one? The playwright's widow expressed her gratitude to "Frank Delius" and felt sure he had worked very hard. Some day they would all have to listen to the results together.

He was comforted, in the spring of 1922, by the announcement of a London choral conductor, Charles Kennedy-Scott, that his *Requiem* was to be produced at last in March. Kennedy-Scott was bravely ready to face the public with the *Requiem's* denunciation of war. But as Delius made plans to go to London his legs began to fail him and he realized he couldn't. With Jelka he traveled by train to the *Kurhaus* at Wiesbaden. Ordinary tonics made him sick and Jelka called in a homeopath. He had to keep his food down, didn't he? He had to write Kennedy-Scott that he was in a wheelchair and couldn't attend the *Requiem's* premiere: *"How disappointed I am!"* Jelka took this down from his dictation. Clare came to him once more. He made jokes to her about the wheelchair when she pushed it, but she knew he "felt his situation very keenly."

The *Requiem's* London debut was a disaster. The audience was middle-aged and conservative. Reviews were blistering. How had Delius dared to ridicule the War To End All Wars? Philip Heseltine, writing as Peter Warlock, was particularly scathing: "Dismally uninspired. It has the stench of the charnel house." "The *Requiem* of Delius has dropped dead on its first performance," said another critic. The conductor himself decided he didn't like it. The thing was too full of death and waste and anger. War should be heroic.

Philip's defection was the cruellest blow. He was even putting his hostility toward the *Requiem* into his otherwise flattering Delius book, now scheduled for publication as an interesting production of the rising musician Peter Warlock. Peter Warlock sported a full beard and talked these days about "poor old Fred." He was noisy, brash, swaggering. In Wiesbaden, while Delius brooded about Philip's desertion, medical fees ate steadily away at his and Jelka's money. Jelka wrote to musicians: in England to Norman O'Neill and to Balfour Gardiner, who had often patronized performances of composers in need and presented concerts of their works. "Of course Fred does not know I am writing this and *must never know.*" She appealed to Sir Thomas Beecham too. She began sending scores to performers like the Russian cellist Alexander Barjansky, who promised to play Delius's cello concerto. She begged Percy Grainger in America to program works like *North Country Sketches* and *A Song of the High Hills*. If Americans refused to listen to the Delius music based on their own folksongs and poets, perhaps they would at least like music that was "foreign." Jelka prodded Delius's publishers in Austria to arrange for *A Mass of Life* in Vienna. After its performance there she and Delius got a letter from a young Hungarian composer who had been deeply moved. His name was Béla Bartók. He also asked a favor. His Hungarian music wasn't covered by international copyright laws. The music of Delius was. Therefore might he print on the title pages of some of his pieces "Revised by Frederick Delius"? Delius consented. He had begun once more to know what it was to struggle. And the *Requiem* had alienated people, he realized. Attendance at Beecham's Delius concerts wasn't capacity any more.

By the summer of 1922, the Wiesbaden sanitarium announced it could do no more for him. He was now able to walk with two canes. His hands were just strong enough to grip them. He and Jelka went to the Gudbrandsdal mountains to spend their first time together in their new chalet. *Høifagerli*, they named it: "high fair meadow." But he hadn't meant Høifagerli to be like this for her. She had to write all his letters. She also took down more piano pieces for his goddaughter, Yvonne O'Neill. Fortunately piano music was easier for her than *Hassan* had been. She enjoyed working with *Mazurka and Waltz for a Little Girl, Lullaby for a Modern Baby*, some preludes and a toccata. Sometimes, to relax, she took walks alone to gather mushrooms for him; he loved them. But the farmer of the adjacent farm, Overli, was angry when she walked through his hay just before his harvesters were to cut it. "Doesn't care *where* she goes!" he muttered.

Delius managed at first with an out-of-tune village piano, but it jangled his nerves. Then he had a piano sent to Høifagerli all the way from Christiania by train, and when the piano arrived in the nearest village, Lesjaskog, he saw the townspeople gaping at him. Two horses began pulling the piano up the mountain, over rocks and ditches, on a cart, and spectators stared at him leaning on his canes while he shouted directions to the driver. The piano was tied to the cart by strong ropes, and two men walked on each side in case it should tip over.

There were days at Høifagerli when he could play piano tunes himself. One of the villagers described his playing as "clunking." On other days his fumbling fingers wouldn't move over the keys. But the air was fresh, and the steep snow-capped mountains on every side of him were dark with trembling firs. He loved them and the panorama they made. "I hope my legs and arms will continue to get stronger gradually," he had Jelka write his worried friends in England.

For a while it looked as if they might. When the concert season of 1923 began, he and Jelka traveled to performances in Germany, and people were very helpful when he had to climb stairs. Jelka supported him on one side and a kindly volunteer on the other. He celebrated his sixty-first birthday on January 29, in Frankfort. Percy Grainger was in Europe on tour and betrayed no shock when he stopped to see him. A German musician wrote a small book about Delius compositions. Even Philip Heseltine sent a birthday present. He had written a *Serenade to Delius* some time ago. It was charming. It was light, of course, and it didn't have the verve his Peter Warlock pieces had, but Delius was touched at his use of Delian refrains, the echoes of American street cries he himself had always woven into his compositions:

Was this Philip's farewell to him or to his own youth? Was it perhaps Peter Warlock's farewell to the personality of Philip Heseltine altogether? Philip didn't write many letters these days. Delius realized in spite of the serenade that he had lost Philip forever. He had lost him to Peter Warlock. Had he been right in urging Philip to give up everything for music? He wondered. Maybe Philip couldn't take the blows. The hardness of Peter Warlock might be only a mask. For ten years Delius had tried guiding Philip to the fulfillment of his gifts. He had literally brought him up. Now Philip's gifts were being fulfilled through Peter Warlock. Soon Peter Warlock was vigorously denouncing the music of Delius once more. People who didn't like it thought Peter Warlock terribly funny. Delius heard about it all, but made no comment.

At last Basil Dean announced *Hassan* and Delius and Jelka went to London for its rehearsals in September, 1923. People were shocked at his canes, his glasses, his stoop. "He's decrepit!" they whispered to each other. When he invited a conductor to visit him later at Grez and said, "We'll go walking together by the river," the conductor stared. Whom was Delius trying to fool—himself?

The rehearsals of *Hassan* were an ordeal. The chorus of pilgrims couldn't keep on pitch.

"I must have a larger *orchester!*" Delius shouted. "They can't hear the *orchester!*"

Exasperated, Basil Dean stepped to the front of the stage. "You can't have a larger orchestra, Mr. Delius. This production is costing enough as it is!" On the first night, the audience chattered incessantly. With Delius and Jelka in their box were Clare and—at his own request—Edward, Prince of Wales. Nevertheless, Delius snapped about the crowd: "Stupid scatterbrains!" He had to have a success; they couldn't spoil it. They simply couldn't. But they went on talking throughout the serenade, and not until the last part of the play were they stunned into quiet by the scene of the lovers' execution. By the final pilgrims' chorus they were rapt. Miraculously the pilgrims stayed on perfect pitch. When the last actor had left the stage singing "We take the golden road to Samarkand!" there was complete silence, then a thunder of applause. This time Delius couldn't take a bow. He could never have managed the steps to the stage.

At their hotel he and Jelka waited for reviews. When they came they were splendid. *Hassan* was the hit of the season. He and Jelka had made it through. Soon they heard that *Nevermore* had a buyer willing to pay the 3,000 pounds they wanted. They could even buy a motor car! Back in Grez they found a yellow Ford that was easy for him to get in and out of. They hired a villager as chauffeur and took long rides into the countryside. Delius looked out the window incessantly. They could even go to Italy, he decided. He wanted to see Italy, and the warmth would surely help his paralysis. He admitted that was what it was, now. But in Italy rain fell endlessly, and tall cypresses loomed narrow and sinister above the rough roads they jogged over in the Ford. In the town of Rapallo he had a relapse. His legs failed him once more. He could climb no stairs at all, and he had to be carried up and down by the chauffeur. His vision grew cloudier. Still he stared hungrily at the broad yellow fields and the rocky hills around him. Was he going blind? That too? How much longer did he have for sight? How could he go on writing music if he couldn't correct Jelka's scores? But he wouldn't think about it, he couldn't. He and Jelka went to visit Henry Clews, the American sculptor who had done a head of him in London during the war.

Clews, who had given up a New York career in banking for art, talked entertainingly; he wrote books on sculpture and literature, and his chateau in southern France was full of his bizarre heads of goblins and animals. Why, he suggested, didn't Delius go to America when Percy Grainger gave his planned Delius performances in New York? Couldn't Delius manage with his canes and Jelka? There were great doctors in America. Briefly Delius thought he might be able, and New York newspapers printed the story that the composer who wrote all that English music—*On Hearing the First Cuckoo in Spring, North Country Sketches, Brigg Fair*—was actually planning to honor the United States with a visit. Also *Hassan* would be opening on Broadway.

The dream of New York was foolish, Delius soon realized. He began to have days when he could scarcely see anything except large objects very close to him. Still he tried to dictate music to Jelka. Remembering Skipton Castle in Yorkshire, he set Tennyson's poem *The Princess*. Would he ever see the splendor falling on the walls of Skipton again? He doubted it. He would write no opera *Wuthering Heights*, either. Jelka refused to face the truth about his eyesight when he tried to break it to her. "You don't see very well today," was all she would say. They would go to another German sanitarium. Everybody said the one at Cassel was splendid.

First he had to see Høifagerli once more. By the time he and Jelka reached Norway in the summer of 1924, he could hardly take a step. Usually he had to be in a wheelchair. The high hills whose song he had sung . . . Day after day he stared out at them from the door. Their gray-blue outlines shifted in clinging mists. The valley of Gudbrandsdal bloomed red and blue and yellow with summer flowers in a vast carpet he could now scarcely make out, but he knew it was there. Thirty-six years ago, in 1886, he had written a song, *At Sunset*:

> What will happen when light is gone
> And the sun is banished? . . .
> Night will enfold us in love,
> 'All terror vanished.

"I want to see a sunset," he told Jelka. "I want to go up there, to the high mountains."

When Percy Grainger came to stay with them, he and Jelka decided they could get a strapping country girl, Zenta, to help. For a part of the way, as long as there was a path, Percy wheeled Delius in his chair. Then he and Zenta improvised a litter. They carried it and Jelka walked alongside. As they climbed higher and higher, a bank of clouds began to enfold them. But they knew they must go on. The air grew sharper, and the mist became cutting. Delius looked carefully at each evergreen bough they passed; he must remember everything. He listened to the calls of distant birds. Greens and grays and the paleness of the boulders: he must fix all the colors in his mind . . . Up Percy and Zenta struggled with him. Several times they had to rest. Jelka herself was breathless. But the little cortege climbed on past the timberline to the scrub and rock of the mountain's crest. When they reached it, the clouds were so thick they could see nothing except the ground beneath their feet.

Delius still refused to use the word "God." He refused to say "prayer." "Meditation," he called it. "Contemplation of All-Being." But now what was in his mind was a true prayer for the last mountain sunset of his life. The vaporous clouds

were still shifting, moving. Let them part. Let him see a glowing sky once more. Let him have that to keep. Somehow he
would go on with his music; he must store up all the loveli-
ness he could to sustain him. In complete silence the group
waited. He knew Percy Grainger understood, Jelka too. Then
he began to feel as if he were slowly losing himself in the
very whiteness and vastness of the mists that surrounded him.
In his mind he heard once more the high hills singing, and the
music softly swelled and ebbed in elusive chords. Music and
mist . . . and then the sky, a patch of it gone gold and orange
and lavender. The clouds parted. He could see every outline
clearly. He could see the red sun dropping behind jagged
peaks and the patches of light on the tundra and gold lying
on the snow of other mountains that were higher still. The
flaming light burned everywhere. All the valley of Gudbrandsdal was a vast expanse of it below deepening mountain
shadows. He listened and he looked and he knew he had
found at last what he had been seeking since Florida. A moment of illumination . . . When the mists finally closed down
he didn't speak. Then the wind was cutting at him again, chill
and damp.

"Thank you," he said finally, turning to smile. "I am ready
to go on now."

17 ❧ The Blue Door

First-time visitors to the Deliuses in Grez-sur-Loing during the late 1920's were always surprised. The cobbled streets of the little village were silent and gray. When the visitors turned down the lane named Rue Wilson after America's wartime president, they came to a wide double-winged stone house with a large blue door in the center. And when the blue door opened, it opened to another world. Everywhere there were flowers and paintings, photographs of the great, piles of music, shelves heavy with books. The living room's tall double doors fronted a garden that, in summer, was a blaze of roses and hollyhocks and marigolds among which butterflies flitted tremulously from bloom to bloom. The river ran crystalline past the dock. Locusts hummed and birds sang. Across the river's water lilies, away from the opposite bank, stretched a wide meadow studded after summer rains with tiny pools of water. Willows bent in gentle winds. Poplars rustled. The smell of phlox was heavily sweet. As the visitors waited on wicker garden chairs, they were brought tea and delicious freshly-buttered cakes by Simone, the curtseying housemaid or, sometimes, by a dignified elderly housekeeper who had been in service with the Deliuses for many years, Madame Gréspier. And who could have dreamed this little Eden lay behind the blue door?

Many of the visitors were musicians, and they didn't know what to expect. They had had letters from Mrs. Delius asking them to come and play for her husband. The man was helpless and they knew they were here on an errand of mercy, but he "refused to hang up his lute." Still, if rarely, he turned out small compositions. He was in his late sixties now. Mrs. Delius had had him at every health resort in Germany. Oeynhausen was supposed to help paralysis; it hadn't helped his. At Cassel there had been a series of electric shock treatments. They had failed. Newspapers had begun to carry reports on his decline. Still he had just managed to publish a *Caprice and Elegy* for cello dictated to his wife. What would he be like in person?

The visitors—perhaps a string quartet, or a group of singers —would hear quick steps from the living room. Mrs. Delius, a tall full-figured woman with wavy gray hair, would fling wide the French doors and then bring out an armchair before anyone had time to help her. She obviously had "great physical strength."

"He is coming now," she would say with a smile. One of the guests, a young soprano, remembered her first sight of Delius. An attendant appeared carrying "a big, stiff doll" over his shoulder. Then he set him down in the chair, arranging his legs under a checked blanket, making sure his arms were straight. Mrs. Delius put a panama straw hat on his balding head to shield him from too much sun. He had clearly been tended with great care; a silk shirt was open at his throat, and his hands were beautifully manicured. On his feet he wore high stiff shoes. His hair was gray-white and just touched his collar in back. When he turned to face the young soprano, she saw he had features like an old Roman's. He was in fact a double of Julius Caesar.

"Can you see her, sweetheart?" Mrs. Delius bent down.

"No."

"He doesn't see very well today," she explained. Was she mad? The man was obviously stone blind. Heavy lids half obscured his vague blue eyes.

He tried to raise his right hand, but only the wrist would

move slightly. Then a deep voice startled with its warmth and its slow Yorkshire broadness. "Well, here we are. I am very happy that you came. Now tell me all about your trip."

Mrs. Delius always described his guests minutely to him. "You are a painter surely," one of them told her.

"No, no, that is all in the past, but you may see my pictures later if you like." What a frightful ordeal for her to have to live with this statue! And yet she looked radiantly happy. She was in bondage, but she appeared to love her chains. While he talked about music—and he was witty, sometimes sarcastic and sometimes full of racy lightheartedness—she beamed at him constantly. The male nurse sat in the distance with a closed book, ready in case Delius tired of talking and wanted to be read to.

At tea time the nurse had to feed him every mouthful. Mrs. Delius first tasted each dish herself to be sure it was seasoned the way he liked it. If it wasn't she sent it back to the kitchen, but she seldom had to. Madame Gréspier was well-trained. "My meat," Delius would murmur. "My tea. Thank you."

Inside the house where he heard his guests perform stood a high console radio. Mrs. Delius called it "our excellent super-heterodyne." On top of it lay heavily red-penciled schedules of concert broadcasts. A table nearby supported a record-player with an immense sound horn. "That was given me by the Electric and Musical Industries of Britain," Delius said proudly. "Sir Thomas Beecham declares it to be the finest he has ever heard." Mrs. Delius in unguarded moments called the great conductor Tommy. Her husband never did. Sometimes Delius asked for a record of his own music. The performance was almost always by Beecham. "Thank you, Thomas!" he would call out to the sound horn when the piece had ended. "That is how I want my music to be played."

Visiting musicians soon learned he was very choosy about what he heard. Once the leader of a quartet announced,

"Master, we shall now play you some early Beethoven."

"Oh, no, you won't!" came a shout.

Mozart, perhaps?

"Bah."

Schönberg?

"The wrong-note craze!"

When Mrs. Delius came to the rescue, she usually suggested Chopin or Grieg or Wagner. When a singer performed well on one occasion, Mrs. Delius whispered after her husband had been taken away, "My dear, he *likes* you!" If he didn't like the artist in question he would call to his nurse at the end: "Begin to read!"

What usually startled musical visitors most of all was that when they had finished, Delius often suggested they listen to a record or two. And what he asked for! One distinguished guest was treated to *Ol' Man River*. Another reported in wonder that Delius had wanted:

> Dinah,
> Is thére anything fi-nah
> In the state of Carolina . . .

When it was over he had been smiling broadly. "*Perr*-fect intonation. Perfect!" That was what The Master preferred to Beethoven? And South American dance bands? Sometimes he asked for jazz. He had a pile of jazz records in his collection. Negroes, he said, had harmonic genius.

When Clare's daughter Margaret came to Grez one summer, she decided that because her uncle understood jazz he must also like musical comedy. Margaret was a young lady, now. Except for fairer hair she looked much as Delius had in his youth: the large blue eyes, long nose, firm chin, very fair skin. Jelka described her in detail. "She even has your hands and feet, Fred." When Margaret began to praise a musical comedy she had seen in London, he cleared his throat.

"My dear Peggy!" The voice was resounding. "Musical comedy is conceived by *vul*garians and executed by *bar*barians for a public that is mentally degenerate." And Margaret didn't mention musical comedy again.

What Frederick and Jelka Delius had endured before they achieved their peace and laughter behind the blue door neither would ever forget. They had had to sell Høifagerli. The constant search for health, the hopes raised and dashed; the time a "cure" had nearly killed him and Jelka and Clare had had him driven back to Grez on the last chance they could bring him around through sheer will . . . Then in the garden he had smiled up at them jauntily: "Well, lasses, here we are!" There had been "Dr. H.," who had sworn he could cure the paralysis completely. Delius had been able to sign his name after a course of treatments. But the control of his fingers had left him as quickly as it had come back. In his disappointment he began to snap irritably at Jelka and when he did the people who heard him were shocked. With "beautiful dignity" she would answer: "Fred, I wonder if you realize how deeply you wounded me. If you did, I don't think you could do it." He did know, and he was sorry. But Jelka's possessiveness, which he had been able to resist gently and subtly as a well man, now enveloped him so thoroughly he had natural moments of longing to be free of it. And he couldn't be, ever again.

Sometimes he had moments of vision. "Jelka, Jelka! I can see my hands!" But they always faded. The trouble was "a general physical breakdown," Jelka wrote Norman and Adine O'Neill. "Mentally he is as fresh and vivacious as ever. But it is a long, weary way." Delius himself was more blunt. "The doctors are donkeys. They don't understand the first thing about my illness."

Norman and Adine brought Yvonne to Grez for him. "Tell me how she looks," he begged. But he felt ill at ease with most children now. He knew they must be staring at him. A blind invalid—repellent, surely. So he said little to them and what he did say was awkward. The children of Grez were frightened of him when his male nurse wheeled him in the street. He could sense their fear like electricity. So he grew more ill at ease with them than ever.

Jelka had written to Philip Heseltine begging him to come to Grez. She was in despair at her inability to cope with orchestral scores. Delius meant to go on composing. His mind was teeming with ideas and he couldn't get them down. The chords and melodies went on haunting him day after day—to no purpose. He couldn't see to correct the mistakes Jelka made when she tried to help ease the burden of his creativity. He had been a father to Philip; now wouldn't Philip come to him in his need? Peter Warlock, who was becoming famous in London for wild parties and wine, women and song, refused point-blank. He was writing his own music at a furious rate. He had no time for Frederick Delius.

It was Percy Grainger who helped him when he could between concert tours. Often he played for Delius by the hour, and Delius afterwards dictated to Jelka his gratitude for Percy's performance: "Your delicate nuancing is quite a revelation to me. For years I have heard nothing but thump, thump, thump! I can only say that you cannot play too often for me, and I'm afraid of abusing your kindness . . . I got such a thrill over Bach the other night and Jelka loved it so much too!"

"How charitable," Percy would say. "But he's always been the most generous of men." At that comment there were other musicians who raised their brows.

What piles of unfinished material there were in the music room at Grez! The old opera *Margot La Rouge* Delius had tried so hard to win Italian money with, for instance; there was good stuff in that. In the midst of a *Poem of Life and Love* his hands and eyes had failed for good. Settings of English verses lay half completed in a stack. He couldn't ask Norman O'Neill to help; Norman had a career of his own. In London his friend Balfour Gardiner tried working from some of the unfinished scores, but felt he wasn't getting their spirit in his orchestrations. Delius realized that if he produced a simple song a year he would be doing well. But he began dictating music to Jelka for a poem by William Ernest Henley, *A Late Lark*:

> My task accomplished and the long day done,
> My wages taken, and in my heart
> Some late lark singing,
> Let me be gathered to the quiet west,
> The sundown splendid and serene,
> Death.

"Yes, that is how I want to go," he said. But still the late lark longed to sing. The end had not come yet. Jelka tried to transcribe the notes one by one, and when Percy Grainger came again to Grez he helped her. But how slow it was! Well, they must all do the best they could, Delius sighed. As a man he hadn't given up, and as an artist he wouldn't and couldn't. He would go on because it was what he had to do. An artist must never betray his gift, "no matter what."

When he and Jelka were able to smile at last, it was because they knew their love had been forged in a purgatory of pain and defeat. She never left him alone to brood. She marshalled her forces and took command. She worked with publishers when they brought out new Delius editions. His music was being played all over the world now. Not often in America; that was a bitter disappointment to him, because so much of it was American, and these days he talked constantly of Florida and Virginia memories. Several letters came to him from Danville. In reply Jelka explained that he didn't see very well, and that he "found great solace in the wireless." She prodded concert managers and she sent to European cities for radio schedules. She ordered records and books. For hours each day she read to him herself. Mostly he wanted to hear Walt Whitman and Mark Twain. To his male nurse fell the duty of reading murder mysteries. Delius loved Edgar Wallace thrillers. He hated novels about psychoanalysis. "My dear fellow," he told a visiting critic, "I can read almost anythin' and everythin' but for heaven's sake don't send me one of those books that begins with the hero lyin' in his leetle cot lookin' up at a spot on the ceiling!" Delius was something of an *enfant terrible*, his visitors agreed. Mrs. Delius spoiled him completely. God knew the poor man deserved some eccentricities. Still, you never knew what he would say next.

"You are very bad!" he burst out when a pianist and a violinist began to butcher one of his sonatas. Always he spoke the truth. "Fred's honesty!" Jelka sighed.

He loved having Clare and Margaret with him when they could come. With his sister and his niece he felt no self-consciousness about his infirmities. "Clare, dear, why didn't you ever give a concert of my songs?" he demanded one evening. Clare started. Was it possible she had heard him correctly? But she was too tactful to remind him or Jelka that he had forbidden her to sing them in London. When after an awkward silence he remembered himself what he had done, he said quietly, "I am sorry." And that was that.

When Jelka was resting, Margaret read to him and she described the view on the Loing: peasant women in blue kerchiefs, farmers in smocks. He told her then about Gauguin, Rodin—the giants. How they had rendered these people and scenes! But Gauguin and Rodin were gone. He often made Margaret laugh with his memories of artistic Paris. He could be caustic and affectionate at the same time about people like Gauguin. Did Margaret know he had advised his Uncle Théodor to buy Gauguin's complete works, and Théodor had said they were worthless? Margaret was fascinated. She listened with him to his records. Sometimes they spoke of the United States. "America must face its problems," he told her. "There will be racial tension there."

When she was in London she made lists of delicacies he liked. Returning to Grez she would bring them with an account. But he would never listen to it. He couldn't stand people who weren't generous, people who itemized things. His doctors wouldn't let him have coffee with caffeine in it; Margaret brought him instead a rare potion from America that was for sale in London gourmet shops. It was called Sanka. He was allowed to have the wines from his cellar, and to his guests he served them lavishly in hollow-stemmed glasses. Margaret found it hard, sometimes, to think of him as helpless. Then in the evening she would see the male nurse and her aunt preparing to take him upstairs, lifting his gaunt stiff form erect from the chair. To remember him as she had seen him at the tea room in Piccadilly Circus years before was nearly unbearable then. She marveled that he was never cross with her. Grandmother Delius was still alive and healthy in England, approaching her nineties. But she had never come to Grez to see her son in his tragedy.

Newspapers began to be full of that tragedy. Often Jelka had to turn away photographers who appeared with their cameras on the doorstep trying to record for what they called his fans his slow wasting-away. It was a death-watch they were keeping, and she and Margaret shivered at their grim persistence. Uncle Fred didn't want his public to remember him this way, Margaret knew. But the photographers lingered until he had to shout in exasperation: "Tell 'em I'm out!" And that everybody found uproariously funny when the story was repeated.

His happiest times were when Sir Thomas Beecham gave Delius concerts in London and the British Broadcasting Corporation presented them over the air. Jelka mobilized Grez villagers ferociously and made them turn off farm motors; there must be no static to interfere. Her reward was seeing Delius smile and nod his head to the music's rhythm. And in her eyes he was handsomer than ever; she begged Edvard Munch to come to Grez to paint him in his gaunt dignity, though Munch couldn't find the time.

Often these days Delius's mail piled up to the point where Jelka was overwhelmed by it. Margaret was startled to hear her say one day, "You have a fluid line in your arm Rodin would have liked." Once she had been an artist, Margaret was reminded; but it was difficult to think of her as one when she spent most of her time at her desk coping with her husband's correspondence. She seemed to have little identity apart from his own, though she eventually painted Margaret's portrait. And Delius made it a point to dictate an answer to every letter.

In May, 1928, one of the letters came from a young Yorkshireman who wanted him to know how grateful he was for Delius's music. As usual, Delius replied. The Yorkshireman wrote again, and the contents of his letter made Jelka draw in her breath. His name was Eric Fenby. He was prepared to come to Grez to live with Delius and learn how to take his music from dictation. He felt he had a mission to perform, and he would give several years of his own life and his planned career in music to it.

"How old is he?" Delius asked. "He must wish to escape the house of his parents!" But Jelka told Eric Fenby to come. He must see the house before he decided definitely. It was a solitary life. Could he sight-read? When her chauffeur drove her in the yellow Ford to the railway station at Bourron, she was amazed at Fenby's youth. Yet he assured her he was in his early twenties. He was small, brown-haired, and wore thick glasses. He was also very shy. But he wasn't escaping from an unhappy house. He had read about Delius's inability to write; it was unthinkable that his music had stopped because of it. Fenby would also be getting invaluable training.

When they arrived at the house Delius was resting. First, beyond the blue door, Jelka led Fenby up to the music room, then to the guest room where he was unpleasantly surprised to see a framed photograph of Nietzsche over his bed. There was also a portrait of crazy Strindberg. Fenby shivered. He was devout. These men were heretics.

When he met Delius, he was apprehensive. Should he shake the drooping hand Delius was struggling to extend to him? A glance from Jelka said yes. He went forward. How emaciated the composer was. Delius began talking about Yorkshire cricket and his old holidays in Filey Bay and Fenby felt more relaxed. But when Delius delivered some musical pronouncements, Fenby was shaken again. Why, if he were to live here he must conceal his own opinions! He loved church music, Bach, Haydn oratorios. Delius, at the moment, didn't. Delius asked Fenby to go to the music room and look at his abandoned composition *A Poem of Life and Love.* He wanted his opinion. When Fenby began to examine the score he felt uneasier than ever. It wasn't Delius at his best. Parts of it were on a level with a student's gropings. How ill Delius must have already been when he tried to write it! Fenby trembled at what he would say when Delius asked him for a verdict. He, too, believed in painful honesty where music was concerned.

Fenby's first test came when Alexander Barjansky, the Russian cellist, arrived with his wife at Grez to play Delius his cello sonata. Fenby had to learn the piano part, which he had never seen. For hours he struggled with it at the Ibach until he felt able to cope with the required chromatics. Barjansky was a tiny man, and Fenby was amused when he discovered that after each piece Barjansky would step inside his cello case to change shirts, his hairy arms darting in and out like a monkey's. When Fenby and Barjansky had finished the sonata Delius shouted: "Bravo!" The first ordeal was over.

Eric Fenby was a hard worker. He also believed his orthodox Christianity was the only possible means of a soul's salvation, and this belief was a little hard to live with on a day-to-day basis. Delius, he repeated to Delius and himself, was a pagan. And Delius, who wanted lively debates instead of shock on Eric's part when he delivered home truths about music and Nietzsche's doubtings, began to see how far he could go taunting Eric's sureness. He gave Eric a copy of *Thus Spoke Zarathustra,* and when Eric protested it was heresy, Delius's response was to tell him Nietzsche's nature was "sublime." Eric finally decided Delius was "stern and untamable."

When at last he criticized *A Poem of Life and Love* to Delius's face, he expected the heavens to fall. At first he thought Delius was "electrified." Then he promptly heard him agreeing with his criticism. Was it possible? Eric must take it apart, Delius said, and isolate the good passages. Then they would work on it together. The time for evolving a method of composition had come.

"I have an idea, a simple little tune. I want you to take it down."

Eric took up his pen over a blank sheet of score paper. He saw Delius throw back his head and heard him begin droning out a harsh monotone: "Ter-te-ter—ter-te-te-ter—Hold it! Ter-te-te-ter—ter-ter-ter—Hold it! Ter-te-te-ter—Hold it!"

There was no melody. There was hardly even a pitch.

"Have you got that? Now sing it!"

"B-but Delius, what key is it in?"

"A minor."

It was useless. Eric bit his lip. Could Delius try naming the notes?

"Well, all right, then!" And he began drawling in the same monotone: "A—BC—BD—E," until Eric, in his confusion, found himself holding his pen upside down. His fingers were black with ink. This genius, whose music had fired all his boyhood dreams, was now unable to get out a simple phrase.

"I'm sorry, I cannot go on! Please excuse me!" Eric leaped up and fled to the garden. When he heard Mrs. Delius's footsteps inside, he also heard Delius tell her, "Jelka, that boy is no good! He is too slow!" Eric was bitterly disappointed. He had wanted to help and now he had made everything worse by giving Delius false hope.

But Delius, reflecting, told Jelka he believed he and Eric could manage. They would have to "show great patience." They must master a technique of communication before they tried composition at all. From then on Delius began to show a new gentleness with Eric, who responded to it by poring over *A Poem of Life and Love*. When he had extracted what he thought good in it, he played it to Delius. Delius began calling out the names of instruments, the time values of notes, the key signatures. The piano, they knew now, was essential to them. To complete a single bar of music took hours. But when they had finished their first session with *A Poem of Life and Love*, orchestrating it from the keyboard, they knew they had a section of manuscript which could be read and played. Delius retitled it *A Song of Summer*. He had written another tone poem, at last. Now he began to organize all the melodic wisps that had bedeviled him for years. Through the house and the garden at Grez week after week echoed the strengthening ring of his voice:

"Eric? What have we got in the basses?"

"F sharp, B, C sharp, F sharp, seven beats," Eric sang.

"Good. Where was I with the upper strings?"

"At the beginning of the third bar."

"The same chord again, and move down to E in the firsts on the last quarter note, then up at A, five beats. Keep the

F sharp in the second fiddles running right through. Now on the fifth beat change the chord . . ."

After months of struggle they had found themselves. Sir Thomas Beecham began to receive new Delius manuscripts in Eric's hand. "Lovely, lovely!" he exclaimed. Delius composed a song for baritone and orchestra, "*Cynara.*" It was by an English poet, Ernest Dowson:

I have been faithful to thee, Cynara, in my fashion . . .
I have forgot much, Cynara, gone with the wind . . .

He also began another violin and piano sonata. *Margot La Rouge*, the discarded opera, he decided to tighten and arrange to suit a Walt Whitman poem, *Idyll: Once I Passed Through a Populous City.*

Frederick Delius, hummed press service wires, was working once more. He was doing it note by note, bar by bar, instrument by instrument. At the end of a few bars he was exhausted and had to be taken to his room to rest. But always he went on. His closest friends, those who came to Grez, were the ones who knew what it cost him. Often at night when the house was dark they would hear his voice: "Jelka? Are you asleep?"

"No, of course not, darling."

"Please come to me. I am in pain."

In January, 1929, just before Delius's sixty-seventh birthday, King George V decorated him with the order of Companion of Honour. It was a high distinction and Delius was pleased. He consented to receive reporters. When they saw him, they were struck by the drama of the moment. He looked like a corpse, gaunt and white; yet he told them he was happy.

"It is good to know they still remember me in England. It is beautiful to know they love my music. Thank them, thank them, it is wonderful."

Here was the story of the year. The reporters began to use

phrases like "The Crippled Genius," "The Blind Composer," "The Valiant Delius," "Years of Neglect—Now Fame!" and when their public ate it up, they kept Delius on their front pages. They ran portraits of Julius Caesar beside his own. They found a distant family connection with Eugénie, romantic last Empress of the French. They linked a Roman Delius with Pontius Pilate's wife. They repeated tales of how Delius worked with Eric Fenby. What they couldn't learn about him they made up: he was sweet and gentle, they said. He was tender and sentimental. When they were admitted on rare occasions to see him, they asked him about his parents. He couldn't resist teasing them then, but they had no idea of it. They simply repeated what he told them. His parents had been "poor but honest," and he had "grown up playing in all Bradford's coal piles." This was a real success story after Britain's heart: coal piles to celebrity. That it hardly squared with the Caesars and the Empress Eugénie bothered nobody.

Delius became a staple item in Sunday supplements. Women's pages described his peach trees, Madame Gréspier's cooking, and Jelka's devotion. Hopeful writers sent him poems about himself. Several letters asked Jelka to send souvenirs, "something he has touched." Soon she ran out of photographs. On one occasion when Margaret was visiting at Grez, a woman managed to get into the garden. When Delius was carried down and put in his armchair, she rushed forward and kissed him before Jelka or Margaret or the male nurse could stop her.

"I am only a poor music teacher from Australia, but I have saved every farthing all my life to cross the world and kneel at the feet of the Master!"

"Well!" the Master exclaimed, bemused. Then he smiled. "Now that you are here, my dear, why don't we all have a glass of champagne?"

All England soon began to clamor for a festival of Delius

works. Beecham had in mind the same project. It would never happen, Delius thought gloomily. But Beecham went ahead with his plans for a series of concerts devoted to every major Delius work except the *Requiem*, and he asked for the help of a London musician—Peter Warlock. Peter Warlock consented to do the organizing and promoting. "Old Fred" was working again, was he? Warlock raised his brows. Well, it was more than he himself was doing these days. He was tormented by the idea that he might be used up as a composer. The festival of Delius's music would be a distraction.

When Beecham wrote to Grez that he was making arrangements for Delius's trip to the festival in London by ambulance and ship, Delius protested. "No! I won't be made a proper show of!" The trip might even kill him, and there was music left in him he had to write. He couldn't die yet.

Eric begged him to reconsider, but Delius was adamant. Early in the summer Eric had to write Beecham he had failed to persuade Delius to go. Beecham reacted by coming to Paris. There he hired a taxi to take him to Grez. He stalked into the garden carrying a sheaf of music; the taxi he directed to wait. He demanded to see Delius. When Delius was brought down, Beecham told him he was definitely coming to London in October and now that that was all settled he would like some refreshment. For nine hours over the local wine of Grez he amused the Deliuses and Eric with sprightly repartee on men and music. When he left, he climbed into the taxi, and Jelka began the task of engineering her husband's return to England. At last she would open the blue door. Eric decided to go to London ahead of them to help Beecham's staff copy scores and parts.

As he was leaving, Delius called to Jelka to put an object in his hand. Supporting his hand on her own he extended it. Eric took a small box, unwrapped it, and then stared. Delius had given him his gold watch and chain.

18 ✐ Samarkand

For Jelka the trip to England in the autumn of 1929 loomed as a formidable ordeal. She would have to protect Delius from too much excitement, care for him on board ship in a cramped stateroom, and never leave his side for fear something would trouble him and she wouldn't be there to explain it. The arrangements were a complex series of shiftings. She knew, too, there might be crowds at the festival concerts, and she dreaded facing them. Still, it was important to back Beecham, who had worked so hard for Delius's music. And it was vital to Delius to hear it again. After all, she thought, there were really few enough serious concertgoers in Britain. Surely the crowds in London wouldn't be so very large.

She and the male nurse brought him by ambulance to the French Channel port of Boulogne. There she was told a storm had been raging over the Channel all day. Waves were crashing on the piers and the wind was moaning. Her heart sank. She could never risk having Delius transferred to his cabin under such conditions. Yet by night the storm had died down, and she and the nurse put him aboard on a stretcher. None of the other passengers had been told of his presence. All during the crossing she stayed in the cabin without emerging; she read to him, and she was delighted at the fresh gaiety of his mood. How he was looking forward to those concerts after all! They reminisced together about their past—Paris, the Griegs, all the early struggles, the enchanted years before the war. At the English port, Folkestone, they intended to wait together until the rest of the passengers had left the ship.

Then Delius would be put quietly into another ambulance. No one would notice him, Jelka thought.

Outside Folkestone, still in the cabin, she was met by the news that there were masses of people on the dock. Reporters were jockeying for position with their cameras. The police had actually been called in to keep order. She couldn't believe what she heard. When she hurried to the porthole, she beheld a mob scene. "They've come to see him," she was told simply. When the ship had reached shore and the other passengers had left, she could hear cheering growing louder and louder. In an agony of shyness and worry she stepped on the deck. The crowd roared its greeting. But the police were efficient and she and the nurse were able to get Delius into a wheelchair and prop him up with cushions. What was all the noise? he kept asking. "They have come to welcome you, sweetheart." When she pushed his chair down the gangway, she saw with relief the heavy cordon of police who were guarding the waiting ambulance.

What reporters saw was "a figure with silvered hair, wearing a grey felt hat, a heavy overcoat, with his sightless eyes shielded by tortoiseshell glasses and a pale, wrinkled, ascetic face." It was "the face of a suffering god," one said emotionally. The nurse "lifted him as if he were a child" onto his stretcher and into the ambulance. Then the nurse and Mrs. Delius climbed in and the police cleared the road ahead to Folkestone's Grand Hotel, where Delius was to rest all day. The reporters had to leave without more of a story, and the crowd dispersed without hearing their idol speak.

Delius himself was stunned. Why on earth had all those people come down? He hated being an object of curiosity. Then he began to smile. At last all of England was asking to hear his music, not just a small group of concertgoers. Already he felt better. "They are too kind," he said. "These are great moments for me, but I don't deserve all this." Next day when

he resumed his journey, the police were there to help on the
way to the ambulance. He managed to raise his right hand
slightly toward the crowd and their cheer was deafening.
"Thank you, thank you." His words were loud and distinct.
On the way to London, Jelka told him people had gathered in
all the towns they were passing through. He himself heard
their cries of welcome. Then she began to exclaim: "Fred!
They are kneeling in the road!"

In London at fourteen he had stayed at the lamplit Langham
Hotel and gone to hear Wagner's *Lohengrin*. He had been a
boy fresh from the provinces then, awed by his nation's
capital. Now at the renovated Langham uniformed police
were ranked in an immovable line, Jelka told him. The street
in front was filled with people who were going down on their
knees. Incredible! He smiled and nodded as he was taken
inside, and in the lobby he smelled the heavy fragrance of a
thousand flowers. Yet whatever had he done except gone on
writing the music he had to write—and could, with Eric
Fenby's help? He was no hero, he repeated. "It is all very
amazing."

London music stores were jammed with angry customers
begging for sold-out Delius recordings. They bought scores
of his music day after day, and harried clerks scurried back
and forth trying to placate their clients and telephone Delius's
publishers for fresh supplies. A newspaper carrying a picture
of him being wheeled to a London rehearsal sold out in
minutes. Painters crowded the Langham lobby begging to be
allowed to see him to make sketches. Most were disappointed,
though when Peter Warlock brought the artist Augustus John,
Delius consented to pose briefly. Eric Fenby was working
night after night with Beecham's musicians. The Queen's and
Aeolian Halls, where the concerts were to be held, had to call
for police help in managing crowds of disappointed ticket-
seekers. The Langham itself was a stormed citadel whose

worried manager felt himself in a nightmare. Traffic outside was jammed at a standstill for blocks.

Beecham had planned six concerts. At the first, in the Queens' Hall, with its decorations of fading cherubs beside tall mirrors on pale gray walls, Beecham conducted *Brigg Fair*, *A Late Lark*, the second *Dance Rhapsody*, *Sea Drift*, and *In a Summer Garden*. He also gave excerpts from *A Village Romeo and Juliet*. When Delius appeared in his wheelchair in a balcony box, the crowd went wild. "They're behaving like mad Italians!" a spectator gasped. With Delius in his box were Jelka and Eric. He smiled at the cheers, but it was his music that really made him happy, and he threw back his head against his pillow to listen when it began, swaying his head to its rhythms.

The second concert in Aeolian Hall featured his songs. When the audience heard *At Sunset*, they began weeping:

> What will happen when light is gone
> And the sun is banished? . . .
> Night will enfold us in love,
> All terror vanished.

They were not too late, they realized. He was still alive in his blindness to receive their love.

At the third concert they wept over Elbert Anderson's slave song in *Appalachia*. The fourth concert consisted of chamber works and more songs; the fifth was devoted to *North Country Sketches*, *Songs of Sunset*, the violin concerto, the first *Dance Rhapsody*, and an excerpt from *Fennimore and Gerda*. The cheering mounted. "We're being besieged!" complained the management of Queen's Hall. By the last Queen's Hall concert the crowd scenes which had plagued officials so far were "made to look of no account." Delius had to be constantly under guard to prevent people from trying to touch his clothes and block his wheelchair by throwing themselves at his feet. During *A Mass of Life* Queen's Hall aisles were jammed with standees. After the last notes had stopped echoing the audience rose to its feet and demonstrated for fifteen minutes. They threw their programs into the air, and several began to throw flowers up to Delius in the balcony. Beecham was bowing repeatedly; the orchestra and chorus were standing in homage to Delius too, shouting along with the spectators.

When Delius asked Jelka to describe it all for him, she couldn't. She was crying too, he realized. The tribute was for her as well. Soon he heard Beecham talking hoarsely into a microphone, and when Jelka did manage to speak, she told him the crowd were now clamoring to hear his own voice. When its roar had died, a complete silence succeeded it. He inclined his head to them, but it wasn't enough. Still they waited. He tried to raise his right hand. When he managed to move it upward a few inches, he heard a quivering breath in the hall. Then he cleared his throat. When his voice came, it wasn't his usual drawl, slow and steady. Now his voice was trembling. Someone nearby whispered that a microphone was ready. He paused, and then spoke.

"Ladies and gentlemen." Another breath sighed in the hall. "Thank you for the very fine reception you have given me. It was," he hesitated, "wholly unexpected." His strength was gathering as he spoke. "I also wish to thank Sir Thomas Beecham for the inspired manner in which he has played my music." Then he smiled broadly. "This festival has been the time of my life. Again I thank you." In the midst of the cheering that began once more he heard a familiar voice close to him. It was Margaret's. She had managed to bring her fiancé upstairs to meet him.

To Clare, listening at home to her radio because her husband was ill and couldn't be left, there was an irony in the scene. Fred, the most collected and restrained of men, wrote music which had a power of exciting crowds. In Christiania long ago they had shot at him. Now they were crying out their tribute. She smiled. Fred had fulfilled himself. Max was dead and so was Ernest, who had ended his days as a wanderer in the Australian Bush. Fred had conquered the obstacles. The strangest thing about his victory was that one person had made no effort to buy a Delius Festival ticket at all. Elise Delius, aged ninety-two and now fond of riding in airplanes, still had no desire to hear her son's music. Julius, her husband, had said he wasn't a composer. To have listened to a note of any of the 200 works Frederick Delius had produced would have been to put Julius in the wrong. And that of course was impossible.

Delius passed his last days in the Langham Hotel in continued wonder. As he rested for the return to Grez he thought of the pilgrims' chorus in *Hassan*: "We take the golden road to Samarkand." Beecham hadn't played that, but the festival had been Samarkand all the same. The glowing Asian dream city was the city Delius himself had built in his work. In his blindness he had seen Samarkand's spires once more. He was thinking too of Irmelin, the princess who had haunted him all his adult life. At Grez with Eric he would write a prelude to be called *Irmelin*, rounding off the cycle of pieces based on her legend. Also he knew he wanted to say good-by to all the people who had given him their homage. How much they understood of his work he wasn't sure. But in the vigorous American words of Walt Whitman he would say a farewell to them in a series of choruses. Their dedication would be given to Jelka. She had organized his existence for more than thirty years. At times he had rebelled at her generalship. But she had made possible his continuing love of life, and he knew it.

"Turn me toward England," he asked her on the Channel steamer bound for France. Then both were silent.

When he was back in Grez with Eric, the English trip seemed a fantastic interlude. They worked at a sonata in the music room when Delius had the strength for it. Jelka read aloud and she also tried to juggle the Delius finances. The accumulated costs of his invalidism had eaten away everything even the festival had earned. Now when she went over her budget again and again, she was faced with a horrifying reality: There was no more money at all. What should she do? She couldn't tell him.

In desperation she wrote to their English friend Balfour Gardiner, a rich man and a lover of Delius's music. Quietly he stepped in to the rescue. He bought the Grez house; the Deliuses could live in it rent free until both died. No one was to know about its sale. Again Jelka had capital on which to manage. The secret lay buried in French real estate records.

During the summer of 1930, an English hypnotist came to Grez. At first he found it impossible to hypnotize Delius, who teased him about his futile efforts. But when he finally succeeded because Delius was tired, he was able to restore some power to his legs. Supported on both sides, Delius could manage the steps into the garden. He was free of pain. In a burst of energy he worked on *Songs of Farewell* with Eric:

> Now finalé to the shore . . .
> Embrace thy friends, leave all in order,
> To port and hawser's tie no more returning
> Depart upon thy endless cruise, Old Sailor.

The hypnotist even tried seating him at his piano. "Play!" he commanded. Slowly Delius raised his arms. But when his hands came crashing down on the keys in a jangled discord, he came to. Eric was near. Even now he had to make a joke. "Eric, the new music!" The hypnotist at last declared he could help no more.

In 1930, Elise Delius died, and she left Frederick out of her will. It was her final condemnation. There was no use evading the reality of death, Delius always insisted; now he knew it would come soon to himself.

"When I die," he told Margaret Harrison, a young violinist who was visiting him, "When I die I will *be* my music." And as he heard it on his record player, she noted, his expression was totally blank, as if already he were lost in a world of shadows.

He had savored life. He had wanted his music, a vital faith he could hold instead of belief in a Victorian tyrant in the sky, and children to love. For Jelka's love he had never even asked, but it had been given him. So had music. His search for a faith was what *A Mass of Life* was about. But children had been denied. That the shouting of childish games in his garden when he wanted to compose would have annoyed him constantly he chose to ignore. Even Philip he had lost. He must watch over Eric.

For Eric, however, life in the house of an elderly sick man was becoming harder and harder. When he went walking with a village girl, Delius lectured him on chaperonage customs in France. When the autumn of 1930 came, Eric knew he was perilously near a nervous breakdown. He would have to get back to England. Delius tried to understand. Eric must return as soon as he could.

God knew the life at Grez must be hard on the poor lad, Delius reflected afterward. Philip Heseltine hadn't even dared to try it. At Christmas news came to Grez that Philip had one night put out his cat, shut the door of his London flat, and turned on the gas. He had committed suicide. No one knew why. "Perhaps Peter Warlock killed Philip Heseltine," people were saying. Delius was plunged into depression. Philip's death dominated his thoughts. The blow weakened him physically, and he was tormented because he had started Philip on the path to music. When Philip's gift had failed, perhaps only momentarily, he hadn't had the strength to stand the failure. Was it Delius's fault?

When Eric returned early in 1931, Delius rallied and they began the *Irmelin* prelude together. But after it Eric felt like a tired veteran again. Once more he had to get away. At the end of the year, in England, he collapsed from strain. Jelka had to break the news to Delius and she was alarmed when she saw him trying without success to hold back tears. For months he was depressed again. When a recovered Eric came back in August, 1932, Delius roused himself to begin dictating. A *Fantastic Dance* was full of Negro blues and whimsical gaiety. He had Eric's help and companionship, and they both followed newspaper accounts of English cricket matches together.

Meanwhile the London musical world began to rock with scandal. Duke Ellington, the American jazzman, was coming for a series of concerts. "Is he very black?" hotel managers wanted to know. "Is he gentlemanly in his bearing?" ART OR DEBAUCHERY? blared headlines. Then Percy Grainger pronounced that Ellington was a great musician and very similar to Delius. There were quick outcries. Delius? Had Grainger been heard correctly? Why, Delius was English! He had just been given the keys to the city of Bradford. When several musicians pointed out that not only had Delius used Negro music as a source but now American popular composers were extracting their harmonic devices from techniques Delius himself had originated, the English public turned a deaf ear. When Ellington said he admired Delius's *In a Summer Garden* particularly, it was considered an insult. The kindest thing one could do for Delius was to squelch any further comparisons of him with Americans. The comparisons were accordingly squelched as an act of homage, and Percy Grainger was denounced as impertinent.

"Trust an American to make money!" sneered an English critic of Ellington after the concert. "The audience sit and clutch hands, gasp, goggle their eyes and jig their knees to the rhythm. They need to be psychoanalyzed."

Only Ellington's press agent continued to quote Grainger's comment. On Ellington's next American tour it appeared on posters everywhere. Most Americans had never heard of Delius, but those who had were surprised because they had always vaguely thought of him as that blind old man fond of writing about English cuckoos in spring.

In the summer of 1933, Eric had to leave Grez once more. His enforced solitude and his musical slavery and Delius's irritability when their work went slowly were becoming more than he could manage to put up with for long, much as he was learning. To replace him came Margaret, whose young husband had died after a tragically short marriage. At Christmas she decorated the house as bravely as she could with pine branches, and she found her uncle as eager as a child for her descriptions of the garlands she had wound down the stair rails. He called for champagne at every pretext.

"Have the servants got champagne too?"

"I think so, Uncle Fred."

"Have they got it in champagne glasses?"

Jelka sent down to find out. No, she learned. But that wasn't the same, he insisted. They were to have champagne glasses immediately.

In January, 1934, he began to sleep more and more during the day. He was seventy-two. He had never really gotten over Philip's suicide, Jelka sometimes thought. When he was awake, she and Margaret read to him. Margaret had begun to write poems of her own and together she and her uncle dreamed of Yorkshire:

> I can only think of the purple moors
> And the springy turf for my feet
> Where the wind tears past with a laughing sound
> And a taste that is bittersweet.

For these lines he asked again and again.

When Margaret had to go back to her newspaper job in London and Delius's nurse had shyly given her a box of chocolates as a farewell present, Jelka managed with him to tend Delius until she herself began to feel ill. But she had to stay with Delius to the end. She could attend to herself later. When she had an attack of pain so violent she couldn't carry on her daily work, she was driven to a doctor's office. Afterward, on a May afternoon in 1934, she demanded the truth. Cancer, he told her. She would have to have an immediate operation.

She wired for Eric. Then she was taken to a hospital in Fontainebleau while Delius remained in the house alone with his nurse. When he knew she had left, he lay rigid. Jelka had never left him. Was she so ill, then? The nurse lied that she wasn't. By the time Eric bounded up the stairs to his room, Delius was calling: "Eric! Eric!" He repeated, "When is she coming back? Where is she?"

Eric tried to read to him. He asked for *Huckleberry Finn*. Then he asked Eric to play him *In a Summer Garden*. Eric turned the record player's sound horn toward the stairway and Delius listened. When Eric went to Fontainebleau to see Jelka, he found her weak but progressing after her surgery. Back at Grez Delius pressed: "Isn't she coming back tomorrow?" It was the shock of losing her that was really killing him. To Delius Eric continued to lie that Jelka's illness hadn't been serious; to Jelka he lied that her husband was getting along fairly well. When he called in additional doctors for Delius, they shook their heads. Soon Delius sank into a coma.

There was a single hope of reviving him. Jelka must be brought back. Her own doctor didn't dare to refuse her pleading. By noon on Friday, June 8, she was sitting by Delius's bed.

"I am here, sweetheart."

He stirred. Slowly at last he turned his head to her. "Jelka?" She could hardly hear him. "I am glad." He smiled. His hand was still in hers when he sank back into unconsciousness. On Sunday, June 10, 1934, before dawn, he died in Eric Fenby's arms. Slowly Eric went into Jelka's room. "My dear, be brave."

That night the regular programing of the British Broadcasting Corporation was interrupted by a news bulletin: "We regret to announce the passing of Mr. Frederick Delius, Companion of Honour." An orchestra began playing *The Walk to the Paradise Garden* from *A Village Romeo and Juliet*. Audiences were told in concert halls. English newspapers saw no need even to mention his name in their headlines: MUSIC'S BLIND HERO IS DEAD; HIS SOUL GOES MARCHING ON.

At Grez he lay in his music room beside the Ibach piano, surrounded by roses Jelka had asked Madame Gréspier to pluck. Because of her own illness he would be buried temporarily in Grez. But Jelka startled the world with an announcement. He had made a last request to her after the 1929 festival. He wanted to lie in an English churchyard.

A churchyard? But he had been an unbeliever, said conventional English churchgoers. Why a churchyard? Jelka was firm, and with the help of violinist Margaret Harrison's family she made arrangements for him to rest among the ancient tombs of St. Peter's, Limpsfield, in Surrey. It was not far from London. Music lovers could visit St. Peter's and put flowers on Delius's grave. He had asked, too, that the flowers they brought be wild. When Jelka was able to travel to London, she made arrangements with lawyers to found a Delius Trust for the future recording of his music. She seemed to be in fair health again. She alone knew she wasn't. Eric spent Christmas with her at Grez. Alexander Barjansky and his wife came later and found her listening to Delius records, following them with a pocket score. "It is so cold," she told them.

"All of life is so cold to me now." A fifteen minute walk to his grave exhausted her. The Barjanskys knew the truth then, too.

In May, 1935, Eric set out for the English Channel with a hearse containing the body of Delius for reburial. Jelka followed with Madame Gréspier. She would stay in London with Adine O'Neill, who was now also a widow. On board ship Jelka developed pneumonia. At the shore she was hurried off to a London clinic. There she begged to be taken on to Limpsfield, but Adine and the clinic authorities refused.

At Limpsfield the body of Delius arrived at midnight on May 23. Oil lamps were fixed to crosses in the churchyard and flickered eerily. Beneath a yew tree a thousand years old, the coffin was lowered while the Vicar of Limpsfield read prayers. Eric disapproved; Delius had been a pagan. The Vicar did not think so; he had read the texts Delius set to music. Afterward the new grave was covered with flowers. The city of Bradford had sent a wreath of Yorkshire heather. The next day automobiles lined the road for miles. Sir Thomas Beecham had come down with a group of musicians. Blackbirds sang beneath a cloudless spring sky.

When Beecham's musicians began playing, the rich oriental strains of *Hassan* echoed in the tiny church among the figures of saints. Some of the spectators who crowded the sloping churchyard among BBC sound trucks under the dark trees remembered then the lines of Ishak the Philosopher to Hassan at the play's end:

> We are the pilgrims, master; we shall go
> Always a little farther . . . We are brave
> Who take the golden road to Samarkand.

When the last notes had faded, the BBC trucks began speeding up to London to process recordings of the ceremony. A young BBC technician was soon startled to receive a call from the BBC's director. He was to take the recordings to Mrs. Frederick Delius in a clinic. The technician promised. He collected *In a Summer Garden*, too, without reading the album's dedication. In the clinic corridor he was met by Adine O'Neill, who ushered him into a tiny darkened room. Instantly he knew the white-haired woman in the bed before him was not merely sick. She was dying. He set up his equipment and began playing the music of *Hassan*. When he had reached Beecham's funeral tribute, she opened her eyes and spoke.

"Dear Tommy."

He paused. Turning to Mrs. O'Neill he murmured: "Do you think she would like to hear more?"

"Yes. I think she would."

He played *In a Summer Garden*. But Jelka Delius didn't stir again. When he left, her eyes were closed, and on May 28, she died.

She had listened, lying in that strange room, in a stranger dream. Perhaps she remembered Fred's gaunt old face and half-closed blind eyes as she heard *Hassan*; perhaps she remembered the cheering of the festival crowds too, and Beecham's voice. But then fresh music brought her back to another time, and she was standing with Fred in the garden at Grez while they both stared up at a large vacant house whose shutters were closed. The younger Fred who had emerged from the mist for her was a laughing man with dark blue eyes and auburn hair, a man who climbed mountains and strode beside crashing seas, a man whose voice was strong and whose steps were purposeful. She had known him that way in the middle of the journey he had made. But she had always known, too, that even before Grez there had been a Fred she could only try to imagine: a young boy named Fritz on an orange grove in moss-hung Florida, listening to Elbert Anderson sing and learning the compassion that had marked his life's music afterwards. That had been the journey's real beginning. She had almost seen Solano Grove herself once. Perhaps it was like all Delius gardens: rich with color, heady with fragrance, fresh with the breath of wind . . . Images began shifting and clashing in her dream. The war: Did she hear the tramping of booted feet on hard-packed French roads again, and the stark chords of the *Requiem* echoing down from the music room?

But her work was done. At last it was safe to sleep.

The death mask and hands of Delius

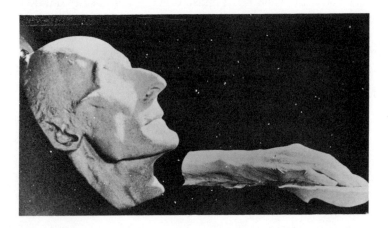

Epilogue

In the autumn of 1935, a few months after Jelka Delius's death in London, New York critics hailed the premiere of George Gershwin's *Porgy and Bess* as original, which it was, and as the first Negro opera, which it was not. In America justice has been slow in coming to the American music of Frederick Delius.

In November, 1965, his *Requiem* was performed in Liverpool Cathedral to an audience who afterwards filled the building with their cheering. Recording arrangements were made and are being concluded as this book is being written. Three more wars and the hydrogen bomb had made a difference.

Some Delius Music

PIANO, VOICE, VIOLIN

Piano Solo

	Publisher
Dance for Harpsichord	Boosey and Hawkes
Three Preludes	Anglo-French Music Co. Ltd.
Five Pieces for Pianoforte:	Boosey and Hawkes
Mazurka and Waltz for a Little Girl	
Waltz	
Lullaby for a Modern Baby	
Toccata	

Piano Arrangements of Orchestral Works

"La Calinda," from the opera *Koanga*	Boosey and Hawkes
"The Walk to the Paradise Garden," from the opera *A Village Romeo and Juliet*	Boosey and Hawkes
Two Pieces for Small Orchestra:	Oxford University Press
On Hearing the First Cuckoo in Spring	
Summer Night on the River	
Air and Dance	Boosey and Hawkes
"Serenade" from the drama *Hassan*	Boosey and Hawkes
Irmelin Prelude	Boosey and Hawkes

Voice and Piano

At Sunset	Augener, Ltd.
Slumber Song	Augener, Ltd.
Longing	Augener, Ltd.
Summer Eve	Augener, Ltd.
The Nightingale	Augener, Ltd.
Homeward Journey	Oxford University Press
Twilight Fancies	Oxford University Press
Cradle Song	Oxford University Press
Sweet Venevil	Oxford University Press
Love Concealed	Oxford University Press
To the Queen of my Heart	Oxford University Press
Indian Love Song	Oxford University Press
Love's Philosophy	Oxford University Press
Il Pleure dans mon Coeur	Oxford University Press
Le Ciel est, par-dessus le Toit	Oxford University Press
Let Springtime Come, Then	Oxford University Press
Autumn	Boosey and Hawkes
Black Roses	Oxford University Press
La Lune Blanche	Boosey and Hawkes
Chanson d'Automne	Oxford University Press
Spring, the Sweet Spring	Boosey and Hawkes
It Was a Lover and His Lass	Boosey and Hawkes
A Late Lark Singing	Boosey and Hawkes
Cynara	Boosey and Hawkes

Violin and Piano

Legende	Forsyth Brothers, Ltd.
Sonata No. 2	Boosey and Hawkes
Lullaby for a Modern Baby	Boosey and Hawkes
Sonata No. 3	Boosey and Hawkes

Violin and Piano Arrangements of Orchestral Works

Violin Concerto	Augener, Ltd.
"Serenade" from the drama *Hassan*	Boosey and Hawkes

PHONOGRAPH RECORDS

Florida Suite
    Royal Philharmonic Orchestra,   Capitol (S)G 7193
    Sir Thomas Beecham

Sleighride
    Royal Philharmonic Orchestra,   Capitol (S)G 7116
    Sir Thomas Beecham

Marche Caprice
    Royal Philharmonic Orchestra,   Capitol (S)G 7116
    Sir Thomas Beecham

Summer Evening
    Royal Philharmonic Orchestra,   Seraphim (S) 60000
    Sir Thomas Beecham

La Calinda from Koanga
    London Philharmonic Orchestra,   Capitol (S)G 7255
    George Weldon

Over the Hills and Far Away
    Royal Philharmonic Orchestra,   Capitol (S)G 7193
    Sir Thomas Beecham

Concerto for Piano and Orchestra
    NDR Orchestra, William Strickland
    Marjorie Mitchell, soloist   Decca (7) 10136

Brigg Fair
    Royal Philharmonic Orchestra,   Capitol (S)G 7116
    Sir Thomas Beecham
    London Symphony Orchestra,   London 9066
    Anthony Collins
    Philadelphia Symphony Orchestra,   Columbia MS 6376
    Eugene Ormandy

Paris: The Song of a Great City
    London Symphony Orchestra,   Decca ACL 245
    Anthony Collins

The Walk to the Paradise Garden
    London Symphony Orchestra,   London 9066
      Anthony Collins
    Hallé Orchestra, Sir John Barbirolli Vanguard SRV 240
    London Symphony Orchestra,   Angel (S) 36415
      Sir John Barbirolli

In a Summer Garden
    London Symphony Orchestra,   Decca ACL 245
      Anthony Collins
    Philadelphia Symphony Orchestra, Columbia MS 6376
      Eugene Ormandy

Intermezzo from Fennimore and Gerda
    Royal Philharmonic Orchestra,   Capitol (S)G 7116
      Sir Thomas Beecham
    Hallé Orchestra, Sir John Barbirolli Vanguard SRV 240

On Hearing the First Cuckoo in Spring
    Royal Philharmonic Orchestra,   Capitol (S)G 7116
      Sir Thomas Beecham
    Hallé Orchestra, Sir John Barbirolli Vanguard SRV 240
    London Symphony Orchestra,   London 9066
      Anthony Collins
    Sinfonia of London, Robert Irving   Capitol (S)P 8659
    Philadelphia Symphony Orchestra, Columbia MS 6376
      Eugene Ormandy

Summer Night on the River
    Royal Philharmonic Orchestra,   Capitol (S)G 7116
      Sir Thomas Beecham
    London Symphony Orchestra,   Decca ACL 245
      Anthony Collins

Double Concerto for Violin,
  Violoncello and Orchestra
    Royal Philharmonic Orchestra,   Pye GGC 4073
      Norman Del Mar
      Raymond Cohen and
        Gerald Warburg, soloists

Concerto for Violin and Orchestra
    Vienna State Opera Orchestra,   Westminster XWN 19045
      Robert Zeller
      Robert Gerle, soloist

A Song Before Sunrise
    Royal Philharmonic Orchestra,   Capitol (S)G 7116
      Sir Thomas Beecham
    Royal Philharmonic Orchestra,   Angel (S) 36285
      Sir Malcolm Sargent

To Daffodils
    Peter Pears, tenor   London Argo RG 349
    Viola Tunnard, piano

Concerto for Violoncello and Orchestra
    Royal Philharmonic Orchestra,   Angel (S) 36285
      Sir Malcolm Sargent
      Jacqueline Du Pré, soloist

Serenade from Hassan
    Cleveland Sinfonietta, Louis Lane   Epic LC 3875

A Song of Summer
    London Symphony Orchestra,   London 9066
      Anthony Collins
    London Symphony Orchestra,   Angel (S) 36415
      Sir John Barbirolli

Sonata for Violin and Piano No. 3
    Ernest Michaelian, violin   Music Library MLR 7047
    Viola Luther Hagopian, piano

Irmelin Prelude
    Hallé Orchestra, Sir John Barbirolli   Vanguard SRV 240
    London Symphony Orchestra,   Angel (S) 36415
      Sir John Barbirolli
    Cleveland Symphony Orchestra,   Epic LC 3330
      George Szell

Idyll: Once I Passed Through a
  Populous City
      Hallé Orchestra, Sir John Barbirolli   Vanguard SRV 240

Songs of Farewell
      Royal Philharmonic Orchestra,   Angel (S) 36285
        Sir Malcolm Sargent

*By Peter Warlock (Philip Heseltine)**

  Serenade to Delius
      Cleveland Sinfonietta, Louis Lane Epic LC 3875

* For other Warlock compositions check current record catalogues.

Index